GERMANY'S HIDDEN CRISIS

Solidarity,

Oli

Solidarity
70.

GERMANY'S HIDDEN CRISIS

SOCIAL DECLINE IN THE HEART OF EUROPE

OLIVER NACHTWEY

Translated by David Fernbach and Loren Balhorn

VERSO
London • New York

The translation of this work was funded by Geisteswissenschaften International—
Translation Funding for Humanities and Social Sciences from Germany,
a joint initiative of the Fritz Thyssen Foundation, the German Federal
Foreign Office, the collecting society VG WORT and the Börsenverein des
Deutschen Buchhandels (German Publishers and Booksellers Association)

First published in English by Verso 2018
First published as *Die Abstiegsgesellschaft. Über das
Aufbegehren in der regressiven Moderne*
© Suhrkamp 2016
Translation © David Fernbach and Loren Balhorn 2018

1 3 5 7 9 10 8 6 4 2

Verso
UK: 6 Meard Street, London W1F 0EG
US: 20 Jay Street, Suite 1010, Brooklyn, NY 11201
versobooks.com

Verso is the imprint of New Left Books

ISBN-13: 978-1-78663-634-8
ISBN-13: 978-1-78663-714-7 (HB)
ISBN-13: 978-1-78663-636-2 (US EBK)
ISBN-13: 978-1-78663-635-5 (UK EBK)

British Library Cataloguing in Publication Data
A catalogue record for this book is available from the British Library

Library of Congress Cataloging-in-Publication Data

Names: Nachtwey, Oliver, author.
Title: Germany's hidden crisis : social decline in the heart of Europe /
  Oliver Nachtwey ; translated by David Fernbach.
Other titles: Abstiegsgesellschaft. English
Description: Brooklyn : Verso, 2018.
Identifiers: LCCN 2018028796| ISBN 9781786636348 (paperback) | ISBN
  9781786637147 (hardback) | ISBN 9781786636362 (United States E Book) |
  ISBN 9781786636355 (United Kingdom E Book)
Subjects: LCSH: Social change. | Social mobility. | Social conflict. |
  Capitalism. | BISAC: POLITICAL SCIENCE / History & Theory. | HISTORY /
  Europe / Germany.
Classification: LCC HM831 .N3313 2018 | DDC 303.4—dc23
LC record available at https://lccn.loc.gov/2018028796

Typeset in Minion Pro by Hewer Text UK Ltd, Edinburgh
Printed and bound by CPI Group (UK) Ltd, Croydon, CR0 4YY

Contents

Introduction

Asked about their professional goals in 2014, a third of all German university students answered that they were looking for a secure position in government service—more than anything, they were seeking stability and security. New, path-breaking occupations, risky start-ups and independent creative activity have lost their attractiveness for many students. Government service, on the other hand, seems to them one of the few areas in which stable employment, security and a predictable social ascent can be expected. This practically bourgeois occupational perspective of young graduates represents only a small cross-section of a society in which collective fear of downward mobility seems to be universal. How did this come about?

Historical memory is often short, and only few of us remember that as recently as 1999, the German economy was still seen as the 'sick man of the euro'; back then the unemployment rate was climbing ever higher. Today the reality looks very different. All over Europe, unemployment is at record levels; in Germany, on the other hand, there have never been so many people in work as in 2016, and never so few unemployed since reunification. While other European states have been mired in a welter of austerity and economic crisis, the German economy has apparently bucked this trend. This is little more than a pleasant illusion, though. Germany is just as much facing the 'crisis of democratic capitalism'[1] as the other European countries.

In this book, I use the example of German development to demonstrate a fundamental social change currently underway in most Western capitalist states. Societies of ascent and social integration, I argue, have become societies of downward mobility, precariousness and polarization.

Since the post-war 'economic miracle', Germany has been seen as a country in which poverty plays only a marginal role. Given the euphoria about the 'new full employment' that is proclaimed in books and newspaper articles,[2] it is all too easy to overlook how great social inequality has become in the country, how strongly the low-wage sector has grown and precariousness has increased. Beneath the surface of a seemingly stable society, the pillars of social integration have long been eroding, while ruin and relegation are spreading.

Literature is a sensitive seismograph for this change, and yearnings for social progress have always found expression in it. Ulla Hahn, in her fictional trilogy of the life of Hildegard (Hilla) Palm, *Das verborgene Wort* (2001), *Aufbruch* (2009) and *Spiel der Zeit* (2014), depicts in fine detail the social mores of an upwardly mobile society in the decades after the Second World War. Her protagonist combines a love of literature with the quest for a self-determined life. Hilla is exceptionally gifted, completes secondary school and—unusually for a 'kid from the proletariat', and a country girl at that—goes on to university. She experiences both the crude and finer distinctions between herself and the class whose sons, even if untalented, regularly end up in dominant social positions. Though her own family unambitiously persists in its simple ways, education grants her an upward mobility that is characteristic of her time.

----

1   Wolfgang Streeck, *Borrowed Time*, London: Verso, 2017.
2   Cf. on this point, the entire section in the *Frankfurter Allgemeine Zeitung* devoted to full employment, faz.net/aktuell/wirtschaft/vollbeschaefti-gung (accessed February 2016).

When literature addresses our social present, on the other hand, it depicts stories of disaster, uncertainty, downward mobility and ruin. In the autobiographical novel *Möbelhaus* (2015), the former journalist who writes under the pseudonym of Robert Kisch recapitulates his own decline from talented writer to furniture salesman. This is the story of a long downward slide, perhaps unique in this particular form. But it attests to the transformation of a whole branch of employment that only a few years ago promised professional prestige, autonomous activity and a good income. This world of journalism no longer exists—or only for a few, if at all. *Möbelhaus* is not the only example. In her reportage *Saisonarbeit* (2014), Heike Geissler relates how she could no longer live from her writing and found herself forced to work as a packer in an Amazon warehouse. Thomas Melle gives a similar account in his novel of the underclass, *3000 Euro* (2014). The story of slipping out of security can also be read in Katharina Hacker's *Die Habenichtse* (2006), Ernst-Wilhelm Händler's *Wenn wir sterben* (2002), Rainald Goetz's *Johann Holtrop* (2012), Wilhelm Genazino's *Fremde Kämpfe* (1984) and *Mittelmässiges Heimweh* (2007), Georg M. Oswald's *Alles was zählt* (2000) and Silke Scheuermann's *Die Häuser der anderen* (2012).

Literature is not a social diagnosis, but nonetheless it often depicts much that is true about the reality that I aim to discuss here from a scientific perspective.

This book attempts to explore certain classical questions of sociology: What kind of society do we live in? What holds groups and individuals together, and what drives them apart? What is the connection between inequality, domination, social integration and social conflict? Many of the arguments that I present here in the spirit of sociological exploration are in a certain sense risky, since in some areas they still lack empirical confirmation. And as they are essentially developed from the example of a single nation state, international and transnational aspects will only be touched on in passing (for example, at the end of the book, a cursory sketch of European trends). In particular, I attempt to present the developments of recent decades historically, and in this way to understand them.[3]

The first chapter focuses on a social constellation that is now past: the heyday of *social modernity*. Social modernity meant the welfare state, the removal of old class barriers, the increase in social and educational opportunities. Above all, children from working-class families attained levels of possibilities for individual development that had previously been unknown. The late German sociologist Ulrich Beck used the concept of a collective 'elevator effect' to describe this.[4] Proletarians became '*Bürger*', citizens—though women far less so, as the model of the man as family breadwinner remained dominant in social modernity.

From the 1970s on, the constellation of social modernity gradually began to fade, primarily because capitalism (as will be shown in Chapter 2) no longer continued the phenomenal growth rates of the 'golden age'. In 1973, Western economies began to decline, constituting a crisis for which no solution has yet been found. No effort has borne fruit—whether Keynesian programmes, neoliberal deregulation or a flood of cheap money. The prevailing tendency, as I argue in Chapter 2, is the rise of a *post-growth capitalism*. The economic crisis that followed the financial crisis is far from over, despite massive intervention by nation states and central banks. On the contrary, global stagnation looms on the horizon.

The long-term weakness of the economy dissolved both the resources necessary for social integration and the will to pursue it. Public companies fell under the pressure of privatization, the

3   C. Wright Mills, *The Sociological Imagination*, Oxford: Oxford University Press, [1959] 2000.

4   Ulrich Beck, *Risk Society: Towards a New Modernity*, London: Sage Publications, 1992. Translator's note: the third chapter of *Risikogesellschaft*, in which the concept of the 'elevator effect' is elaborated, is omitted from Mark Ritter's 1992 English translation; for this reason, the German original is cited when necessary.

welfare state was dismantled and social rights were reduced. In almost all areas of society—and this is the hallmark of our time— competitive market mechanisms were introduced. Finally, many achievements of social modernity were subjected to a renewed, now *regressive*, modernization (Chapter 3), which frequently combines social liberalization with economic deregulation. Horizontally, between groups with different sexual orientations, between genders and in certain respects even between ethnic communities, society has become more egalitarian and inclusive—but vertically, this egalitarianism is tied to greater economic inequalities.

As Ulrich Beck diagnosed in his influential book *Risk Society*, the old industrial society 'exits the stage of world history on the tip-toes of normality, via the back stairs of side effects'.[5] Aside from the fact that industrial society has still not completed this exit, we can formulate the following findings for the society of downward mobility: since it has gradually emerged on tip-toes and via the back stairs, it has not yet reached the main lobby. True, the proliferation of poverty, precarity and social inequality is ever more frequently a subject of political debate, but so far the new inequalities have not been dealt with in an adequate manner. Social ascent remains the object of desire, the behavioural norm, the political model, to be reached through achievement, through equal opportunity, through education. As far as equal opportunity is concerned, it is now well known that children from working-class families often do not have the same educational prospects. In the social competition for opportunity, despite formal equality, those with less cultural capital ultimately remain behind, while those who are better placed from the very start achieve success, sometimes even without special effort on their part.

Do we perhaps speak so much about social ascent because in reality it is ever more rare? This is one of the arguments made in this book. The shift to a society of downward mobility is taking

---

5 Ibid., 11.

place in several dimensions. There still are of course large zones of social stability, yet the central fact is that the developmental dynamic of German society has changed. Until the early 1990s, for example, real incomes rose, and so-called 'normal labour relations' (permanent jobs with protection from dismissal, affording a certain degree of security) were the general rule. In the last thirty years, the social dynamic has shifted against those dependent on employment. Precarity, a marginal phenomenon in social modernity, has expanded and is now institutionalized as a relevant sector of the labour market. As far as occupational mobility is concerned, though there is still clearly more upward than downward mobility, the outlook has worsened. Besides, the broad middle class has contracted and a proportion of its members have slid downward—something new in German post-war history. If ever more women are in employment, this may mean a gain in emancipation, but in many cases women have been forced to take low-wage jobs because their spouse's income is no longer sufficient to meet family needs.

Modernity is continuing to develop, but likewise going into reverse. Problems that were long seen as overcome have again become relevant. The dismantling of the welfare state and the withdrawal of social rights have again made the 'structuration of class relationships' the focus of social inequality.[6] At the same time, social classes do not present themselves today as they did in the late nineteenth century, as collective milieus with organizations tested in struggle. There is therefore no 'repeat' of the traditional class struggle, despite a large number of new social conflicts. In a society of downward mobility, there is tension and conflict between capitalism and democracy, between freedom and equality. A new kind of revolt breaks out, a democratic class conflict essentially driven by the struggle for political and social rights. New civic protests are a by-product of political alienation

---

6   Anthony Giddens, *The Class Structure of the Advanced Societies*, London: Unwin Hyman, [1973] 1989.

in post-democracy. However, and this is a great danger, there is also a spreading of apathy, social exclusion and anti-democratic sentiment. On the one hand, fears of downward mobility produce—especially among the middle class—a need for social Darwinist or xenophobic distinction, expressed for example in the debates as to whether Germany is 'abolishing itself' and whether the culture of the underclass is unproductive. The rise of the Islamophobic 'Pegida' movement and the success of the right-populist Alternative für Deutschland in the 2017 elections are expressions of this development.

On the other hand, a new kind of protest emerges from time to time, involving both social issues and democratic participation. Whether among women cleaners, care workers, in Amazon warehouses or hospitals, there has been a rise in the number of strikes, and by groups that were traditionally seen as difficult to organize into trade unions, as their jobs are often temporary and precarious. With Occupy, we saw an unconventional protest movement that took possession of public spaces for several months. This was a grassroots democratic movement, which generally, though not always, acted outside of the established left organizations such as trade unions and parties, these being perceived by the protesters as part of the establishment, part of the problem. Both the new strike movements and Occupy are new forms of protest characteristic of a society of downward mobility. Fear of relegation and precarity are no longer perceived as an individual fate, but are rather a collective experience. The German Occupy camps saw a new type of protester—similar to those in New York's Zuccotti Park, where the movement started, or that play an important role within the Spanish *Indignados*: young graduates with precarious jobs, dim prospects and blocked channels of upward mobility. Their number so far may still be small, but they find great resonance in public opinion. After all, their parents and grandparents experienced the decades of ascent, and cannot fail to recognize how their children are threatened with collective relegation. 'We are the 99 per cent'—the very slogan of the Occupy movement was emblematic of a post-democratic society of downward mobility, combining questions of fair distribution with those of democratic participation.

What has been absent from all these protests, however, is the idea of a successful future. People look back in vain at the seemingly better age of social modernity, not least because revolt remains spontaneous and episodic. Periods of increased social protests are rapidly followed by unusual calm. Yet so long as the problems to which these protests react are not resolved, social tension will in all probability persist. Hopefully these revolts will not themselves turn regressive at some point.

If the diagnosis presented here proves correct, we could be facing a new cycle of social conflicts, in which once again the battle is for a better society. And it is in these conflicts that the future of our democracy may well be decided.

I could not have written this book without the support of many colleagues and friends. They are too many for me to name here. And so I would like to thank three institutions that gave me space, time and possibilities of discussion such as are hardly possible in regular university work: the DFG Research Group on Post-Growth Societies in Jena, the Hamburg Institute for Social Research, and especially the Institute for Social Research in Frankfurt. I would also like to thank my friends and colleagues Loren Balhorn and Sebastian Budgen for their efforts in bringing this book to an English-speaking audience.

1

Social Modernity

Viewed with hindsight, the post-war decades in the Federal Republic of Germany were marked by a unique economic, social and political constellation. The politically polarized society of the Weimar Republic, riven by class conflict, had been followed by the Nazi dictatorship. After its collapse, a relatively stable democracy arose in the Federal Republic, and above all, it was one that was secured socially. In this book I refer to this epoch as *social modernity*.

The material foundation for this was economic prosperity. In the short period from 1950 to 1973, the annual growth rate in Western Europe averaged 4.8 per cent—the result of Keynesian capitalism. This steady growth made possible a breakneck social modernization, which embraced work, life, culture and politics, and restructured all of these fields.[1]

1 Johannes Berger, 'Modernization Theory and Economic Growth', in Waltraud Schelkle, Wolf-Hagen Krauth, Martin Kohli and Georg Elwert (eds), *Paradigms of Social Change: Modernization, Development, Transformation, Evolution*, New York: St Martin's Press, 2000, pp. 31–48. Focusing on bureaucratic organization, trade-union penetration and standardization in this period, Wagner also speaks of an 'organized modernity' (Peter Wagner, *A Sociology of Modernity: Liberty and Discipline*, London: Routledge, 1993).

THE SIGNIFICANCE OF THE WELFARE STATE

The roots of the welfare state in Germany stretch back to the Bismarck era, with the first legislation on sickness and accident insurance in 1883, followed by contributory pensions in 1889. This was Bismarck's reaction to the growing strength of the workers' movement, and at the same time a project of modernizing early capitalism. Under the Weimar Republic, further centralized welfare measures were introduced, particularly unemployment insurance in 1927, but it was only through post-war democracy that the welfare state was comprehensively achieved—not least because even large sections of the social and political elites had lost confidence in an unregulated laissez-faire capitalism that obeyed only the laws of the market. The 'great transformation' that the Austro-Hungarian economic historian Karl Polanyi had predicted in 1944, even before the end of the Second World War, basically came into being. Polanyi argued that the idea of a self-regulating market—as would later be propagated again by neoliberalism—was bound to remain a 'stark utopia'.[2] If such a utopia were to be realized, this would mean as a final consequence the total dislodgement of the economy from society. According to Polanyi, a society subjugated to the market in this way could not exist without dissolving its own substance—in other words, human beings and nature.[3] All attempts to approximate the optimal market society would ultimately produce counter-moves seeking to re-embed the economy in society.[4] For example, in the United States after the crash of 1929, urban workers, the poor and socialists, as well as farmers and conservatives, worked together for a new social policy. The welfare state established after the Second World War, not just in Germany but also in other (West)

---

2   Karl Polanyi, *The Great Transformation: The Political and Economic Origins of Our Time*, Boston: Beacon Press, [1944] 2002, 3.

3   Ibid., 3, 39.

4   Ibid., 79.

European countries, was close to the institutionalized form of a counter-movement as analysed by Polanyi.[5]

The characteristic feature of the proletarians, for Marx, was that they possessed neither capital nor means of production. This meant that they had no alternative to selling their labour-power.[6] Under capitalism, labour is a commodity that is bought and sold on the labour market, and workers are consequently exposed without defence to the dangers of this market—poverty, sickness, old age and unemployment. The welfare state succeeded in limiting the degree to which labour has this commodity character; it is a 'de-commodifying' institution, since it socializes the aforementioned risks.[7] French sociologist Robert Castel therefore refers to the complex of claims to social security, pensions, public goods and services as 'social property'.[8] The welfare state does not function the same way everywhere: some of its expressions are widespread and universally applied, others are conservatively oriented at maintaining stability, while others again offer scarcely more than a social minimum.[9]

5   Later we shall see how the pendulum has swung back in the direction of market liberalism.

6   Karl Marx, *Capital* Volume One, Harmondsworth: Penguin, [1867] 1973.

7   Following the English word 'commodity' and the Latin '*commodum*'; cf. also the discussions in Claus Offe, *Contradictions of the Welfare State*, London: Hutchinson, 1984; Gøsta Esping-Andersen, *The Three Worlds of Welfare Capitalism*, Cambridge: Polity Press, 1990, Chapter 1; Robert Castel, *From Manual Workers to Wage Laborers: Transformation of the Social Question*, Rutgers: Transaction, 2002; idem, *L'Insécurité sociale: qu'est-ce qu'être protégé?* Paris: Éditions du Seuil, 2003; idem, *La montée des incertitudes. Travail, protections, statut de l'individu*, Paris: Éditions du Seuil, 2009; and Stephan Lessenich, *Die Neuerfindung des Sozialen. Der Sozialstaat im flexiblen Kapitalismus*, Bielefeld: transcript, 2008.

8   Castel, *From Manual Workers to Wage Laborers*, 247–302.

9   In *The Three Worlds of Welfare Capitalism*, Danish political scientist Gøsta Esping-Andersen establishes a typological distinction between liberal (e.g., Great Britain), conservative (Germany in particular) and social-democratic (e.g., Sweden) welfare states.

Besides, the welfare state is not a philanthropic agent, but contains a productivist dualism. It seeks, on the one hand, to attenuate the life risks of wage earners, but on the other hand, to ensure that those able to work actually do so. By health and work protection, welfare policy creates a basic precondition for a sufficient supply of healthy labour-power to be available. No one, however, is to lie back and do nothing. Those able to work are to seek it, or else be subject to sanctions.[10]

The idea of who exactly forms part of the potential labour army has changed time and again in the course of history. In the early stage of capitalism, it was taken for granted that women and children belonged to this group. The struggle against child labour was long, and lasted into the early twentieth century. During this time, the image of women's roles changed, insofar as they were now given primary responsibility for children and household. They were to be chiefly housewives, while their husbands earned money.

The essential point remains, however: the welfare state was a central instance of social progress in social modernity. Wage earners were visibly able to expand their social property and their share of social wealth, while social welfare and health care legislation was extended. The poor and an underclass certainly continued to exist, but the extent and nature of their deprivation had changed. Both absolute and relative poverty declined, and the glaring pauperism of certain sections of workers belonged to the past.[11] Social need,

10   Cf. Claus Offe and Gero Lenhardt, 'Staatstheorie und Sozialpolitik. Politisch-soziologische Erklärungsansätze für Funktionen und Innovationsprozesse der Sozialpolitik' [1977], in Jens Borchert and Stephan Lessenich (eds), *Strukturprobleme des kapitalistischen Staates*, New York: Campus, 2006, 153–80; cf. also Jens Borchert and Stephan Lessenich, ' "Spätkapitalismus" revisited. Möglichkeiten und Grenzen adaptiver Selbsttransformation der Wohlfahrtsstaatsanalyse', in Anna Geis and David Strecker (eds), *Blockaden staatlicher Politik. Sozialwissenschaftliche Analysen im Anschluss an Claus Offe*, Frankfurt: Campus, 2005, 83–97.

11   Serge Paugam, *Les formes élémentaires de la pauvreté*, Paris: Presses Universitaires de France, 2005.

where it still existed, was at this time above all *outside* the sphere of paid employment. This is precisely what is changing in today's society of decline (see Chapter 4).

NORMAL LABOUR RELATIONS

The upheaval of social modernity was not confined to the introduction and expansion of the welfare state; it was both wider and deeper in scope. The whole system of paid employment was transformed, leading to an age of industrial mass production. The first decades of the twentieth century saw the rise of gigantic chemical, steel and automobile factories. Henry Ford was the first to systematically introduce the assembly line in his workshops. He took up the basic idea of scientific management that Frederick Taylor had developed: he systematically separated mental and manual work, and applied a strict division of labour to all processes, which were standardized and hierarchically managed. Regulation theory, following Italian Marxist Antonio Gramsci, characterized this mode of production as 'Fordism'. Though developing in the 1920s, it reached its maximum scope only after 1945.[12] This economic model is characterized by a long-term logic of production and less by the external demands of the market. Mass production meant simultaneous participation in mass consumption. Rising wages and falling prices for consumer goods enabled German working-class families for the first time to afford automobiles, televisions and washing machines, which had previously been only within the means of a privileged minority.

12 Cf., among others, Michel Aglietta, *A Theory of Capitalist Regulation: The US Experience*, London: Verso, 2001; idem, *Le capitalisme de demain*, Paris: Fondation Saint Simon, 1998; Robert Boyer, *The Regulation School: A Critical Introduction*, New York: Columbia University Press, 1990; Joachim Hirsch and Roland Roth, *Das neue Gesicht des Kapitalismus*, Hamburg: VS, 1986; Werner Abelshauser, *Deutsche Wirtschaftsgeschichte seit 1945*, Munich: C. H. Beck, 2004.

These developments culminated in the establishment of so-called 'normal labour relations'.[13] Under pre-Fordist industrial capitalism, labour had basically been almost completely flexible and insecure. Normal labour relations, on the other hand, typically included permanent full-time employment, with job security and social insurance, as the precondition for a self-directed life; they also included the possibility of collective participation in the shaping of labour relations themselves. A condition in which workers were subject to insecurity, anxiety and disorder was replaced by the basic pillars of certainty, predictability and relative social security. Work was now endowed with a certain degree of dignity. The Bavarian-Saxon *Zukunftkommission* ('Committee on the Future') reported that in 1970, 84 per cent of all jobs were subject to normal labour relations.[14]

All of this, of course, took place against the backdrop of an extremely low rate of unemployment. In those years, the supply of labour power was scarce, and in many countries, Germany in particular, there was almost full employment. Trade unions gained new strength, and almost 80 per cent of employees were covered by collective wage agreements. Low unemployment induced employers, who at that time were not yet driven by principles of 'shareholder value', to apply particular personnel strategies. Even in areas of low-skilled work, this phase saw so-called 'closure processes' in company labour markets.[15] This means that companies offered even unskilled workers long-term employment prospects, with the possibility of gaining skills and promotions within the company— not least in exchange for their know-how and loyalty.

---

13 Ulrich Mückenberger, 'Die Krise des Normalarbeitsverhältnisses', *Zeitschrift für Sozialreform* 31(7–8), 1985, 415–34.

14 Cf. Kommission für Zukunftsfragen Bayern-Sachsen, *Erwerbstätigkeit und Arbeitslosigkeit in Deutschland. Entwicklung, Ursachen, Maßnahmen*, Bonn, 1996, 96.

15 Werner Sengenberger, *Struktur und Funktionsweise von Arbeitsmärkten. Die Bundesrepublik Deutschland im internationalen Vergleich*, Frankfurt: Campus, 1987.

Even at this time, however, there existed forms of atypical employment, principally among women. Insofar as they were not housewives, they worked in less protected jobs with lower skill levels, or as supporting family members in small enterprises.[16] Shortly before the end of Germany's economic miracle, in 1966–67, the first recession of the post-war years, part-time workers only represented 6.5 per cent of all workers.[17] By 1970, this proportion had already risen to 9.3 per cent. The main forms of precarious employment today, however, either did not exist at that time, or did so very little. Subcontracted work was completely banned until 1972, and still after this was strictly regulated. Until 1985, dismissal was possible only under very strict conditions, and part-time employment existed only to an extremely negligible extent.[18]

THE DEVELOPMENT OF SOCIAL AND ECONOMIC CITIZENSHIP RIGHTS

The changes in working conditions sketched out above, along with the development of the welfare state, amounted to a fundamental change in class society. In pre-capitalist societies, classes such as patricians and plebeians, or lords and serfs, were based on a clearly defined status hierarchy. Each class possessed its own customs and allocated rights, which in turn

16 Cf. Nicole Mayer-Ahuja, *Wieder dienen lernen? Vom westdeutschen 'Normalarbeitsverhältnis' zu prekärer Beschäftigung seit 1973*, Berlin: Edition Sigma, 2003.
17 On these figures, cf. Walter Müller-Jentsch and Peter Ittermann, *Industrielle Beziehungen. Daten, Zeitreihen, Trends 1950–1999*, Frankfurt: Campus, 2000. In 1970, 90 per cent of part-time workers were women—an indication that for many women, part-time work was a way of emancipating themselves from their role as just housewives (cf. Mayer-Ahuj, *Wieder dienen lernen?*).
18 Unfortunately there is scarcely any firm historical data on 'normal labour relations'. Among other things, this is because their significance only reached the awareness of social scientists and statisticians when they were diagnosed to be in crisis—around the mid-1980s.

divided it from other classes. In modern class society, legal inequality and its privileges gradually disappeared. The Declaration of the Rights of Man and of the Citizen, proclaimed in 1789 in the wake of the French Revolution, marked the birth of modern state citizenship and its corresponding rights. Men were now free and equal before the law, but not yet citizens with equal rights of participation. English sociologist T. H. Marshall described this as the emergence of 'civil rights'.[19] These rights were not in conflict with capitalist society, being even 'indispensable to a competitive market economy'.[20] Civil or citizenship rights initially included such fundamental liberal rights as freedom of speech, thought and belief, free elections, freedom of contract and the right to property, along with the introduction of a legal system before which all were equal. According to Marshall, civil rights developed in stages, the attainment of one such right providing the basis for the achievement of the next. Thus, civil citizenship rights were followed by political ones, including the right to participate in and influence political power. In particular, their kernel was the introduction of free and secret elections, along with universal suffrage. Marshall called the wider group of rights that arose in the twentieth century with the formation of the social state 'social citizenship rights'.[21] As a member of society, every citizen now could claim a basic level of security and participation (for example, through systems of social insurance that provided for sickness, unemployment, poverty and old age, as

19   T. H. Marshall, *Citizenship and Social Class*, London: Pluto, [1950] 1992.

20   Ibid., 20. Below, the concept 'citizenship rights' and 'civil rights' will be used as synonyms.

21   Heinz Bude has quite correctly noted that the evolutionary process, as T. H. Marshall analysed it with a view to British history, is not applicable to the German case. Here social rights partly preceded political ones (cf. Bude, *Die ironische Nation*, Hamburg: Hamburger Edition, 1999, 21).

well as education and health systems) that was 'not proportionate to the market value of the claimant'.[22] 'Surreptitiously',[23] Marshall also introduced the idea of 'industrial citizenship'. This is based less on a general citizenship status than on the collective rights of the employee; it involves a system of 'secondary industrial citizenship'[24] achieved by trade unions. In Germany's post-war period, this citizenship was expressed through workers' rights of participation and co-determination, in free collective bargaining and in the institutionalization of works councils.[25]

With the legal guarantee of collective bargaining, trade unions and employers became contracting parties. While this has led to conflict, it also established norms and achieved such things as the right to health and safety measures in the workplace, protection from arbitrary decisions on the part of management, paid holidays and sick leave,[26] as well as a minimum wage and of course the autonomous representation of workers' interests. Through works councils, workers became 'company citizens'.[27]

Social and economic citizenship moderate the tension between the political equality of citizens in the democratic state

22 Marshall, *Citizenship and Social Class*, 28.

23 Walther Müller-Jentsch, *Arbeit und Bürgerstatus. Studien zur sozialen und industriellen Demokratie*, Wiesbaden: VS, 2008, 18.

24 Marshall, *Citizenship and Social Class*, 40.

25 The legislation on collective bargaining was passed in 1949; it considerably reduced the influence of the state in comparison with the Weimar Republic.

26 In Germany, this was even regulated by compulsory payment of wages in case of sickness, which is a good historical example of the relationship between industrial and social rights. In 1956–57, these payments were won by the IG Metall trade union in one of the longest strikes of the post-war era.

27 Hermann Kotthoff, *Betriebsräte und Bürgerstatus. Wandel und Kontinuität betrieblicher Mitbestimmung*, Munich: Rainer Hampp, 1994, 179; Colin Crouch, 'The globalized economy: End to the age of industrial citizenship?' in Ton Wilthagen (ed.), *Advanced Theory in Labour Law and Industrial Relations in a Global Context*, Amsterdam: North-Holland, 151–64.

and the social inequality of a market society.[28] Civil rights do not underpin the market—they are not traded, they result from status. According to Marshall, the welfare state is not simply a useful market-correcting institution—it benefits and integrates the working class, endowing them with a new status in society: proletarians become citizens. Class society was not abolished by the development of civil rights, but a foundation of equal social rights was introduced. What arose was not a society of equals, but a society of people on equal terms.[29]

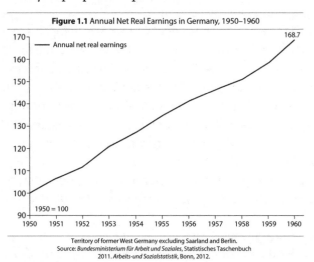

Figure 1.1 Annual Net Real Earnings in Germany, 1950–1960

Territory of former West Germany excluding Saarland and Berlin.
Source: *Bundesministerium für Arbeit und Soziales*, Statistisches Taschenbuch 2011. *Arbeits-und Sozialstatistik*, Bonn, 2012.

28   Dahrendorf is not wrong to call civil rights 'the key to the modern world' (*The Modern Social Conflict: The Politics of Liberty*, New Brunswick, NJ: Transaction Publishers, [1988] 2012, 35). A developed citizenship status, according to Axel Honneth, is a precondition for 'freedom's right', a social freedom that should 'guarantee the material conditions under which all individuals can exercise their freedoms more effectively' (*Freedom's Right: The Social Foundations of Democratic Life*, translated by Joseph Ganahl, Cambridge: Polity Press, 2014, 78).

29   Castel, *From Manual Workers to Wage Laborers*; idem, *L'insécurité sociale: qu'est-ce qu'être protégé?*; idem, *La montée des incertitudes. Travail, protections, statut de l'individu*; Axel Honneth, *Freedom's Right: The Social Foundations of Democratic Life*. Pierre Rosanvallon speaks of 'a society of similar individuals', *The Society of Equals*, Cambridge, MA: Harvard University Press, 2013.

Figure 1.2 Net Real Earnings and Labour Productivity in Germany, 1960–1969

——— Annual real net earnings
---- Labour productivity (GDP per employed person, constant prices)

1960 = 100

Territory of former West Germany.
Source: *Bundesministerium für Arbeit und Soziales*, Statistisches Taschenbuch
2011. *Arbeits-und Sozialstatistik*, Bonn, 2012.

SOCIAL ASCENT, THE ELEVATOR EFFECT, AND INDIVIDUALIZATION

As mentioned, post-war West Germany—like most European societies of that time—was also, in material terms, a society of social ascent. National income per head had tripled between 1800 and 1950, but from 1950 to 1989 it grew thirteen times faster than in the previous fifty years.[30] Net real wages tripled between 1950 and 1970. The average gross hourly wage of an industrial worker rose almost fivefold in the same time span.[31]

Diagrams 1.1 and 1.2 show the development of real wages from 1950 to 1969. What is striking here is not just the tremendous increase, but also how wages and labour productivity rose in parallel during the 1960s.[32] In this period, workers were able to

30   Rainer Geißler, *Die Sozialstruktur Deutschlands*, Wiesbaden: VS, 2014, 59ff.

31   Walther Müller-Jentsch and Peter Ittermann, *Industrielle Beziehungen. Daten, Zeitreihen, Trends 1950–1999*, Frankfurt: Campus, 2000.

32   Unfortunately no data exist for the 1950s.

increase their living standard almost in strict proportion to the growth of the value that they added.[33]

As standards of living improved, the differences between workers and white-collar employees tended to disappear and, as a consequence, so did the proletarian way of life. Dwellings became larger and more comfortable, people could afford refrigerators and televisions; from 1950 to 1965 the number of automobiles in West Germany rose from 2 million to 12 million. Working-class families were in a position for the first time to take long-distance holidays, whereas in previous decades—inasmuch as they had paid leave at all, a right that only existed from 1963— they had to remain at home or take holidays close by. Free time also rose continuously in these decades; particular milestones here being the introduction of the five-day week and the limitation of the working week to forty hours in the early 1970s.

Taken together, this amounted to de-proletarianization in terms of consumption, lifeworld, and even mentality.[34] By the end of the 1970s, 43 per cent of skilled workers already owned their own home. Rising material prosperity, above all the acquisition of consumer goods that had previously been reserved for the middle and upper classes and thus had an almost luxurious air, changed workers' self-valuation. 'This better life was also a collective rise into respectability'.[35]

---

33   This development was also seen as completely reasonable in the wage conflicts of that time (cf. Schulten 2004, 112ff.). These focused above all on the extent to which inflation should be taken into account in the evolution of wages.

34   On this, see Josef Mooser, *Arbeiterleben in Deutschland 1900– 1970*, Frankfurt: Suhrkamp, 1984; Hans-Ulrich Wehler, *Die neue Umverteilung. Soziale Ungerechtigkeit in Deutschland*, Munich: C. H. Beck, 2008, 153ff; Geißler, *Die Sozialstruktur Deutschlands*, 215ff.; and Werner Abelshauser, *Deutsche Wirtschaftsgeschichte seit 1945*, Munich: C. H. Beck, 2004, 327ff.

35   Mooser, *Arbeiterleben in Deutschland*, 227. This does not mean, however, that they perceived themselves as part of the middle class, particularly because within the workforce there continued to be great

Despite these developments, class barriers remained visible in many ways. The incomes of certain groups of workers fell in relation to the overall average, in some cases even considerably.[36] The Federal Republic's distribution of wealth has historically been extremely unequal. It may well have been possible for even the lower classes to put a little money aside, but essentially wealth remained concentrated in the topmost stratum.[37] General upward mobility, however, meant that differences of income and wealth lost their subjective significance now that it was possible for more people to lead a respectable life.

In conditions of social modernity, occupational and social mobility increased substantially. Opportunities for ascent multiplied, and paths of descent declined. In 1971, 41 per cent of the children of skilled workers rose into higher occupational classes, and by 1978 this figure had increased to 63 per cent.[38] Suddenly it was possible not just to climb out of the lower classes by a degree or two, but to jump several steps at once. The Federal Republic experienced a relative social opening, and this development continued until the turn of the century.[39] The expansion of the educational system in the 1960s and '70s was a central factor in this development. For the first time, large numbers of children from the working class were able to

---

differences in social situation and lifestyle (cf. Geißler, *Die Sozialstruktur Deutschlands*, 218ff.; Hans-Ulrich Wehler, *Bundesrepublik und DDR 1949–1990*, Munich: C. H. Beck, 2008, 153ff.).

36 Geißler, *Die Sozialstruktur Deutschlands*, 72ff.
37 Wehler, *Bundesrepublik und DDR 1949–1990*, 120ff.
38 Ibid., 161.
39 Reinhard Pollack, 'Soziale Mobilität', in Statistisches Bundesamt/ Wissenschaftszentrum Berlin für Sozialforschung, *Datenreport 2013. Ein Sozialbericht für die Bundesrepublik Deutschland*, Bonn: Bundeszentrale für politische Bildung, 2013, 189–97. At the same time, the increased frequency of occupational promotion should not be underestimated. The likelihood of remaining in the social class in which one was born continued to be high. Besides, social mobility is also a result of industrial change; simple occupations have become less common and knowledge-intensive jobs more frequent. This trend practically enforces (at least nominal) upward mobility. I shall return to this point in Chapter 4.

complete secondary and even university education. Nevertheless, there were limits to this educational ascent. Inequalities typical of social strata remained in place, as the number of working-class children who attended *Gymnasien* and universities remained below the numbers from the middle and upper strata. Compared with offspring of the middle and upper strata, working-class children generally lacked the requisite cultural capital—in other words, the ability learned already at an early age to appropriate and appear to exude a certain form of cultivation.[40] And higher educational qualifications in particular form the basis for a further professional ascent.[41] In other words, though such advances were widespread, they also remained restricted by social class.

The cumulative developments of social ascent marked a significant shift in working-class history.[42] Diagnosing this break has been the object of intense reflection from a number of perspectives. Ulrich Beck may be seen as one of its most prominent interpreters, coining the concept of the 'elevator effect' in the 1980s to describe the new social mobility.[43] In a society of economic growth—according to this metaphor—all strata, from wage earners through to the wealthy, stand together in an elevator and rise together. Inequalities between strata or social classes, in this scenario, are certainly not abolished, but they play a less significant role when everyone becomes more prosperous: 'Class society as a whole is taken a stage higher. There is a collective rise in income, education, mobility, rights, science, mass consumption—despite all the new and persisting inequalities.'[44]

40   Pierre Bourdieu, *Distinction: A Social Critique of the Judgement of Taste*, Cambridge, MA: Harvard University Press, [1979] 1996.

41   Geißler, *Die Sozialstruktur Deutschlands*, 313ff.

42   Wehler, *Bundesrepublik und DDR 1949–1990*, 154ff.

43   Ulrich Beck, *Risikogesellschaft*, Frankfurt am Main: Suhrkamp, 1986; idem, *Risk Society: Towards a New Modernity*, translated by Mark Ritter, London: SAGE, 1992.

44   Beck, *Risikogesellschaft*, 122; cf. Steffen Mau, *Lebenschancen. Wohin driftet die Mittelschicht?* Berlin: Suhrkamp, 2012.

Beck linked this diagnosis with one of the most influential social developments of modernity: individualization. In his view, the very foundations of society were being modernized: traditional class allegiances and identities were weakened and even almost dissolved. If, in early modernity, the labour market was the place where classes were constituted and collective experiences generalized into a class consciousness, in social modernity this effect was reversed: the collective success of the workers' movement paradoxically led to the rise of new and more individualist modes of behaviour. The regulated labour market and the welfare state, which neoliberals have repeatedly stereotyped as undermining freedom, was in actual fact a central precondition for the realization of the modern individual.[45] Each individual wage earner palpably profited from successful collective bargaining (a success that could be read on their payslip), even if they did not take part themselves in collective actions. Unemployment insurance and protection from dismissal were collective rights, but they were generally claimed individually—you went to the job centre or to court by yourself, for example. Previously, people who grew up in the working class adopted its mentalities, values and lifestyles, and spent their time in its political organizations. Each person's biography was marked out for them by their family, neighbourhood or trade union, in which they were socialized into their class fate. Under social modernity, on the other hand, 'this overall experience and controlling tie of a class-culturally marked social milieu was frequently broken . . . New material and temporal development possibilities coincide with the seductions of mass consumption, and cause the contours of traditional life forms and social milieus to disappear.'[46]

But Beck exaggerated a diagnosis of his time that was on

45   Lutz Leisering, 'Sozialstaat und Individualisierung', in Jürgen Friedrichs (ed.), Die Individualisierungs-These, Opladen: Leske+Budrich, 1998.
46   Beck, Risikogesellschaft, 129, 124.

the whole very pertinent. He maintained that, basically, 'capitalism *without* classes' had arisen.[47] Though social inequality continued to exist, this was in a certain sense 'beyond status and class', and hence simply between individuals and groups.[48] Beck was not alone in this assessment, and not even the first to formulate it. As far back as 1949, Theodor Geiger had spoken of a 'class society in the melting pot',[49] and later, Helmut Schelsky believed he had identified a 'levelled middle-class society'.[50] Generally in German sociology, however, and in stark contrast to the situation in the English-speaking countries, the twentieth century saw a pronounced tendency to deliver obituaries of class society—as if classes would vanish with the dismissal of the concept.

The working class as it had existed for more than a century found itself in the late twentieth century in a period of dramatic change, even long-term erosion. Yet this was not simply a result of social ascent and change in lifestyle; many other factors came into play. Traditional industries successively lost importance. Classical factories still existed, yet an increasing number of people worked in the public sector or in service companies where white-collar jobs were dominant. Even in manufacturing plants, holistic concepts involving the autonomy of individual workers or teams began to replace hierarchically organized, heteronomous activities.[51] Class society as such, however, did not disappear; it remained, precisely

47   Beck, *Risk Society*, 88.
48   Ibid., 91.
49   Theodor Geiger, *Die Klassengesellschaft im Schmelztiegel*, Köln: Kiepenheuer, 1949.
50   Helmut Schelsky, *Auf der Suche nach Wirklichkeit: Gesammelte Aufsätze*, Düsseldorf/Köln: Diederichs, 1965.
51   Horst Kern and Michael Schumann, *Industriearbeit und Arbeiterbewusstsein. Eine empirische Untersuchung über den Einfluss der aktuellen technischen Entwicklung auf die industrielle Arbeit und das Arbeiterbewusstsein*, Frankfurt: Suhrkamp, 1985; Claus Offe, *Contradictions of the Welfare State*, London: Hutchinson, 1984.

through changing—in a differentiated form and now with individualist characteristics.[52]

THE TRANSFORMATION OF SOCIAL CONFLICT

The extension of citizenship rights, the elevator effect, and the visible integration of the working class led Beck to a further radical thesis, which followed directly from his diagnosis: if there were no classes, then there was no class conflict. For Beck, the focus of conflict was no longer vertical, between above and below; its new forms rather involved both the side effects of industrialization (above all, environmental pollution and ecological risk) and the results of individualizing the lifeworld. His diagnosis was, in this respect, a theoretical foundation for new social movements (see below, Chapter 5), which challenged the notion of the workers' movement as the central emancipatory or oppositional collective actor.

Beck's view of the transformation of social conflict was shrewd and precise, recognizing and describing as he did the new ecological risks and new social movements; yet he strikingly failed to recognize the continued relevance of class structures. It is true that he frequently mentioned the continuity of social inequalities, yet the class foundation of these was, in his view, abolished by the elevator effect.[53] He threw

---

52 Cf. Klaus Dörre, *Risikokapitalismus. Zur Kritik von Ulrich Becks 'Weg in eine andere Moderne'*, Marburg: Verlag Arbeiterbewegung und Gesellschaftswissenschaften, 1987; Michael Vester, Peter von Oertzen, Heiko Geiling, Thomas Herman and Dagmar Müller, *Soziale Milieus im gesellschaftlichen Strukturwandel. Zwischen Integration und Ausgrenzung*, Frankfurt: Suhrkamp, 2001.

53 But Beck left a back door open: 'The factors that individualized classes yesterday and today, may also tomorrow or the day after, under other circumstances—such as radically sharpening inequalities [. . .] turn into new kinds of "class formation processes" that presuppose the individualization attained, now however precisely no longer understandable in traditional terms' (Beck, *Risikogesellschaft*, 134).

the baby out with the bathwater, as it were, by extrapolating his analysis too far.

Ralf Dahrendorf, one of the doyens of post-war German sociology, took a different view. Dahrendorf was concerned above all with the *transformation* of social and class conflicts. The essential point of his theory is that in every society class conflicts exist, since in every society there is domination.[54] As neither a Marxist nor a leftist of any description, he was much less inhibited in devoting himself to such questions.

The panorama that Dahrendorf sketched was very different from that of Beck, despite significant concurrence in their basic approach.[55] Dahrendorf did indeed find that class conflict had lost its 'absolute quality' as a result of the construction of social citizenship rights, since there were no longer qualitative differences between people, only quantitative ones.[56] Collective bargaining, co-determination and trade union participation had led to an 'institutionalization of the class antagonism'.[57] This was

54   Ralf Dahrendorf, *Class and Class Conflict in Industrial Society*, Stanford: Stanford University Press, 1959; idem, *The Modern Social Conflict: The Politics of Liberty*.

55   Dahrendorf formulated his analytical starting point in the form of a simple question, which accepted Marx's finding that while the wage earner is a free legal subject, he only possesses his own labour-power (*Capital* Volume One, 280): 'What does "free and equal" mean if one party needs labor to survive whereas the other can pick and choose, hire and fire?' (*The Modern Social Conflict*, 36).

56   Jürgen Habermas argued similarly. As the 'political content of mass democracy' (*The Theory of Communicative Reason, Volume Two: Lifeworld and System: A Critique of Functionalist Reason*, translated by Thomas McCarthy, Boston: Beacon Press, 1987, 347), the welfare state partially pacified the antagonism between capital and labour, and legitimized the market-economy order. By way of the welfare state, said Habermas, social-integrative forces are focused 'at the point of the structurally most probable conflict—in order all the more effectively to keep it latent' (Jürgen Habermas, *Legitimation Crisis*, London: Heinemann, 1976, 37f).

57   Dahrendorf, *The Modern Social Conflict*, 105–08. As early as 1949, Theodor Geiger formulated this similarly ('institutionalization of class opposition'; *Die Klassengesellschaft im Schmelztiegel*, Cologne: Kiepenheuer, 182ff.).

pivotal in the dialectic of the development of social citizenship rights. The more effective workers were in liberating themselves from the risks of the market, the more the motor of this liberation, class position and class conflicts lost importance:

> Once citizenship rights are almost general, disparities of realms of life take the place of generalized demands for civil, political or social rights. People fight for the recognition of comparable worth for women, or against pollution, or even for disarmament, but they do so from a common basis of citizenship.[58]

Similarly, in *The Modern Social Conflict*, Dahrendorf warned that it would be premature to declare class antagonism as overcome: 'It is not easy (yet?) to tell what form the conflicts arising from a new exclusion will take.'[59] Even basic civil rights that are formally guaranteed by law and constitution can in the end be restricted in their individual exercise by economic weakness and lack of education. Against the backdrop of the neoliberal policies that began with Ronald Reagan and Margaret Thatcher in the 1980s, though Dahrendorf still saw social modernity and social citizenship as stable, he maintained that the 'great historical force for change' in social modernity 'at some point in the 1960s or '70s . . . lost its momentum because the principle which it strove to

---

58 Dahrendorf, *The Modern Social Conflict*, 154. Neo-Marxist authors including Claus Offe had already argued similarly to the liberal Dahrendorf. They also proceeded from the assumption that class conflict had been partially appeased but was not obsolete. In what continued to be a class-rooted society, however, disparities tended to increase in scale (Joachim Bergmann, Gerhardt Brandt, Klaus Körber, Ernst Theodor Mohl and Claus Offe, 'Herrschaft, Klassenverhältnis und Schichtung', in Theodor W. Adorno (ed.), *Spätkapitalismus oder Industriegesellschaft? Verhandlungen des 16. Deutschen Soziologentages vom 8. bis 11. April 1968 in Frankfurt am Main*, Stuttgart: Enke, 1969; Offe, *Strukturprobleme des kapitalistischen Staates*, 1969.

59 Ralf Dahrendorf, *The Modern Social Conflict*, 46.

establish had become widely accepted'.[60] In short, with the disappearance of this historical force, questions of class may again become relevant for social conflicts.

THE DIALECTIC OF SUCCESS AND THE
EXHAUSTION OF SOCIAL MODERNITY

For the majority of wage earners, social modernity was an era of progress, yet melancholic nostalgia for a lost normality ('everything used to be better') ignores its ambivalent character. In almost all spheres of society—work, family and state—contradictions ran deep.

The state had taken on an *interventionist* role. As theorists had discussed as early as the 1970s, the state increasingly saw itself as protecting society from the destructive power of the market. In their view, the state under social modernity was a 'late capitalist' one,[61] functionally necessary because the logic of the market led firms to strategies that would destabilize the whole system unless counter-measures were taken. The increasing differentiation and rising socialization of production and reproduction thus made necessary an arrangement that undertook essential social coordination over and above a market allocation that was inadequate.[62] Authors such as Claus Offe and Jürgen Habermas counted among these the elaboration of infrastructure,

---

60 Dahrendorf, *The Modern Social Conflict*, 108f; Claus Offe, *Strukturprobleme des kapitalistischen Staates*, revised edition, Frankfurt: Campus, 2006.

61 Cf. on this the discussion in Jens Borchert and Stephan Lessenich, 'Lang leben die Strukturprobleme!', introduction to Offe, *Strukturprobleme des kapitalistischen Staates*. revised edition, 11–22, and Oliver Nachtwey, 'Legitimationsprobleme im Spätkapitalismus revisited', in Karina Becker, Lars Gertenbach, Henning Laux and Tilmann Reitz (eds), *Grenzverschiebungen des Kapitalismus: Umkämpfte Räume und Orte des Widerstands*, Frankfurt: Campus, 2010, 359–79.

62 Cf. Offe, *Strukturprobleme des kapitalistischen Staates*, revised edition, Chapter 3; Jürgen Habermas, *Legitimation Crisis*, 50ff.

welfare-state obligations, the creation of opportunities for the investment of surplus capital, countercyclical policy and—an increasingly urgent task from the 1970s—measures of environmental protection. Yet such permanent intervention by the state produced side effects, especially problems of legitimation.[63] Social security also included social control, the reorientation of reproduction brought social inequalities, and integration involved the normalization and standardization of social life. The welfare state also engendered a new bureaucracy, in which individual problems such as unemployment or sickness were 'generalized, formalized, and turned into impersonal cases in a filing system'.[64] Conflicts between state, employers and trade unions were settled in the context of 'corporatist' regulation. This consensus-oriented procedure brought the conflicting parties to the negotiating table, where common interests (above all, Germany's economic competitiveness) were discussed and social exchange deals brokered. For example, trade unions were willing to accept a moderate wage policy in exchange for welfare state expansion. Corporatism was frequently successful in securing social peace and economic development, but it also drained life away from the democratic process; deals took the place of debates, consensus the place of conflict, and so on.[65] The rule of employers' associations, trade unions and the welfare-state bureaucracy also endangered democracy, since citizens increasingly tended to remain outside the decision-making process.

Another excluded group were the so-called 'guest workers', who are underscored as having played a crucial role in Germany's spectacular social and economic ascent that was possible for the majority of working people at this time. This ascent ultimately

---

63   Here the analyses of Beck, Dahrendorf and the representatives of critical theory largely coincide (cf. Beck, *Risk Society*; Habermas, *Legitimation Crisis*; Offe, *Strukturprobleme*).

64   Dahrendorf, *The Modern Social Conflict*, 128.

65   Cf. ibid., 104ff.

rested in large part on an 'underclass' of migrant workers,[66] who had been brought to Germany for repetitive and dirty work in a prospering industry, and then later, once the long economic boom was over, were coolly sent back home. Without them, there would not have been 'normal labour relations' in the form that we knew.

These normal labour relations were above all to be found in medium and large firms, in which—compared with today—there was a relatively homogeneous workforce. Work here was still hard, standardized and authoritarian, but those employed accepted it as adequately compensated by increased social security. The sharper separation between work activity and private life even made this alienated work seem bearable.

Both inside and outside the firm, normal labour relations contributed to normalizing capitalism. 'Nonconformist' ways of work and life, the option to work creatively, less or even not at all, initially appealed only to a small minority.

Women remained in an underprivileged position under social modernity. The 'male breadwinner model'[67] brought with it new inequalities. Since housewives were not employed, they were excluded from many insurance benefits, or minimally covered by these. The care and reproductive work that women performed in the household was neither paid nor integrated into the official order of social modernity.

In other words, while social modernity attenuated the conflicts and risks induced by vertical inequalities (between classes), it reproduced new inequalities on the horizontal level— weighing especially on women and migrants. This brought to light a paradox of equality or equal rights. Never before had the overwhelming majority of people under capitalism attained such

---

66   Abelshauser, *Deutsche Wirtschaftsgeschichte seit 1945*, 315ff.

67   Jane Lewis, 'The Decline of the Male Breadwinner Model: Implications for Work and Care', *Social Politics: International Studies in Gender, State and Society* 8(2), 152–69.

a secure position. Yet precisely through this increased equality, inequalities between women and men emerged more sharply, becoming, as Beck formulated it, 'inextinguishably visible'.[68] As we shall see, in today's society of downward mobility the struggle against the disadvantaging of women has induced a certain complicity with a new structuration of class. Never before have women had such equal rights on the labour market, yet at the same time the vertical class differences between women are growing ever greater.

Until well into the second half of the twentieth century, social modernity appeared vital and imbued with an inner dynamic; the 1960s saw 'the greatest push forward of an historically unmatched rise in standard of living, the convergence of forms of life between social strata, and increased social mobility'.[69] The welfare state further expanded, and the late 1970s marked its 'historical zenith'.[70]

At that point in time, the welfare state was even accepted well within the ranks of Christian Democrats and Liberals as the natural complement to Keynesian capitalism. Social expenditure and higher wages were ultimately also seen as economic stimulants.[71] From that point on, however, social modernity increasingly eroded. Its institutions, compromises and norms, and above all the features we have just analysed—the welfare state, normal working conditions, social citizenship and social ascent—were hollowed out, and are still being so.

68   Beck, *Risikogesellschaft*, 129.

69   Mooser, *Arbeiterleben in Deutschland*, 228.

70   Stephan Lessenich, *Die Neuerfindung des Sozialen. Der Sozialstaat im flexiblen Kapitalismus*, Bielefeld: transcript, 2008, 18.

71   Cf. Christine Buci-Glucksmann and Göran Therborn, *Der sozialdemokratische Staat. Die 'Keynesianisierung' der Gesellschaft*, Hamburg: VSA, 1982; George Vobruba (ed.), *Der wirtschaftliche Wert der Sozialpolitik*, Berlin: Duncker & Humblot, 1989; idem, *Politik mit dem Wohlfahrtsstaat*, Frankfurt: Suhrkamp.

2

Capitalism (Almost) without Growth

No lesser figures than former World Bank president and US treasury secretary Larry Summers and Nobel Prize economist Paul Krugman recently chose the dramatic term 'secular stagnation' to characterize the present phase of capitalist development. They feared that the industrial countries of the West were faced with a persistent period of very low economic growth. Capitalism (almost) without growth could in their view become the 'new normal'.[1] This diagnosis did not come from nowhere; almost a

---

1 Lawrence Summers, 'Why stagnation might prove to be the new normal', *Financial Times*, 15 December 2013, Paul R. Krugman, 'Secular stagnation, coalmines, bubbles, and Larry Summers', *New York Times Blog*, 16 November 2013, krugman.blogs.nytimes.com (accessed February 2016). Wolfgang Streeck has recently offered a similar opinion (see *Buying Time*, translated by Patrick Camiller, London: Verso, 2014). On the neo-Marxist side, this diagnosis—generally ignored, of course, in the mainstream media—had already been proposed by John Bellamy Foster and Fred Magdoff, *The Great Financial Crisis: Causes and Consequences*, New York: Monthly Review Press, 2009; Gopal Balakrishnan, 'Speculations on the Stationary State, *New Left Review* II(59), 2009; Karl Beitel, 'The Rate of Profit and the Problem of Stagnant Investment: A Structural Analysis of Barriers to Accumulation and the Spectre of Protracted Crisis', *Historical Materialism* 17(4), 2009, 66–100.

decade into its greatest crisis, the global economy has still not completely recovered.[2] Scepticism is growing even among economic actors: the head of HSBC, one of the world's largest banks, forecasts that there will be no return to a self-sustaining growth path in the foreseeable future. He rather sees the industrial countries as having reached the end of a long era of expansion, and likewise expectts a period of stagnation. The impulse of the past few decades—given by the liberalization of world trade, technological innovations, better educated 'human capital' and the integration of women into the workforce—has been exhausted.[3]

The concept of secular stagnation originally goes back to followers of John Maynard Keynes, who discussed the perspectives of 'mature economies' in the context of the Great Depression of the 1930s.[4] Authors such as Alvin Hansen, Josef Steindl and Michał Kalecki[5] assumed that economic growth in industrial

----

2   As far as the crisis of recent years is concerned, there have been several excellent analyses. Since this is not the central project of the present book, I refer to the following as important treatments of the subject: Elmar Altvater, *Der große Krach—oder die Jahrhundertkrise von Wirtschaft und Finanzen von Politik und Natur*, Münster: Westfälisches Dampfboot, 2010; David McNally, *Global Slump: The Economics and Politics of Crisis and Resistance*, Oakland: Spectre, 2011; Klaus Dörre, 'The New *Landnahme*: Dynamics and Limits of Financial Market Capitalism', in Klaus Dörre, Stephan Lessenich and Hartmut Rosa, *Sociology, Capitalism, Critique*, London: Verso, 2014; David Harvey, *Seventeen Contradictions and the End of Capitalism*, London: Profile Books, 2014; John Bellamy Foster and Fred Magdoff, *The Great Financial Crisis*, New York: Monthly Review, 2009; Graham Turner, *No Way to Run an Economy: Why the System Failed and How to Put It Right*, London: Pluto, 2009.

3   Stephen D. King, *When the Money Runs Out: The End of Western Affluence*, New Haven: Yale University Press, 2013.

4   Cf. Karl Pribram, *A History of Economic Reasoning*, Baltimore: Johns Hopkins University Press, 1983, 509ff.

5   Alvin Hansen, *Full Recovery or Stagnation?* New York: W. W. Norton, 1938; Josef Steindl, *Maturity and Stagnation in American Capitalism*, Oxford: Oxford University Press, 1952; Michał Kalecki, *Theory of Economic Dynamics*, New York: Monthly Review, [1954] 2008.

societies would gradually come to a halt. They saw the reasons for this in demographic developments, the exhaustion of natural resources, a slowdown in technical progress, a lack of readiness for risky entrepreneurial initiatives, political frictions, and not least a factor that Keynes described in his *General Theory of Employment, Interest, and Money* as the 'marginal efficiency of capital'.[6]

The idea that the economy can stagnate for very long periods of time, however, is still older. It is already found with the fathers of political economy, thinkers such as Adam Smith, David Ricardo, Thomas Malthus, John Stuart Mill and Karl Marx. Notions of equilibrium also played a central role for them, though they had a different view of themselves than do present-day economists, who present their profession as an exact science. They considered their discipline 'political economy', which required analysing the stages of capitalism and its crises. Before we turn to the historical genesis of post-growth capitalism, we need first to sketch out an alternative political economy of stagnation.

THE POLITICAL ECONOMY OF POST-GROWTH CAPITALISM

The early classics of political economy were particularly concerned with the conditions of production and distribution of goods and incomes, the role of labour, the investment of technology and resources, the evolution of population, and models of

---

6   John Maynard Keynes, *General Theory of Employment, Interest and Money*, Cambridge: Cambridge University Press, [1936] 2013, 135. Other writers of quite different provenance have developed similar theories: Marxist authors such as Paul A. Baran and Paul M. Sweezy, *Monopoly Capital: An Essay on the American Economic and Social Order*, New York: Monthly Review, [1966] 2009, but also Joseph Schumpeter, the sceptical admirer of capitalism (*Capitalism, Socialism and Democracy*, London: Routledge, [1942] 2010).

capital accumulation.[7] Whereas the models of neoclassical theory that arose later (and were basically statistical) expected technological progress to yield an unending impulse for economic growth, the classics were far more sceptical about long-term economic development—a fact that is often ignored today. Independently of the particular reasons that they adduced (general satiation of the market, over-rapid population growth, exhaustion of available agricultural land), Smith, Ricardo, Malthus, Mill and of course Marx all expected in some form or other a transition to a stationary state. They all shared the assumption of diminishing returns, which would lead to a slowdown in capital accumulation.[8]

The most famous and still-influential approach came from Marx. Marx admired capitalism for its internal dynamism, the way it had unleashed economic forces to a degree previously unknown. He also assumed, however, that the rate of profit—in other words, the relationship between profit and capital advanced—tended to fall, bringing recurrent crisis and stagnation. The reason for this, according to Marx, lies in the competition between firms, which forces them to rationalize production, raise productivity, and economize on labour-power in relation to the investment of capital. This is completely rational from the standpoint of the firm, but has damaging effects on the economy

7 Cf. Mark Blaug, *Economic Theory in Retrospect*, Cambridge: Cambridge University Press, 1992; Pribram, *History of Economic Reasoning*.

8 Whereas Malthus analysed the long-term perspectives for growth with gloomy pessimism, Mill looked forward to the 'stationary state', the concept used at this time, believing that such a situation would finally provide the opportunity to consider the qualitative aspects of growth. In this way he foreshadowed the modern critique of growth (Gareth Dale, 'Critiques of growth in classical political economy: Mill's stationary state and a Marxian response', *New Political Economy* 18(3), 2012). David Ricardo predicted a fall in the rate of profit on the basis of an increasing scarcity of land, a theme that Marx later took up from the perspective of the labour theory of value.

as a whole. In the end, all firms are forced to bow to this logic, and the number of workers employed rises more slowly than the investment of capital. For Marx, labour is the origin of profit, the source of surplus-value, without which the system cannot survive.[9] If the labour performed and the resulting profit decline in relation to capital, then in the end the rate of profit falls.[10]

Controversies about the internal logic, coherence and validity of Marx's theory of the falling rate of profit continue to this day.[11] For present purposes, however, it is irrelevant whether Marx's theory is correct, in whole or in part. Analysis of postgrowth capitalism is an empirical question, not a scholastic one. The falling rate of profit was also recognized as a tendential development by Smith, Ricardo, Mill, and later by Keynes and Schumpeter, even if described with other concepts.[12] Marx was simply the writer who elaborated this assumption systematically and made it central to his theory of crises. More recent studies conducted in the English-speaking world, as I shall show in the next section, indicate that since the 1960s profit rates have indeed declined.[13]

9   Cf. Marx, *Capital* Volume One, Harmondsworth: Penguin, [1867] 1976.

10   At the same time, Marx recognized a series of countervailing forces at work, such as a rise in the rate of exploitation, technological progress, and the falling cost of machinery, which could lead the rate of profit to rise (cf. Marx *Capital* Volume Three, Harmondsworth: Penguin, [1894] 1981).

11   Cf., among many others, Michael C. Howard and John E. King, *A History of Marxian Economics, Vol. 1: 1883–1929*, Basingstoke: Macmillan, 1989; idem, *A History of Marxian Economics*, Vol. 2: *1929–1990*, Basingstoke: Macmillan, 1992; Michael Heinrich, *Die Wissenschaft vom Wert. Die Marxsche Kritik der politischen Ökonomie zwischen wissenschaftlicher Revolution und klassischer Tradition*, Münster: Westfälisches Dampfboot, 1999.

12   Pribram, *History of Economic Reasoning*; Blaug, *Economic Theory in Retrospect*.

13   Actual economic development has therefore led to new attention being paid to Marx's crisis theory, even on the part of non-Marxian

THE LONG RISE OF NEOLIBERALISM

The first thirty years after the Second World War were the golden age of post-war capitalism—a period of previously unknown prosperity. Social modernity was able to develop, based on a broad consensus around the embedding of the market.[14] Growth rates above 5 per cent were not rare in this period. Between 1950 and 1973, the world economy grew by an average of 4.9 per cent, and in Western Europe by 4.79 per cent.[15] Only later would it become clear how exceptional this historical constellation truly was.[16]

It is impossible to give an exact date when all of this began to change, but if one point stands out as marking the turn, it was 15 August 1971. On that day, US president Richard Nixon buried the post-war economic order by abolishing the convertibility of the US dollar into gold. The result was an end to the Bretton Woods system of fixed exchange rates. The whole international order of currency and trade had to be reorganized, and the new system of flexible exchange rates produced repeated instabilities. There was already a cyclical economic downturn in the late 1960s, and in 1966–67 Germany witnessed a recession for the first time since the Second World War. In 1973–74, a new crisis affected the global economy, and in 1975 the greatest post-war recession struck the whole of Europe (see Diagram 2.1). These years saw the start of what the American historian Robert Brenner has called the 'long downturn' of the world economy.[17]

writers such as Wolfgang Streeck (*Buying Time*, 11ff.) and Hans-Werner Sinn, '300 Milliarden Euro Verluste durch Niedrigzinsen' (interview), *Frankfurter Allgemeine Zeitung*, 5 December 2014.

14   Tony Judt, *Postwar: A History of Europe Since 1945*, New York: Vintage, 2010.

15   Angus Maddison, *The World Economy: Historical Statistics*, Paris: OECD, 2003.

16   Werner Plumpe, *Wirtschaftskrisen: Geschichte und Gegenwart*, Munich: C. H. Beck, 2010.

17   Robert Brenner, *The Boom and the Bubble: The US in the World Economy*, London: Verso, 2003; idem, 'The Economics of Global

Average growth fell from around 4 per cent in the early 1970s to below 2 per cent in the recent past (cf. Diagram 2.2). The German economy, which in 2003 the *Economist* called 'the sick man of the euro', is no exception, despite having been elevated in the last fifteen years as the new superstar. In the long run, it has performed only marginally better than the European average (cf. Diagram 2.1).

The first response to the growth problems of the 1970s was the Keynesian instrument of boosting demand. In 1971, President Nixon even famously declared, 'We are all Keynesians now!' Yet within a few years this recipe had a steadily decreasing effect, and the consensus began to crumble. Even social democratic proponents admitted that the increasing international integration of markets meant that Keynesian policies could no longer produce long-term effects[18] Economic theory, social interpretations and political preferences all underwent an epochal change, eventually becoming a 'landslide':[19] the gradual erosion of social modernity. A 'revolt of capital' began against the social and democratic embedding of capitalism, marking the start of the 'long turn to neoliberalism'.[20] The complex institutional regulation of post-war capitalism, with its dense network of labour legislation and state insurance, an embedded financial market along with comprehensive state-run sectors, now appeared to business as the 'main obstacle to capital accumulation'.[21]

Turbulence', *New Left Review* I (229), 1998.

18   Fritz Scharpf, *Crisis and Choice in European Social Democracy*, Ithaca: Cornell University Press, 1991. Crisis theorists of the early 1970s still assumed that Keynesianism had made economic fluctuations a relic of the past (Claus Offe, *Strukturprobleme des kapitalistischen Staates*, Frankfurt: Campus, [1972] 2006; Jürgen Habermas, *Legitimation Crisis*, Cambridge: Polity Press, [1973] 1988).

19   Eric Hobsbawm, *Age of Extremes: The Short Twentieth Century, 1914–1991*, London: Abacus, 1995.

20   Streeck, *Buying Time*, 26ff.; cf. also David Harvey, *A Brief History of Neoliberalism*, New York: Oxford University Press, 2007.

21   Dörre, 'The New *Landnahme*', 37.

Figure 2.1 GDP Development in Germany and the EU 15 (constant prices)

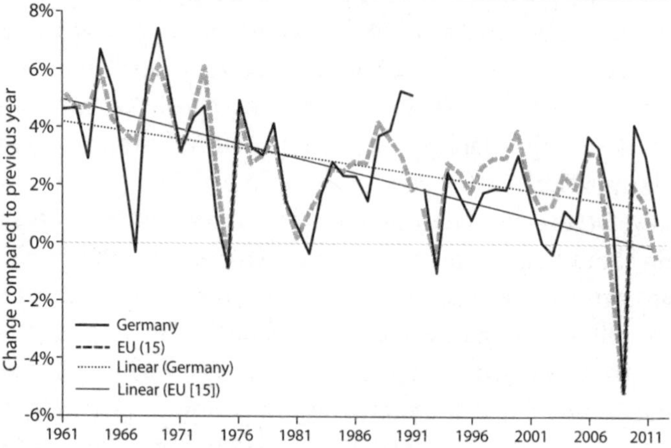

Source: Ameco, author's representation

Figure 2.2 GDP Development in the OECD countries (constant prices)

Source: OECD, author's representation

Instead of regulation, state intervention and demand adjustment in the Keynesian tradition, neoliberal economic ideas now gained traction—market-centred, with deregulation and supply-side policies following the ideas of Milton Friedman and Friedrich von Hayek. Capital now set itself a new goal: the 'expansion of its markets at home and abroad'.[22] External expansion involved a stronger integration of the global economy, and internal expansion a policy of what German sociologist Klaus Dörre calls *Landnahme* (land grabbing):[23] the opening of new markets in areas of society—health care, for example—that had previously not been subject to the logic of profit maximization. The results, however, were limited. The neoliberal strategy, as pursued, did bring about a rise in profit, but has been unable to halt the trend of post-growth capitalism.

Neoliberalism had a material foundation that played into the hands of the market fundamentalists: the internationalization of production and the global restructuring of the financial system. Many firms had of course long been active on international markets, selling their goods there or obtaining raw materials, and the crisis of the 1970s reinforced this activity. The majority of firms, however, retained a national base—not least because they were closely involved with the politics of their own countries and because the spatial fixing of capital is not easily undone—whereas international value production chains and market access both expanded and intensified.

As well as this, after the end of the Bretton Woods system, financial markets, particularly Wall Street, became the new central agents of economic power[24]—precisely *because* they were deregulated. This gave them massive manoeuvrability vis-à-vis nation states.[25] The financial sphere also underwent a tremendous acceleration: transactions were compressed in both time and space. Trade between Tokyo, Frankfurt and New York was

22   Streeck, *Buying Time*, 27.
23   Dörre, 'The New *Landnahme*'.
24   Peter Gowan, *The Global Gamble: Washington's Faustian Bid for World Dominance*, London: Verso, 1999.
25   Cf. David Held, Anthony McGrew, David Goldblatt and Jonathan Perraton, *Global Transformations: Politics, Economics and Culture*, Cambridge: Polity Press, 1999.

carried out in a few minutes, soon in nanoseconds. As the volume of trade steadily increased, actors and especially instruments traded diversified.

Value creation in financial markets differs from the traditional production economy by the outlay of money for means of production and labour-power, so as to obtain profit from the sale of the goods produced—the cycle that Marx described with the formula M–C–M'. Instead, financial instruments are bought in the expectation that they can later be sold at a higher price. The production of goods disappears, and money leads directly to more money (M–M').[26] The volume of transactions on financial markets is now more than 100 times greater than the turnover of goods and services. Meanwhile, these financial markets have partly become self-reinforcing cycles. By the generation of derivatives and bundled securities (what Marx called 'fictitious capital'), what are in practice simply betting slips can be bought and sold on the stock exchange.

The Austrian-born economist Rudolf Hilferding, Social Democratic finance minister under the Weimar republic of the 1920s, published the 1910 book *Finance Capital*,[27] which generalized the development of German banks. His diagnosis— according to which in the course of capitalist development, finance capital will increasingly dominate the productive economy and in the end also determine politics—has regained a certain plausibility today.

---

26   Foster and Magdoff, *The Great Financial Crisis*, 45. Thus, the financialization of capitalism leads to a return of the coupon clipper (Beitel, 'The Rate of Profit'; Costas Lapavitsas, 'Financialised Capitalism: Crisis and Financial Expropriation', *Historical Materialism* 17(2), 2009, 114–48). For the 'small saver', however, such an existence is scarcely possible, given persistently low interest rates.

27   Rudolf Hilferding, *Finance Capital: A Study in the Latest Phase of Capitalist Development*, London: Routledge, [1910] 2007.

WEAK INVESTMENT

In OECD countries over the last forty years, the average rate of growth has fallen significantly. If the global economy is still able to prosper to a certain extent, this is due above all to developing countries such as China, India and Brazil, which pull the average growth rate up.

According to Robert Brenner, the fall in the rate of profit in developed industrial countries is responsible for the 'long downturn' of the global economy.[28] There are still only a negligible number of empirical studies of the rate of profit.[29] Most of these, however, find that this rate has in fact fallen sharply since the 1960s. In the early 1980s it recovered somewhat, yet did not reach the level of the golden age.[30] Depending on the method of

---

28   Robert Brenner, *The Economics of Global Turbulence*, London: Verso, 2006.

29   The great majority of these study the rate of profit in the United States, since the world's largest and most advanced economy is taken as exemplary for the other industrial countries; the good data base for the United States also favours this focus. Robert Brenner was also able to demonstrate a falling rate of profit in Germany (see *The Boom and the Bubble*).

30   Results differ according to whether machinery is costed on the basis of the historical acquisition price or replacement price (Deepankar Basu and Ramaa Vasudevan, 'Technology, Distribution and the Rate of Profit in the US Economy: Understanding the Current Crisis', *Cambridge Journal of Economics* 37(1), 2013, 57–89). This controversy particularly bears on the effects of a long-term historical trend. Some authors expect a secular diminution in the rate of profit and also see this as the essential cause of the economic crisis since 2008 (Andrew Kliman, *The Failure of Capitalist Production*, London: Pluto, 2012). Others diagnose a stabilization of the rate of profit, and attribute the crisis above all to neoliberal policy (e.g., deregulation) (Gerald Duménil and Daniel Lévy, *The Crisis of Neoliberalism*, Cambridge, MA: Harvard University Press, 2011; David Harvey, *The Enigma of Capital—and the Crisis of Capitalism*, Oxford: Oxford University Press, 2010). It is unnecessary to come down on one side here, as for the long run they all more or less agree: profit rates have tended to fall since the golden age, even if they then stabilized. Only the extent of this decline is in dispute.

calculation, most studies find that the rate of profit, after recovering, began to fall again, and reached its lowest level since 1985 in 2001 following the bursting of the dot-com bubble. From 2001 it then rose strongly for a short while, even temporarily regaining the level of the 1950s. In this brief phase, firms could again show fantastic returns, as profits rose faster than GNP. After the crisis of 2008, however, the rate of profit again fell steeply (cf. Diagram 2.3).

Despite the mentioned brief rises in profit rates, as far as the long-term development of capitalism is concerned it is impossible to speak of structural recovery. Even in those periods in which profits rose, the rapid growth spurts of the past were absent. The reasons for this did not lie directly in the long-term fall in profit rates; rather, in an intermediate quantity—the problem of 'over-accumulation' of capital.[31]

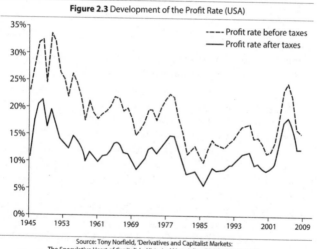

Figure 2.3 Development of the Profit Rate (USA)

---- Profit rate before taxes
—— Profit rate after taxes

Source: Tony Norfield, 'Derivatives and Capitalist Markets:
The Speculative Heart of Capital', in *Historical Materialism* 20 (1), 103–32, 2012.

Marx had declared the capitalists' motto to be: 'Accumulate, accumulate! That is Moses and the prophets! . . . Therefore save, save, *i.e.*, reconvert the greatest possible portion of surplus-value,

---

31   Cf. David Harvey, *The Limits to Capital*, London: Verso, 2006; idem, *The Enigma of Capital*.

or surplus-product into capital!'[32] According to several authors, they did this so comprehensively in recent decades that they have almost taken the bread from their own mouths, so to speak. Over-accumulation means that the owners of capital can no longer find any long-term investment possibilities in which to accrue the expected returns. There is in a certain sense *too much* capital. Even if sufficient profit can be obtained in the present, economic agents do not find it rewarding to reinvest for future business.[33]

At first sight, it seems strange that ever less investment would take place precisely today. All firms face significant pressure to innovate. At the same time, however, there are many reasons to harbour reservations in terms of long-term investment in productive capacity. Markets may be saturated, there may be too many suppliers, monopolistic or oligopolistic competition may prevent success in the market, or insufficient demand reduces the prospect of eventual *realization* of profits.

In contrast to the situation with the rate of profit, the decline in investment has been almost unbroken, once we abstract from fluctuations of the trade cycle.[34] This in turn has resulted in declining growth.

Diagram 2.4 shows how gross investment as a share of GDP surged during the golden age, globally but in the OECD countries as well. Since the start of the long downturn in 1973, on the other hand, it has continuously declined—most strikingly in the OECD countries. While the level of investment has fallen generally,

32   Marx, *Capital* Volume One, 742.

33   Against the neoclassical assumption, investments depend above all on expected profits. Cf. José A. Tapia Granados, 'Does investment call the tune? Empirical evidence and endogenous theories of the business cycle', *Research in Political Economy* 28, 2012, 229–40. Cf. Harvey, *The Enigma of Capital*; Alex Callinicos, *Bonfire of Illusions*, Cambridge: Polity Press, 2010.

34   In *The Failure of Capitalist Production*, economist Andrew Kliman assumes that the unbroken fall in profit rates simply means too little in the way of resources for investment. This approach, however, applies a constricted production paradigm that fails to include the gigantic financial wealth seeking profitable opportunities on the financial markets.

'mature' economies have particularly suffered. In Germany since the 1990s, net investment in relation to profits has also fallen considerably.[35] The next section analyses why firms still invest too little, despite increased competitive pressure.

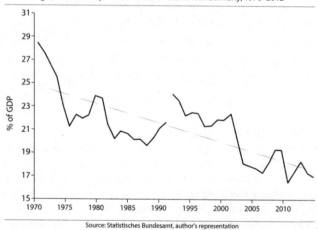

Figure 2.4 Development of the Gross Investment Ratio around the World and in the OECD countries, 1960–2012

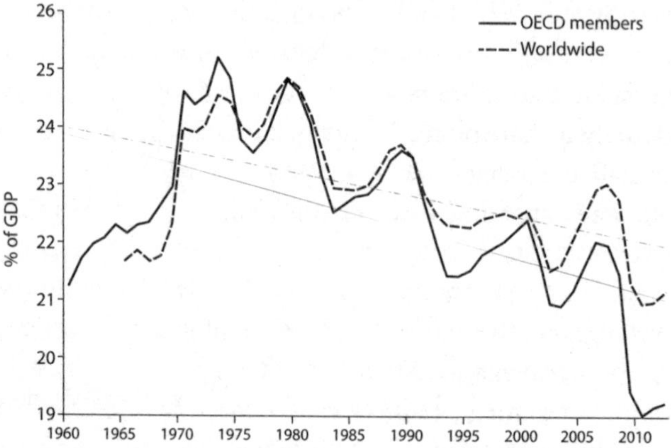

Source: World Bank, author's representation

Figure 2.5 Development of Gross Investment in Germany, 1970–2012

Source: Statistisches Bundesamt, author's representation

35   Diagram 2.5; see also Jan Priewe and Katja Rietzler, *Deutschlands nachlassende Investitionsdynamik 1991–2010. Ansatzpunkte für ein neues Wachstumsmodell*, Bonn: Friedrich-Ebert-Stiftung, 2010.

FINANCE CAPITALISM AND THE GROWTH CRISIS

In liberal capitalist countries (the UK, the US), firms used to finance themselves chiefly on the capital market, but from the 1980s, even in more strongly regulated economies, especially Germany, they also increasingly depended on the financial market, as the traditional model of close long-term connection between a firm and its bank eroded. As a result, large companies in particular became subject to a 'shareholder value' orientation in order to maximize their share price.[36] In the old, pre-finance capital model, an alternative strategy was still open to firms—growing the company and expanding its sales volume. This logic then changed substantially[37]—the culture of the long term broke down, and firms increasingly oriented themselves to securing maximum returns in the short term. If yields were previously seen as the *result* of economic performance, they have since become a *target*, presupposed by management, that steers the organization. The instruments of this new form of management are profit valuations, budgeting, indicators and the setting of profit aims, which are oriented to capital productivity and broken down by top managers according to division, factory, profit or cost centre, and even by individual work group. Major divisions of firms are outsourced. Small and medium-sized firms not directly dependent on the

36   Cf. Martin Höpner, *Wer beherrscht die Unternehmen? Shareholder Value, Managerherrschaft und Mitbestimmung in Deutschland*, Frankfurt: Campus, 2003; Paul Windolf (ed.), *Finanzmarkt-Kapitalismus. Analysen zum Wandel von Produktionsregimen. Sonderheft der Kölner Zeitschrift für Soziologie und Sozialpsychologie 45*, Wiesbaden: VS, 2005. There are certainly still a significant number of firms in family ownership, or otherwise escaping the logic of the financial markets. In recent decades, however, institutional actors have frequently obtained direct or indirect influence over these.

37   Cf. Klaus Dörre, 'Krise des Shareholder Value? Kapitalmarktorientierte Steuerung als Wettkampfsystem', in Klaus Kraemer and Sebastian Nessel (eds), *Entfesselte Finanzmärkte. Soziologische Analysen des modernen Kapitalismus*, Bielefeld: transcript, 2012.

financial markets have even applied this mechanism,[38] since many corporations directly transferred this competitive pressure to their suppliers. In short, financialization, meaning the encroachment of the logic of credit and capital markets onto the productive economy, is a totalizing aspect of the present-day economy, which in the end generalizes accounting standards (the power of statistics) as the basis of control.[39] Firms in almost all sectors have been gripped by the silent compulsion of finance capitalism.

I shall go on to show that the 'shareholder value' orientation became a major driving force in the growth of precarious work. Firstly, however, it is necessary to show how this contributed to a decline in investment, as long-term investment in the productive economy was eschewed as risky and capital was no longer patient, so stock market value had to be hiked up in the short term.[40]

It was precisely in key areas of production that profit rates were too low in terms of the new logic. Corporations then sought to increase their returns more relentlessly by trading in innovative financial products. Soon some of them drew a major part of their turnover from speculation outside their original trade: 'Even automobile companies became banks with ancillary automobile production.'[41] For many of them, this was 'the most convenient way of earning money'.[42] The expanding financial

38   Karina Becker, *Die Bühne der Bonität. Wie mittelständische Unternehmen auf die neuen Anforderungen des Finanzmarkts reagieren*, Berlin: Edition Sigma, 2009.

39   Cf. Colin Crouch, *The Knowledge Corrupters: Hidden Consequences of the Financial Takeover of Public Life*, Cambridge: Polity Press, 2015; Uwe Vormbusch, *Die Herrschaft der Zahlen: Zur Kalkulation des Sozialen in der kapitalistischen Moderne*, Frankfurt: Campus, 2012.

40   Systems of managerial reward were a driving force in this change, as salaries were linked not to the long-term development of the firm, but rather to present profit.

41   Christoph Deutschmann, 'Warum tranken die Pferde nicht', *Frankfurter Allgemeine Zeitung*, 25 September 2013.

42   Tony Norfield, 'Derivatives and capitalist markets: The speculative heart of capital', *Historical Materialism* 20(1), 2012, 103–32, 124.

markets were the place where, despite the problem of over-accumulation, money could still be made, since capital there was not fixed for long, but could be moved relatively frictionlessly to the next good investment, or even to developing countries. This also contributed to low investment in the OECD world, and hence to post-growth capitalism.

In the light of the analysis developed here, the frequently made criticism that recent economic problems have their cause above all in the 'uncoupling' of financial markets from a supposedly healthy 'real economy' proves largely false, or at least imprecise. The maximization of so-called 'arbitrage profits' by taking advantage of short-term price differences on financial markets has certainly been above all the business of hedge funds, banks or individual speculators, but the logic of finance capital also spread to productive firms. The underlying situation was the other way around: finance capitalism arose because profit rates in the real economy had fallen.

Another factor in the slowing of investment activity has to do with the 'shareholder value' orientation. Companies were mandated to report profits and pay dividends that were both as high as possible. This means that some of the profits from their own value creation were pumped into the financial markets rather than being reinvested. Over recent decades, this share of profits moved from production into the markets has steadily grown, particularly in the United States.[43] And since management likes to reduce risk wherever possible, the creative and cumulative innovation processes that are necessarily bound up with renewal and growth have weakened, since these come with a certain degree of uncertainty.[44] Finance capitalism was originally born as a reaction to the crisis of growth, before itself becoming a cause of this crisis in its own right.

43 Beitel, 'The rate of profit'; Foster and Magdoff, *The Great Financial Crisis.*

44 Deutschmann, 'Warum tranken die Pferde nicht?'

Even the emergence of new markets and technologies were unable to stop the decline in investment. High technology and microelectronics have transformed economic and social processes to an almost revolutionary degree.[45] But it remains an open question whether we are at the start of a 'new machine age', in which technological change, digitalization and economic connectivity will generate long-term advances in productivity that have a persistent effect on growth.[46] Machines will supposedly communicate with one another directly in the future, while 3D printers increasingly individualize production and robots take over more human activities. Moreover, it is suggested that new technologies will emerge every few years that act as 'game changers' on markets and often even expand on these.

It is wise to be cautious here.[47] So far, the value creation of the Internet economy remains around 3 per cent of GDP. This can and will change. Yet the contribution of digitalization to productivity and growth remains unclear. The Internet is a classic example, as it was invented as far back as 1969. Cell phones appeared in the 1990s, and for a long time now computers have been commonplace in both offices and homes. Today almost everyone owns a smartphone. The real qualitative leap in communication, however, took place many decades ago, with the general spread of telephone connections. In 1962, only 14 per cent of private households in West Germany had telephones, but that figure rose to 88 per cent in twenty years. By comparison, the

45   Cf. Anselm Doering-Manteuffel and Lutz Raphael, *Nach dem Boom: Perspektiven auf die Zeitgeschichte seit 1970*, Göttingen: Vandenhoeck & Ruprecht, 2012.

46   Erik Brynjolfsson and Andrew McAfee, *The Second Machine Age. Work, Progress, and Prosperity in a Time of Brilliant Technologies*, New York: W.W. Norton & Company, 2014; Jeremy Rifkin, *The Zero Marginal Cost Society*, New York: Palgrave Macmillan, 2015.

47   Already in the 1970s and '80s, there was the idea that what was then known as 'computer-integrated manufacturing' would soon largely displace living labour. That was forty years ago.

spread of mobile phones has been less decisive in qualitative terms. Another example is the idea of the paperless office in the age of the Internet. Many people expected that all processes would be sped up by email, and use of paper would rapidly decline. Yet the opposite has been the case—there is more useless communication, which is often printed out anyway.

The technological revolutions connected with the smart-phone, Internet, email and other electronic tools have so far failed to give the economy a productivity boost comparable with the innovations of the second Industrial Revolution, such as automobiles and washing machines. These developments, so obvious and almost banal, had a far greater effect on productivity than have the innovations of the digital economy.[48] The growth impulse of recent years has resulted rather from the innovative monetary and credit policies of central banks.

Since the 1990s, persistent attempts have been made to reflate the economy through a policy of cheap money. In the end, however, it turns out that this growth has been a product of asset price inflation and snowballing indebtedness.[49] Rising debt was also an element in what has been called 'privatized Keynesianism'.[50] The classical Keynesian/Fordist mechanism for stabilizing demand through wages no longer functions under finance capitalism, since growth in real wages does not keep pace with the expansion of markets and productivity (see Chapter 4). Privatized Keynesianism served as a temporary compensation instrument; in functional terms, individual debt replaced the absent public

48   Robert J. Gordon, 'Is U.S. Economic Growth Over? Faltering Innovation Confronts the Six Headwinds', NBER Working Paper No. 18315, Cambridge, 2012; Ha-Joon Chang, 23 Things They Don't Tell You About Capitalism, London: Allen Lane, 2010.

49   Robert Brenner, 'New Boom or New Bubble? The Trajectory of the US Economy', New Left Review II(25), 2004, 57–100; Altvater, Der große Krach.

50   Colin Crouch, 'What Will Follow the Demise of Privatised Keynesianism?', Political Quarterly 80(1), 2009, 302–15.

demand and even made it possible for workers on very low wages to carry on consuming—though this could not continue forever.[51] It was Elizabeth II who asked, at a meeting of the UK's top economists at the London School of Economics, 'Why did no one see the crisis coming?' She received no answer.[52]

Even shortly before the collapse of the housing market, the economic and political elites, in an act of sedative autosuggestion, convinced themselves that modern economic policy had brought an end to the cyclical recurrence of recessions—an assertion maintained by, among others, Gordon Brown. In 2007, after a remarkable boom lasting more than ten years, the former British chancellor and short-lived prime minister announced that boom and bust were a thing of the past. With this audacious prediction he followed a familiar pattern, frequently observable in periods of upturn. If the trade cycle has been stable for a longer period than usual, it fuels the illusion that this time things will be quite different, that this boom will not be followed by a downturn. Until finally, just like every other time, a great crisis breaks.[53]

....

51   For consumers, cheap credit was so accessible that personal creditworthiness was almost not even a consideration, which finally led to the financial dispossession of many private households (Lapavitsas, 'Financialised capitalism').

52   The answer, even if it might not have pleased the Queen, would have to run something like this: modern economics is above all a theory of exchange and markets, in which the balance of competition and equilibrium ends up in an 'ecodicy' (Joseph Vogl, *Specter of Capital*, Stanford: Stanford University Press, 2014): the idea that despite crises, or even through these, markets are self-regulating and tend toward equilibrium. Given these unrealistic and ideological assumptions, the majority of highly paid economists are not in a position to recognize crises in good time.

53   Carmen M. Reinhart and Kenneth S. Rogoff, *This Time Is Different: Eight Centuries of Financial Folly*, Princeton: Princeton University Press, 2011; cf. also Charles P. Kindleberger, *Manias, Panics and Crashes: A History of Financial Crises*, Basic Books: New York, 1989; Hyman Minsky, *Can 'It' Happen Again? Essays on Instability and Finance*, Armonk: M. E. Sharpe, 1984.

This latest great crisis began in 2007 with the bursting of the US housing bubble, and rapidly developed into a full-blown financial crisis. In 2008, the US bank Lehman Brothers failed, followed by other financial institutions, insurance companies and hedge funds. Housing markets collapsed worldwide, while financial markets stood on the brink of meltdown. As before, the financial crisis was followed by a global economic crisis. Germany saw its greatest recession of the post-war years. Taking such key indicators as the growth of production, the stock exchange index and trade, the crisis that began in 2007 was comparable to the crash of 1929 and the ensuing Great Depression; indeed, the recent collapse was more drastic in some respects. The parallels are striking: financial bubbles, structural imbalances, the dispossession of many savers and, not least, greed, deception, and above all the illusion of the system's stability.[54]

During the Great Depression of 1929, international economic and political elites followed the economic policy consensus of non-intervention. There was no attempt to master the crisis by either monetary policy or expansionary fiscal measures; instead, the economic malaise intensified via the consolidation of state budgets.[55] This was an early form of the strategy today known as austerity. Now, eighty years later, it initially seemed that something had been learned. In both the United States and Europe, central banks and governments coordinated measures designed to prevent further slippage in asset prices and the threatening credit crunch. Above all, the collapse of the real economy led to states in 2008–09 having not only to rescue the banks, but also support the economy with countercyclical measures.[56] Previously unimaginable sums were 'made available', in the euphemism of

54   John Kenneth Galbraith, *The Great Crash*, London: Penguin, [1954] 2009.

55   Cf. Peter Gourevitch, *Politics in Hard Times. Comparative Responses to International Economic Crises*, Ithaca: Cornell University Press, 1986.

56   Cf. Altvater, *Der große Krach*.

the time. The volume of state stimulus amounted to more than 2 per cent of GDP in many countries. And indeed, the global economy did overcome the depression phase after a year or so—though without returning to pre-crisis levels in global terms.[57]

It is remarkable how quickly such immense sums were obtained—after all, it had previously been said in tones of utter conviction that the coffers were empty. And yet, against all expectations, the bankers and financiers did not have to pay for their hegemonic position. Almost without exception they were rescued by funds from taxation or government credits, even if this involved a fundamental restructuring of rules governing capital ratios, ownership and management structures. The international financial markets were only moderately regulated.

The crisis finally revealed itself as an opportunity for neoliberalism, as in many countries bank rescues led to an explosion in state debt.[58] As a result, history took a new turn, as suddenly the major institutional investors, banks and hedge funds found themselves back at the helm. In conjunction with the ratings agencies, they were able to exert unprecedented pressure on all governments, which were forced to refinance themselves on the capital markets. Heads of government and finance ministers were compelled to orient their policies more strongly than ever to 'the markets'. The hour of austerity policy had arrived. Its key measures involved consolidating state finances, reducing bureaucracy and privatizing public services to commercial operators. Policies of this kind had indeed been implemented already—states had long been spending more than they took in taxation—but now this approach was radicalized.[59] This time, in contrast to the

57   Cf. Barry Eichengreen and Kevin Hjortshøj O'Rourke, 'A tale of two depressions redux. What do the new data tell us?' 2012, voxeu.org (accessed February 2016).

58   Cf. Philip Mirowski, *Never Let a Serious Crisis Go to Waste: How Neoliberalism Survived the Financial Meltdown*, London: Verso, 2014.

59   Armin Schäfer and Wolfgang Streeck (eds), *Politics in the Age of Austerity*, Cambridge: Polity Press, 2013.

situation after 1929, consolidation followed a certain distance behind the outbreak of crisis.[60] At the same time, efforts were made to stabilize financial markets and promote investment using expansionary monetary policy. The first aim succeeded remarkably well, the second hardly at all. Budgetary cuts and the loosening of monetary policy had contrary effects, cancelling one another out. Austerity policies meant that many countries lacked the necessary growth.[61] The economic policy of these years could be compared with the attempt of a driver to simultaneously accelerate and apply the handbrake.

Even independently of austerity policies, financial capitalism continued to remain a time bomb. There was no effective re-regulation of banks, credit or capital markets. Any learning from the experience of the great crisis was scarcely implemented; financial speculation, bubbles created by low interest rates (particularly again in the housing sector), as well as financial market imbalances continued to risk great instability and even a new crash. The financial alchemy of derivatives, shorting, hedging, and so on was in theory supposed to minimize risks and increase transparency.[62] In actual fact, the opposite has proven to be the case: these new instruments and operations generalize risk, since today financial markets and products are highly integrated and mutually dependent on one another. There is therefore a higher probability that crises here will spread to other parts of the system. Major crises have generally become more likely.[63]

60   In the United States, the crisis of 1929 led to the New Deal—in other words, to the extension of social policy measures and a strengthening of trade unions. Europe today seems especially far from any policy of this kind.

61   Mark Blyth, *Austerity: The History of a Dangerous Idea*, New York: Oxford University Press, 2015.

62   Neoclassical theory even assumes that financial markets are particularly effective in this respect.

63   Callinicos, *Bonfire of Illusions*.

In the end, neither neoliberalism nor financialization has been able to stop the wellsprings of growth from drying up. Of course, the real economy has recovered. This is only partly based on new value creation, and instead produced a renewed acceleration of asset price inflation. The European Central Bank continues to function as a filling station with almost unlimited reserves; its monetary policy has had only limited success, however, inasmuch as the European economy is still spluttering. The Bank's policies only feed the monster of finance capitalism, which could be well described by a line from Dante's *Divine Comedy*: 'It pants more hotly after feeding than before.'

A new era began in 1973: the years 'after the boom'.[64] The global economy came off the rails, and since that time, discussions of stagnation and growth have generally been conducted from one of two basically normative perspectives. On one hand, people stoically insist on the necessity of dynamic growth, perhaps the only point on which liberals, social democrats, conservatives and left trade unionists have agreed. 'Without growth, everything is nothing in the capitalist economy.'[65] Liberals such as Karl-Heinz Paqué see growth as a key social imperative, not only for the creation of prosperity, but basically as a solution to almost all social problems.[66] This approach is not new, but a variant of the so-called 'trickle-down' theory—meaning that, if there is more growth and thus more wealth created, in time this will seep through to all social groups.

On the other hand, the ecological critique of growth sees continued economic expansion as fatal.[67] If unrestricted growth continues, say growth critics, everything in the future will be

---

64 Doering-Manteuffel and Raphael, *Nach dem Boom.*

65 Altvater, *Der große Krach*, 39.

66 Karl-Heinz Paqué, *Vollbeschäftigt. Das neue deutsche Jobwunder*, Munich: Carl Hanser, 2012.

67 The crisis of industrialism and growth was already a major theme in the 1970s—often in similar tones as today (cf. Fred Luks, *Die Zukunft des Wachstums*, Marburg: Metropolis, 2001).

worthless as the planet will no longer be inhabitable. Champions of a 'post-growth economy'[68] attack the wastage of resources and call for a society without economic growth. Both positions, however, miss the nub of the problem. Post-growth capitalism is increasingly a reality, albeit not in the ecological variant that critics desire. Instead, everything is done to generate new growth—including the continued depletion of natural resources. With today's post-growth capitalism, questions of ecological sustainability, qualitative criteria of growth and the good life are not obsolete; on the contrary, efforts made in all industrial countries to generate more growth generally contradict the growing awareness of the need for sustainability. What is rarely emphasized in policy debates, however, is the social question. In the past, growth provided the key resource for moderating structural inequalities, as rising productivity facilitated employment and social integration through upward mobility. In the absence of growth, though, social tensions increase, as the progress and distribution of income and wealth becomes a zero-sum game.[69] As we shall see in the next chapter, processes of regressive modernization set in, and downward mobility becomes more frequent.

68   Nico Paech, *Befreiung vom Überfluss. Auf dem Weg in die Postwachstumsökonomie*, Munich: Oekom, 2012. *The Limits to Growth*, the 1973 report by Dennis Meadows et al., is an early document from this perspective.

69   Stephan Voswinkel, *Was wird aus dem 'Fahrstuhleffekt'? Postwachstum und Sozialer Aufstieg*, der DFG-Forscher-gruppe Postwachstumsgesellschaften 08/2013, Friedrich-Schiller-Universität Jena.

3

Regressive Modernization

Modernity is frequently equated with democracy; it stands for reason and enlightenment, for the institutionalization of freedom, autonomy and human rights. It is characterized by belief in progress, in evolution to a higher stage of society by way of social differentiation. Free markets, rationalization and bureaucracy are supposed to guarantee the freedom of the individual, independent of one's social rank.[1] This, at least, is the normative and functional narrative that modern societies like to depict.[2] After

1   Both the concept of modernity and its chronology have been subject to diverse interpretations. Cf., among others, Johannes Berger, 'Modernitätsbegriffe und Modernitätskritik in der Soziologie', *Soziale Welt* 39(2), 1988, 224–35; Klaus von Beyme, *Theorie der Politik im 20. Jahrhundert. Von der Moderne zur Postmoderne*, Frankfurt: Suhrkamp, 1991, Peter Wagner, *A Sociology of Modernity: Liberty and Discipline*, London: Routledge, 1993; Uwe Schimank, 'Die Moderne: eine funktional differenzierte kapitalistische Gesellschaft', *Berliner Journal für Soziologie* 19(3), 2009, 327–51. However, the underlying optimistic and evolutionary tone of many of these blinded them to the catastrophes of the twentieth century.

2   Jürgen Habermas, *The Philosophical Discourse of Modernity*, Cambridge: Polity, 1990; Johannes Berger 'Was behauptet die Modernisierungstheorie wirklich—und was wird ihr bloß unterstellt', *Leviathan* 24(1), 1996, 45–62; Thomas Schwinn (ed.), *Die Vielfalt und Einheit der Moderne. Kultur- und strukturvergleichende Analysen*, Wiesbaden: VS, 2006.

the Second World War, modernization theorists assumed that prosperity and democracy were inseparable, and that they would continue expanding together.[3]

These authors initially had reality on their side: in the present OECD countries, income inequality had declined since the late nineteenth century.[4] Yet a cautious note soon followed this optimism. The 1970s saw a major turning point in Western societies; from then on, income differentials again began to widen.[5] Since the 1990s, another contention of modernization theory has been thrown into question: the seemingly indissoluble nexus between democracy and growth is suddenly no longer self-evident, as countries such as China are prospering even in the absence of democracy. In Western societies, moreover, doubts have arisen as to whether modernization can continue endlessly without at some point consuming its own foundations. Since the 1970s, it is not just economic crises, but social, political and ecological ones that have changed political semantics. If the previous decades were still characterized by socially planned progress, these guiding concepts have now almost completely disappeared from political discourse.[6]

---

3   Seymour Martin Lipset, 'Some social requisites of democracy: Economic development and political legitimacy', *American Political Science Review* 53(1), 1959, 69–105.

4   Modernization theorists assume that inequality initially rises in transitional societies. But if a society modernizes and develops further, this process is supposed to bring growing equality (cf. Simon Kuznets, 'Economic growth and income inequality', *American Economic Review* 45(1), 1955, 1–28; Talcott Parsons, *The System of Modern Societies*, New York: Prentice Hall, 1971; Reinhard Bendix [1969], 'Modernisierung in internationaler Perspektive', in Wolfgang Zapf (ed.), *Theorien des sozialen Wandels*, Cologne: Kiepenheuer & Witsch, 1980.

5   Stephan Hadril, 'Warum werden die meisten entwickelten Gesellschaften wieder ungleicher?', in Paul Windolf (ed.) *Finanzmarkt-Kapitalismus. Analysen zum Wandel von Produktionsregimen. Sonderheft der Kölner Zeitschrift für Soziologie und Sozialpsychologie 45*, Wiesbaden: VS, 2005.

6   Anselm Doering-Manteuffel and Lutz Raphael, *Nach dem Boom: Perspektiven auf die Zeitgeschichte seit 1970*, Göttingen: Vandenhoeck & Ruprecht, 2012, 85.

Modernization no longer sounds entirely positive, and if people speak of progress today, this is above all because they see it as threatened. As far back as the early 1980s, Jürgen Habermas warned of a 'colonization of the lifeworld' by the growing dominance of systemic imperatives.[7] At the same time, he maintained that the continued existence of the welfare state and democracy depended on 'the capitalist dynamics of growth' not becoming 'weak'.[8]

Ulrich Beck likewise adopted this new scepticism about the path of modernity in his concept of a 'second modernity'.[9] Beck differentiated between the 'simple modernization' that led to the first modernity, and the 'reflexive modernization' that introduced the second modernity. Simple modernization was defined by the transformation into industrial society, while reflexive modernization denoted the 'self-transformation' of modernized industrial society.[10] The traditional modernization of industrial society threatened to turn partly against itself—for example, when new energy technologies such as nuclear power involved life-threatening risks. The logic of wealth production had become quite divorced from the logic of risk production.[11] An important

7   Jürgen Habermas, *Theory of Communicative Action, Volume Two, Lifeworld and System: A Critique of Functionalist Reason*, Boston: Beacon Press, 1987, 332ff.

8   Ibid., 350ff. At this time, belief in Keynesianism was only a little shaken in circles of left intellectuals, not yet completely.

9   Ulrich Beck, *Risk Society: Towards a New Modernity*, London: Sage Publications, 1992; idem, 'The Age of Side-effects: On the Politicization of Modernity', in *The Reinvention of Politics: Rethinking Modernity in the Global Order*, London: Polity Press, 1997. Reactions to Beck's *Risk Society* were rather mixed when it first appeared, yet scarcely any other book from the 1980s analysed social change and its new risks with such pertinent suggestiveness. Today this book is seen as a 'key text' of its time (Doering-Manteuffel and Raphael, *Nach dem Boom*, 85ff.).

10   Beck, 'The Age', 15.

11   In this respect, Beck's diagnosis shows many similarities with Zygmunt Bauman's concept of 'liquid modernity' (*Liquid Modernity*, Cambridge: Polity Press, 2000).

driver of reflexive modernization processes was the 'side effects of side effects'. Environmental pollution resulting from industrialization had the side effect of creating new political actors, such as the ecology movement, which would again drive new modernizations.

In the second modernity, moreover, existing institutions such as the nation state, existing forms of paid employment, and democracy are transformed and often hybridized. For example, the nation state still exists, but it has lost national effectiveness by simultaneously appearing as a transnational actor. Beck's theory of this second modernity,[12] however, is exaggerated, inasmuch as he hypostasizes existing trends and treats it as an epochal break.[13] Transformative change has not been quite so radical as Beck assumed. His postulated loss of the significance of paid employment (more on this in Chapter 4) has not continued, but actually reversed. The complete disappearance of class society, supplanted by individual inequalities, was a chimera. There have always been class structures, and in the era of social modernity they were simply held in check.

And yet, if we abstract from its tacit theoretical purpose, Beck's theory of reflexive modernization is highly topical and

----

12   Beck, *Risk Society* and 'The Age'; Ulrich Beck, Wolfgang Bonß and Christoph Lau, 'The Theory of Reflexive Modernization: Problematic, Hypotheses and Research Programme', *Theory, Culture and Society* 20(2), 2003, 1–33.

13   This idea of an epochal break has recently been revived by Anselm Doering-Manteuffel and Lutz Raphael in their book *Nach dem Boom*. These two historians go so far as to speak of a 'change of revolutionary quality', embracing work, production, life and politics (*Nach dem Boom*, 12ff.); cf. Robert Castel, *La montée des incertitudes. Travail, protections, statut de l'individu*, Paris: Éditions du Seuil, 2009. The French historian Pierre Rosanvallon likewise diagnoses a 'spectacular break with the past, reversing the trend' of a steadily reducing inequality (*The Society of Equals*, 4). Such contentions may sound catchy and plausible, yet their champions are often blind to immanent contradictions that do not fit their assessment so readily.

extremely useful for grasping contemporary developments. As distinct from Beck, who described the self-transformation of modernity,[14] the procedure I shall adopt here is rather one influenced by critical theory, which emphasizes internal contradictions and contrary developments with the paradoxical formula of 'regressive modernization'.[15] The adjective 'regressive' refers to the circumstance that present-day societies have fallen behind the level of integration reached in social modernity. 'Modernization' implies that we are not witnessing an unambiguous retreat to a situation below that attained in supposedly better times. This counter-modernization (expressed, for example, in increased material inequality) is in fact accompanied on other levels by an emancipatory modernization (for example, a decline in discrimination against certain groups).[16] Yet this is in no way the basis of a new dynamic, even if in more than a few cases regression takes place with the simultaneous implementation of basically emancipatory norms.[17] It is a progress that bears

14   In a work world rich in productive ambivalences, Beck also reflected this aspect. The modernization of modernity, he argued, was not a linear process: 'types of counter-modernization' ('The Age', 14) were possible, often amounting to a 'dialectic of modernization and counter-modernization' (34).

15   Cf. on this, Theodor Adorno and Max Horkheimer, *Dialectic of Enlightenment*, London: Verso, [1944] 2016. These authors find this a basic aspect of modernity: 'the curse of irresistible progress is irresistible regression' (28).

16   To a certain extent, regressive modernization follows the story that Colin Crouch developed for 'post-democracy'. According to Crouch (cf. *Post-Democracy*, Cambridge: Polity, 2004, 1ff.), from the early twentieth century onward, democracy experienced a rise that reached a peak in the 1960s and '70s. This was followed by a downward movement—albeit within the structures of modernity. The decline occurs within modernity, there is no restoration of pre-modern conditions. What Crouch overlooks, however, is that there have at the same time been further signs of progress, which may still continue, leading to a developing self-contradiction.

17   Recent critical theory of the Frankfurt School treats this process as 'normative paradoxes of the present' (cf. Michael Hartmann and Axel Honneth, 'Paradoxes of Capitalist Modernization: A Research Programme',

retrogression within it,[18] and this retrogression generally if not always affects the lower classes.

Various symptoms of regressive modernization are found in almost all the fields of society discussed in this volume—in parliamentary democracies, in the labour market, as well as in the educational system. For example, in recent decades access to education has massively expanded. Populations whose educational progress used to stop at secondary school can now attend university. However, this extension also devalues the qualifications earned, as today there are ever fewer prospects of secure employment with only a school-leaving certificate. As far as the political system is concerned, if the opportunities for citizens to participate are greater than ever before, the actual influence of the lower classes has substantially declined (more on this in the final chapter). Political participation in democracy is replaced by economic participation on the (labour) markets, as analysed in the following section.

Regressive modernizations frequently arise in the wake of liberal equalizations. One of the most important achievements of recent decades has been the growing equality of rights between the sexes. To a lesser extent this is also true in relation to ethnic origin. In both respects many social barriers are lower, and

---

in Axel Honneth (ed.), *The I in We: Studies in the Theory of Recognition*, translated by Joseph Ganahl, London: Polity, 2012; Alex Honneth and Ferdinand Sutterlüty, 'Normative Paradoxien der Gegenwart—eine Forschungsperspektive', *Westend. Neue Zeitschrift für Sozialforschung* 8(1), 2011, 67–85). This approach has the great advantage of enabling the endogenous transformation of capitalist societies to be studied. It thereby avoids structure-determining explanations of '*self-destructive*' economic processes characteristic of descriptions of "late capitalist" social formations' (Martin Hartmann and Axel Honneth, 'Paradoxes of Capitalist Modernization', 177).

18 Sighard Neckel describes this as a 'cogwheel mechanism with reverse movement, which drives its object forward by itself moving backward' ('Refeudalisierung—Systematik und Aktualität eines Begriffs der Habermas'schen Gesellschaftsanalyse', *Leviathan* 41(1), 2013, 47).

discrimination less frequent. But whereas in theory such advances are universal, they have different effects in particular fields and on particular groups, so that their implementation may have unintended regressive effects. For example, women's participation in the labour market has generally risen—but above all as cleaners, cashiers and nursing staff. Competition in the labour market has increased overall in the wake of increased gender and ethnic rights. The traditional sexual division of labour in the home, based on the model of the male breadwinner, has declined in favour of equal participation in the labour market (the dual-income model). However, and we shall return to this, in lower segments of the labour market *both* partners now earn less, so that total household income has fallen.

Frequently, therefore, (economic) inclusion produces more inequality rather than greater equality. The idea of Agenda 2010, according to its champions, was to simplify participation in the labour market for everyone, to facilitate access and allow people to take responsibility for their own lives.[19] The result was that more people could join the labour market more rapidly and directly, yet with fewer rights, less security and lower incomes.

The consequences of regressive modernization cannot simply be removed by an act of will. Although there certainly are forces that would like to see women withdraw from the labour market and return to the domestic sphere, this restoration would be neither socially acceptable nor would it raise men's incomes again.

The findings presented below relate to developments in key areas of German society. So far, we can only recognize certain *processes* of regressive modernization, which have not yet condensed into characteristics of a new epoch. Whether these trends will affect the whole of society or whether they will lead to a real caesura remains unclear for the time being.

---

19 Cf. Thomas Meyer, 'Die Agenda 2010 und die soziale Gerechtigkeit', in *Politische Vierteljahresschrift* 45(2), 2004, 181–90.

NEOLIBERAL COLLUSION

Modern capitalism cannot function without cooperation, without the willing participation of individuals. It has repeatedly managed to mobilize new motivations and system-conforming behaviour. The at least partial acceptance of the market mechanism by the population is the basis for social stability.[20] And even regressive modernization functions only on the basis of conscious or unconscious agreement. At the end of the day, this is an overdetermined phenomenon, one not reducible to a single factor; it results from a chain of different micro-transformations. At the same time, it is possible to identify certain important influences: people act on the basis of social norms and ideas, but it 'is always the case that the day-to-day activity of social actors draws upon and reproduces structural features of wider social systems.'[21] These systems, according to Giddens, 'structure' the action of individuals.[22] Their actions, in other words, depend on the options presented. For example, for many wage earners, pension prospects have not really improved in recent decades. If someone is concerned for their pension, then they have the option (subsidized by the state) of taking out additional private insurance (in Germany, a so-called 'Riester pension'). Regressive modernization in this sense may well be based on the exertion of political power, but precisely in such a way as to involve people as subjects in this change, to make them accomplices.

Only occasionally has open class struggle been launched from above with the intention of directly curtailing the claims

---

20   The social hegemony of a particular group and its thinking, however, rests on a combination of consensus and compulsion (cf. Antonio Gramsci, *Prison Notebooks*, New York: Columbia University Press, [1929–35] 2011; Benjamin Opratko, *Hegemonie. Politische Theorie nach Antonio Gramsci*, Münster: Westfälisches Dampfboot, 2012).

21   Anthony Giddens, *The Constitution of Society: Outlines of the Theory of Structuration*, Cambridge: Polity, 1984, 24.

22   Ibid., 16.

and rights of citizens. In these cases, as with Agenda 2010 (or, largely forgotten, the struggles over sick pay in 1996),[23] the 'interest of capital'—reforms designed to increase competitiveness, to attract foreign investment—is blatant. More frequently, however, regressive modernization is realized by the neoliberal confluence of the interests of capital, liberalizations and subjectifications. Neoliberalism is fundamentally an ideology in the sense that economic theories are above all rationalizations of interests.[24] Radicalized ideas of free markets basically conceal a modern form of 'class politics', which principally serves the interests of the owners of capital.[25] Yet, in the end, this perspective only explains why businesspeople and a particular kind of conservative politician have found their interests articulated in neoliberalism; it blinds us to the crux of neoliberal success. For neoliberalism has been extremely successful in creating a (secret) collusion with a chiefly emancipatory critique of social modernity, by latching onto this modernity's paradoxes: on the one hand, social modernity restrained the distress and uncertainty of capitalism, while on the other hand, the social-bureaucratic mechanism to which this gave rise—one of standardization, normalization and homogenization—prevented individual autonomy from developing.[26] After the demise of Keynesianism, the market appeared as a more effective mechanism for

23   When the Kohl government tried to abolish this in 1996, it failed due to resistance from the trade unions (Wolfgang Streeck, 'No Longer the Century of Corporatism. Das Ende des "Bündnisses für Arbeit"', MPIfG Working Paper 03/4, Cologne, 2003).

24   Adam Przeworski, Capitalism and Social Democracy, Cambridge: Cambridge University Press, 1985, 206.

25   David Harvey, A Brief History of Neoliberalism, New York: Oxford University Press, 2007.

26   Cf. Peter Wagner, Modernity: Understanding the Present, Cambridge: Polity Press, 2012; Klaus Dörre, 'The New Landnahme: Dynamics and Limits of Financial Market Capitalism', in Klaus Dörre, Stephan Lessenich and Hartmut Rosa (eds), Sociology, Capitalism, Critique, London: Verso, 2015.

distributing social resources. The state and state intervention could be branded as bureaucratic, inefficient and defective. Competition and market oversight of the state were now seen as the modern form of 'governmentality'.[27] The values of neoliberalism had to be internalized, as Margaret Thatcher expressly indicated: 'Economics are the method, the object is to change the heart and soul'.[28] This succeeded principally by establishing a new subjectivity aimed at a new way of governing the self.[29] Neoliberalism's power was secured from below and from inside, by the creation of incentives for people to see themselves as naturally autonomous and entrepreneurial subjects, and to view collective social solutions and institutions as suspect.

Neoliberalism is totalitarian in what it claims, despite its constant promise of freedom. The market serves as final reference for all spheres of life: it is seen as the central mechanism both of social processes and of individual modes of thought and action.[30] Spheres of society that were previously more or less protected from the logic of the market ('de-commodified') are subjected to it again ('re-commodified'). This policy has been expressed in a variety of forms—for example, in the deregulation and liberalization of the labour market and welfare state (more

27   Michel Foucault, *The Birth of Biopolitics: Lectures at the Collège de France, 1978–1979*, translated by Graham Burchell, New York: Palgrave Macmillan, 2008.

28   Pierre Dardot and Christian Laval, *The New Way of the World: On Neoliberal Society*, London: Verso, 2013, 263.

29   Cf. Thomas Lemke, Susanne Krasmann, Ulrich Bröckling, 'Gouvernementalität, Neoliberalismus und Selbsttechnologien. Eine Einleitung', in Ulrich Bröckling et al. (eds), *Gouvernementalität der Gegenwart. Studien zur Ökonomisierung des Sozialen*, Frankfurt am Main: Suhrkamp, 2000, 7–40.

30   Cf. Dardot and Laval, *The New Way of the World*; Ulrich Bröckling, *The Entrepreneurial Self: Fabricating a New Type of Subject*, translated by Steven Black, London: Sage, 2016. This is often quite contradictory in practice, as mistrust of the state and recourse to the primacy of 'freedom' often require state application of market principles, sometimes by force.

on this below). Another dimension was the privatization of public goods and companies, which were now placed on the stock market. David Harvey calls this process 'accumulation through dispossession',[31] as communal goods originally financed by taxation have come into the hands of private entrepreneurs, thus withdrawn from public or democratic control.[32]

And yet neoliberalism found acceptance among broad sections of the population—particularly in the upwardly oriented middle class—as well as in parties and associations that had previously been critical of the market. Many social groups and milieus that sought individual sovereignty welcomed social liberalizations, or were at least able to adapt to them. This led, however, to side effects: old-age provision by private pensions simultaneously legitimizes the de-collectivization of the welfare state. Another example is that of tax reductions. These are generally welcomed by the middle and upper classes, despite the fact that they contribute to decreasing the resources of the state for redistribution, infrastructure, and so on. Other side effects can be observed on the financial markets. The wealth of the upwardly mobile and upper middle class has risen visibly in social modernity, yet instead of the previous habit of saving, this money has increasingly been placed on financial markets, creating a 'collective Buddenbrooks effect'.[33] Like Thomas Buddenbrook in Thomas Mann's famous novel, people leave the trusted path of conservative economic action in the hope of gaining a higher and quicker return through speculative deals. By purchasing stocks

31   David Harvey, *Seventeen Contradictions and the End of Capitalism*, London: Profile Books, 2015, 141.

32   These ideas also found their way into the models of political interpretation adopted by social democratic parties (cf. Donald Sassoon, *One Hundred Years of Socialism*, New York: New Press, 1996; Oliver Nachtwey, *Marktsozialdemokratie: Die Transformation von SPD und Labour Party*, Wiesbaden: VS, 2009).

33   Christoph Deutschmann, *Kapitalistische Dynamik*, Wiesbaden: VS, 2008.

and making financial investments, today's middle classes have contributed to financial markets having gained such great importance, yet they are now themselves caught up in the volatility of these, for better or worse.[34]

The movement of the 1968ers and their successors saw itself as championing an 'artistic critique', which emphasized autonomy, self-determination and individual responsibility in the face of established regulations.[35] The actual political impetus of the 1968ers, however, was originally based on this artistic critique being combined with a social critique directed at inequality. In the 1970s, though, neoliberalism managed to untie this link, to emphasize the artistic critique and neutralize the social critique from the trade unions that targeted vertical inequalities.[36] The artistic critique thereby became an important source of neoliberal collusion. It particularly helped to undermine the core realms of work and the welfare state.

In social modernity, wage labour was humanized and partly withdrawn from market pressure, as discussed in Chapter 1. Establishing normal labour relations was an important step for wage earners, allowing them far greater scope for shaping their own lives—despite women and migrants frequently remaining excluded. These normal labour relations, however, continued to be a means of regulation. From working hours to labour protection, from job classification to career path—everything seemed planned and regulated. The situation with the welfare state was

---

34   The US automobile workers' unions ended up in a particularly unpleasant situation. As a result of the crisis, they often took over control of large company pension funds. The yields on these, however, frequently depend on the reduction of wage costs in the companies in which they plan to invest.

35   A paradigmatic form of this artistic critique is Herbert Marcuse's *One-Dimensional Man: Studies in the Ideology of Advanced Industrial Society*, London: Routledge, [1967] 2002.

36   Cf. Luc Boltanski and Eve Chiapello, *The New Spirit of Capitalism*, London: Verso, 2005.

similar. Before this was criticized from the conservative side as too expensive and inefficient, it was alternative left milieus in particular that saw it as an agency of discipline.[37] The welfare state was never an 'easy chair'; it rather served as a more or less concealed instrument to create fitness for work, social control and conformity.

The artistic critique viewed regulated employment as pallid and even stifling. The new networked, project-based company organization, in contrast, appeared as a kind of liberation. Self-determination and individual responsibility now formed part of the arsenal of labour policy inspired by the artistic critique just as much as project-based group work, job rotation, flexible hours and the expansion of direct participation. Many highly skilled employees welcomed such initiatives on the part of management, or even demanded these if companies did not offer them. Under the 'new spirit of capitalism', bureaucratic modes of control of social modernity and the Fordist mode of production seem to belong to the past. Security was exchanged for autonomy, social justice for participation.[38]

Wage earners were forced into a Faustian pact in order to gain greater individual freedom at work. Companies did indeed offer their employees greater autonomy, yet at the same time they seduced them into higher performance. Work became less well defined and more subjective—the market was literally

---

37 Cf. Thomas Schmid, 'Nichtsnutz und Robot: Über einige Schwierigkeiten, die Verstaatlichung des Sozialen rückgängig zu mache', *Freibeuter* 11/1, 1982. The author of this left-libertarian argument later became editor-in-chief of *Die Welt*.

38 Boltanski and Chiapello, *The New Spirit of Capitalism*. However, their argument is exaggerated and stunted. For example, they assume the trade unions are never bearers of the artistic critique and ignore the critique of Taylorism from the trade unions and industrial sociology (cf. Sarah Nies and Dieter Sauer, 'Arbeit—mehr als Beschäftigung? Zur arbeitssoziologischen Kapitalismuskritik', in Klaus Dörre et al. (eds), *Arbeitssoziologie und Kapitalismustheorie*, Frankfurt and New York: Campus, 2012, 34–62.).

introduced into companies themselves.[39] For example, work groups were now supposed to act as cost or profit centres, as if they were autonomous entrepreneurial segments on fictitious markets.[40] Management not only handed over work organization to the employees, but also rational calculation of cost and efficiency. They were encouraged to think and act entrepreneurially themselves. This often had practical side effects for companies. My research (for example, among employees whose work had a project character) found silent and undocumented overtime: at the end of the official working day employees formally clock out, but return right away to their desks. In order to complete their projects they have to perform voluntary overtime—secretly and on top of their formal working hours.

It is apparent from the new forms of business management that perspectives of a post-industrial, knowledge-based and humanized service society, as developed in the 1970s by Alain Touraine and Daniel Bell, have failed to materialize.[41] The idea of an interactive and communicative service logic, which would humanize the world of work by way of reflexive and self-determined activity, has proved an illusion. Humanization through service work has failed precisely because personality and

39   Ulrich Brinkmann, *Die unsichtbare Faust des Marktes. Betriebliche Kontrolle und Koordination im Finanzmarktkapitalismus*, Berlin: Edition Sigma, 2011.

40   Cf. Nestor D'Alessio and Anne Hacket, 'Flexibilität und Kapitalmarkt. Neue Formen der Arbeitsorganisation und Unternehmenskontrolle', in Forschungsverbund Sozioökonomische Berichterstattung (ed.), *Berichterstattung zur sozioökonomischen Berichterstattung in Deutschland. Teilhabe im Umbruch. Zweiter Bericht*, Wiesbaden: VS, 2012; Klaus Dörre, 'Krise des Shareholder Value? Kapitalmarktorientierte Steuerung als Wettkampfsystem', in Klaus Kraemer and Sebastian Nessel (eds), *Entfesselte Finanzmärkte. Soziologische Analysen des modernen Kapitalismus*, Bielefeld: transcript 2012.

41   Alain Touraine, *Post-Industrial Society*, London: Wildwood House, 1974; Daniel Bell, *The Coming of Post-Industrial Society*, New York: Basic Books, 1976.

interpersonal interactions have become a new resource of domination. So-called 'emotional labour', in which empathy with the client is part of the activity (as, for example, with care work), serves domination in the work process.[42] Closeness to clients does not automatically make the activity more human; in fact, the very opposite can be the case: the employee has to 'serve two masters'—the employer and the client.[43] The image of the 'worker-entrepreneur' demonstrates the ambivalent constitution of modern subjectivity. Behind the supposedly entrepreneurial gain in freedom, employees face a new method of oversight, in the form of an imperative to permanent 'self-control' and 'self-economizing'.[44]

---

42   Cf. Arlie Russell Hochschild, *The Managed Heart: Commercialization of Human Feeling*, Berkeley, CA: University of California Press, [1983] 2012.

43   Horizontal relations with clients have deteriorated in the service sector, in parallel with vertical power relations in the firm. Moreover, flat, supposedly egalitarian and non-hierarchical structures in the firm lead to conflicts over power being perceived as conflicts among the personnel (cf. Friederike Bahl and Philipp Staab, 'Das Dienstleistungsproletariat. Theorie auf kaltem Entzug', *Mittelweg 36* 19(6), 2010, 90ff.).

44   G. Günter Voß and Hans J. Pongratz, 'Der Arbeitskraftunternehmer. Eine neue Grundform der "Ware Arbeitskraft"?', *Kölner Zeitschrift für Soziologie und Sozialpsychologie* 50(1), 1998; cf. Manfred Moldaschl and Dieter Sauer, 'Internalisierung des Marktes—Zur neuen Dialektik von Kooperation und Herrschaft', in Heiner Minssen (ed.), *Begrenzte Entgrenzungen. Wandlungen von Organisation und Arbeit*, Berlin: Edition Sigma, 2000. It is also doubtful how far the subjectification of work extends. The real changes in work organization are frequently exaggerated in the literature, while heteronomous work processes actually remain firmly established (cf. Christoph Deutschmann, *Postindustrielle Industriesoziologie. Theoretische Grundlagen, Arbeitsverhältnisse und soziale Identitäten*, Weinheim: Juventa, 2002; Manfred Moldaschl, 'Organisierung und Organisation von Arbeit', in Fritz Böhle, G. Günther Voß and Günther Wachtler (eds), *Handbuch Arbeitssoziologie*, Wiesbaden: VS, 2010.

THE SATANIC MILL OF LIBERALIZATION[45]

Neoliberal politics means creating corridors for collusion with the market. This has frequently happened by way of economic liberalization. Margaret Thatcher privatized social housing in order to convert its occupants into owners with corresponding interests and behaviours. Privatization, however, is only part of the general policy of liberalization that began in the 1980s and is still under way. This involves the transfer of state competencies to markets, the deliberate creation of markets, the general strengthening of competition, autonomy and individual responsibility, along with the decentralization of decision-making.[46]

Liberalization has particularly affected public services. During the second half of the twentieth century, these steadily expanded. It was part of the post-war consensus that society should not be completely given over to the market. In Germany, as in most European states,[47] many fields that were regarded as social infrastructure became state-controlled common property: education, health, post and telecommunication, transport, and water and power supply. While a number of these remain in public hands, far greater parts of the state and public sector have been privatized since the 1980s. On one hand, the state needed the proceeds to

45   Karl Polanyi (*The Great Transformation: The Political and Economic Origins of Our Time*, Boston: Beacon Press, [1944] 2002) used the term 'satanic mill' to refer to the first great wave of market creation, which eroded social institutions and embedding, finally leading to the free-market capitalism of the nineteenth century.

46   Martin Höpner, Alexander Petring, Daniel Seikel and Benjamin Werner, 'Liberalisierungspolitik. Eine Bestandsaufnahme des Rückbaus wirtschafts- und sozialpolitischer Interventionen in entwickelten Industrieländern', *Kölner Zeitschrift für Soziologie und Sozialpsychologie* 63(1), 2011. In this reading, 'deregulation' simply means the reduction of regulative density.

47   In some of these, state intervention was still more comprehensive (cf. Andrew Shonfield, *Modern Capitalism*, Oxford: Oxford University Press, 1965).

reduce its debts; on the other, public companies were no longer seen as adequate agencies for meeting basic requirements. Many citizens initially welcomed these privatizations—they saw public institutions such as the postal service not as democratic providers of common goods, but rather as bodies with a Prussian-authoritarian tradition that were unprofessional and unhelpful. Beneath the surface, this was accompanied by a tectonic shift in the mentality of large groups of the population. Public services were now seen chiefly from the standpoint of the 'client'. Against the anonymous institution of bureaucracy, the no less anonymous market generally appeared friendlier, even emancipating.

What interests us here in particular are the effects of privatizations. Socially regulated public services had been the sector that embodied social modernity in an almost ideal form. Collective bargaining guaranteed wages, along with the welfare of the personnel. Workers could count on lifetime employment, with regular even if moderate wage increases, and the representation of their interests was firmly anchored. Advancement within the company was possible through experience, qualification or performance.[48] Privatization did away with the public sector as the guardian of social modernity. In no other branch did standards erode so dramatically, or were labour relations and structures of co-determination that had been uniformly regulated so greatly fragmented. The wave of privatizations, particularly since the 1990s, thus represented a 'fundamental break with the modus operandi of the post-war interventionist welfare state'.[49] Frequently, a new 'dirty competition' also arose in the

48   At least it was supposed to be, in theory. In practice, the public sector had for a long time been not so democratic in the eyes of citizens and consumers—for example, because too many positions, in particular at managerial levels, were filled less on the basis of skill and performance, but rather by party affiliation.

49   Cf. Wolfgang Streeck, *Re-Forming Capitalism: Institutional Change in the German Political Economy*, Oxford: Oxford University Press, 2009, 71.

form of entire branches of industry without trade union bargaining. A similar pressure developed in institutions such as universities and hospitals, where rudiments of classic public service had survived. Here, principles of competition were introduced and many services outsourced, transferred to external and generally private suppliers—again with the consequences of low wages and lack of union representation.[50] In this way, liberalization and especially privatization became driving forces of downward mobility.

POST-DEMOCRACY—GOVERNMENT BY MARKETS

The crux of modern democracy originally lay in its egalitarian opposition to the inequalities that capitalism produced. 'Democracy requires certain rough equalities in a real capacity to affect political outcomes by all citizens.'[51] It is therefore not surprising that social modernity and democracy should have initially developed in harmony. Nor was it accidental that the popular Social Democratic chancellor Willy Brandt came up with his famous slogan to 'dare more democracy' in 1969, the precise moment that social modernity was approaching its zenith.

A little later, however, a clear note of increased doubt about future democratic perspectives appeared in critical opinion. In the 1970s, the talk was particularly of the 'legitimation crisis' of

---

50   Cf. Thorsten Brandt and Thorsten Schulten, 'Liberalisierung und Privatisierung öffentlicher Dienstleistungen', *WSI-Mitteilungen* 61(10), 2008, 570–76. For case studies of the German railways and health sector, cf. respectively Tim Engartner, *Die Privatisierung der Deutschen Bahn*, Wiesbaden: VS, 2008, and Nils Böhlke, Thomas Gerlinger, Kai Mosebach, Rolf Schmucker and Thorsten Schulten (eds), *Privatisierung von Krankenhäusern. Erfahrungen und Perspektiven aus Sicht der Beschäftigten*, Hamburg: VSA, 2009.

51   Colin Crouch, *Post-Democracy*, 16ff.; cf. Rosanvallon, *The Society of Equals*.

late capitalism, which Habermas identified in his much-discussed book of this title published in 1973 (1976 in English). According to Habermas, the growing administrative interventions of the state resulted in a similarly growing deficit of democratic legitimacy. Habermas's diagnosis of this legitimation crisis was empirically flawed, though not completely wrong. It is true that the general level of protest had markedly risen, and its scope had extended. Yet the prevailing mood among the population in general was different: West German citizens showed contentment with the social market economy, the welfare state and democracy. Even if increasing numbers of people were involved in citizens' initiatives outside of parliament, they continued to display great confidence in democratic institutions; never had more people gone to the polls, or voted for the two main parties, than in the 1970s. A relative majority of citizens even judged social conditions to be 'by and large fair'. In 1973, this figure was 44 per cent, whereas 42 per cent deemed them unfair. In 1979, the positive figure even rose to 50 per cent, while the negative one declined to 36 per cent—figures that would be almost completely reversed in the 1990s.[52] Habermas and his like-minded colleague Claus Offe, whose book *Strukturprobleme des kapitalistischen Staates*[53] ('Structural Problems of the Capitalist State') had a similar effect, were mistaken in their concrete diagnosis. Yet they were far-sighted in recognizing certain problems that democracy would reveal later. They diagnosed forms of de-ideologization, growing bureaucratization and oligarchy in major political organizations. This resulted in parties abandoning their original aims in favour of broader, cross-class coalitions

---

52 Cf. Oliver Nachtwey, 'Legitimationsprobleme im Spätkapitalismus revisited', in Karina Becker, Lars Gertenbach, Henning Laux and Tilmann Reitz (eds), *Grenzverschiebungen des Kapitalismus*, Frankfurt: Campus, 2010.

53 Claus Offe, *Strukturprobleme des kapitalistischen Staates. Veränderte Neuauflage des Buches von 1972* (eds Jens Borchert and Stephan Lessenich), Frankfurt: Campus, 2006.

and becoming parties for everyone, which in the end simply competed for power. They had cut themselves so far adrift from their original bases that they were now only loosely linked to them.[54] A consequence was a structural change in the public sphere, which now sought 'diffuse mass loyalty—but avoids participation'.[55]

The diagnosis of de-democratization that Offe and Habermas formulated in the 1970s can claim greater plausibility today. Politics has become increasingly disconnected from the agreement and influence of citizens. This is the nub of the debate that Colin Crouch opened with his book *Post-Democracy*. Crouch saw modern parliamentary and representative democracy as a system in which there are still formally free elections and governments can be voted out of power. Post-democracy does not apply a restricted suffrage that would exclude the lower classes. The process is subtler; the democratic edifice is hollowed out from within. Citizens lose influence on political decisions, while lobbyists, economic elites and especially global corporations build up their power. Wage earners and trade unions become marginal social actors, while elites obtain ever more privileges.

The degree to which parties are anchored within the wider population has declined dramatically in post-democracy. They have become actors who continue to govern but are increasingly less representative; they exert power, but articulate less in the way of social protest.[56] In place of parliamentary representation of the interests and needs of the population, we frequently have 'the presentation of policies already decided by the executive and

54 Cf. Otto Kirchheimer, 'The Transformation of the Western Party Systems', in Joseph LaPalombara and Myron Wiener (eds), *Political Parties and Political Development*, Princeton, NJ: Princeton University Press, 1966, 177–200.

55 Jürgen Habermas, *Legitimation Crisis*, Cambridge: Polity Press, 1980, 36.

56 Peter Mair, 'Ruling the Void? The Hollowing of Western Democracy', *New Left Review* II(42), 2006, 25–51.

corporations.[57] Taken to its conclusion, post-democracy thus becomes a 'democracy *after* the demos', in which the state machinery governs by itself.[58] Political conflict in a 'post-political' consensus is conducted by way of expertise, legal regularization and the construction of material constraints, with contradictions and social antagonisms being increasingly ignored.[59]

As a result, democracy becomes a paradoxical arrangement. Though citizens cling strongly to democracy as an idea, they expect ever less from actually existing democratic process. Outside parliamentary forms, opportunities for democratic participation have even increased, and democratic norms have been radicalized.[60] Citizens' initiatives and the expansion of referenda and critical public opinion have greatly supplemented traditional democratic procedures in many areas.[61] What is problematic about this formal expansion of participation, however, is that it has been highly asymmetrical. The chorus of concerned citizens sings the songs of the middle class: it is chiefly groups with solid incomes and a high level of education that participate, whereas underprivileged groups tend to abstain. Those with precarious employment vote less often than others; in other words, inequality leads to an asymmetrical gain in influence by the better off.[62] This amounts to a reversal in

57 Stephan Lessenich and Frank Nullmeier, 'Einleitung: Deutschland zwischen Einheit und Spaltung', in Stephan Lessenich and Frank Nullmeier (eds), *Deutschland. Eine gespaltene Gesellschaft*, Frankfurt: Campus, 2006, 24.

58 Jacques Rancière, *Disagreement: Politics and Philosophy*, Minneapolis, MN: University of Minnesota Press, 2004, 102.

59 Chantal Mouffe, *On the Political*, London: Routledge, 2005.

60 Cf. Danny Michelsen and Franz Walter, *Unpolitische Demokratie: Zur Krise der Repräsentation*, Berlin: Suhrkamp, 2013; Ingolfur Blühdorn, *Simulative Demokratie: Neue Politik nach der postdemokratischen Wende*, Berlin: Suhrkamp, 2013.

61 Cf. John Keane, *The Life and Death of Democracy*, London: Pocket Books, 2009; Paul Nolte, *Was ist Demokratie? Geschichte und Gegenwart*, Munich: C. H. Beck, 2012.

62 Armin Schäfer and Harald Schoen, 'Mehr Demokratie, aber nur für wenige? Der Zielkonflikt zwischen mehr Beteiligung und

the developmental trend of social modernity, in which democratic participation was a vehicle to create greater social equality.[63]

In the end, post-democracy, just like neoliberalism, is a cover for class politics. The lack of participation of the lower classes is simply the reverse side of the 'new dominant, combined political and economic class' of the privileged.[64] The class basis of post-democracy is often overlooked, as in public debate social classes are generally equated with particular outward cultural characteristics. But the 'contemporary political orthodoxy that social class no longer exists is itself a symptom of post-democracy.'[65] Class is a relational concept, which focuses on economic position and asks what access certain groups have to political power (see Chapter 4). And it is precisely this connection between economic position and political power that has grown stronger. We could also say that politics has been transformed from a 'democracy of the centre' into an 'elite democracy'. A statistically normal distribution is the implicit starting point of most models of democracy.[66] In these models it is the median voters, those defining the centre, who decide the government and accordingly, the policy direction. This political centre ought to stand for equilibrium and balance. By the early 1900s, however, Italian liberal economist Vilfredo

politischer Gleichheit', *Leviathan* 41(1), 2013, 94–120; Armin Schäfer, 'Liberalization, Inequality and Democracy's Discontent', in Armin Schäfer and Wolfgang Streeck (eds), *Politics in the Age of Austerity*, Cambridge: Polity Press, 2013.

63   Cf. Dirk Jörke, 'Re-Demokratisierung der Postdemokratie durch alternative Beteiligungsverfahren?' *Politische Vierteljahresschrift* 54, 2013, 485–505.

64   Crouch, *Post-Democracy*, 52.

65   Ibid., 53. This diagnosis is certainly plausible on the basis of Crouch's international perspective; however, something similar could already have been said of the situation in post-war West Germany.

66   Classically, Anthony Downs, *An Economic Theory of Democracy*, New York: Harper & Row, 1957; cf. Manfred G. Schmidt, *Demokratietheorien*, Opladen: UTB, 2000.

Pareto argued that 80 per cent of wealth was concentrated in 20 per cent of the population (from today's perspective, this would be an underestimate). He also saw true representative democracy as an illusion; in the end, a ruling elite would always emerge.[67] Pareto's democracy is a democracy of the elites for the elites.

This is why we are experiencing a fundamental structural change in politics, a change from *genitivus objectivus* to *genitivus subjectivus* that can be expressed as government by markets. The political appeal of popular parties in social modernity, particularly after the 1929 crisis and its sequels, lay in the regulating and limiting of markets. Social democratic parties may well have stopped dreaming of a socialist transformation, but they still believed in the possibility of successful *policies against the markets*.[68] In the face of neoliberalism and the revolt of capital, globalization and competition for location, politics has increasingly been forced to see itself as government in service of the markets, as representative of their interests.[69] Democracy has become 'market-conforming', to quote an expression used by Angela Merkel.

THE WELFARE STATE AND SOCIAL RIGHTS

Scarcely did the welfare state reach its zenith when it began to decline. The turning point was the economic crisis of 1973. Until shortly before this time, the welfare state had been expanding,

67 Cf. Gottfried Eisermann, *Vilfredo Pareto. Ein Klassiker der Soziologie*, Tübingen: Mohr Siebeck, 1987.

68 Gøsta Esping-Andersen, 'Die drei Welten des Wohlfahrtskapitalismus', in Stephan Lessenich and Ilona Ostner (eds), *Welten des Wohlfahrtskapitalismus: Des Sozialstaat in vergleichender Perspektive*, Frankfurt: Campus 1998.

69 Adam K. Webb, 'The Calm before the Storm? Revolutionary Pressures and Global Governance', *International Political Science Review* 27(1), 2006, 73–92.

and it absorbed an unprecedented share of the total budget. But as unemployment began to rise again, social expenditure rose in parallel. This accelerated state debt until finally a new era began in which the welfare state came under permanent pressure to consolidate.[70]

Neoliberalism identified the welfare state as one of the most serious obstacles to renewed growth. It was now seen not just as too expensive, but also as ineffective, as it supposedly sedated people with its welfare services and took away the impulse to behave responsibly. The middle class grew hostile to benefit recipients; they should not depend on the welfare state, but could look after themselves privately. As an institution, therefore, the welfare state was no longer interpreted as collective insurance for all employees and citizens, but rather as a gift from the strong and active to the weak and passive.[71]

Changes in the 1980s brought two decades of successive cuts and reductions. At first the welfare state was clipped only at its margins, while the basic structure remained remarkably stable.[72] In the 1990s, however, the burden of long-term unemployment on state coffers significantly increased pressure to reform.[73] The turning point to a new era of social policy in Germany was under the 'red-green' coalition of 1998–2005. The 'socio-political

70   Cf. Jens Alber, 'Germany', in Peter Flora (ed.), *Growth to Limits. The Western European Welfare States since World War II*, New York: Walter de Gruyter, 1986; Paul Pierson, *Dismantling the Welfare State? Reagan, Thatcher, and the Politics of Retrenchment*, Cambridge: Cambridge University Press, 1994; Streeck, *Buying Time*.

71   Cf. Stephan Lessenich, *Die Neuerfindung des Sozialen. Der Sozialstaat im flexiblen Kapitalismus*, Bielefeld: transcript, 2008; Robert Castel, *La montée des incertitudes. Travail, protections, statut de l'individu*, Paris: Éditions du Seuil, 2009.

72   Stephan Lessenich, *Dynamischer Immobilismus. Kontinuität und Wandel im deutschen Sozialmodell*, Frankfurt: Campus, 2003.

73   Timo Fleckenstein, 'The Politics of Labour Market Reforms and Social Citizenship in Germany', *West European Politics* 35(4), 2012, 847–68.

counter-reformation' began in the coalition's first term, with the introduction of partly privatized retirement insurance.[74] But the true transformation of the welfare state started in 2003, when the then chancellor Gerhard Schröder delivered a speech announcing his Agenda 2010, the overture to 'the greatest reduction in welfare services since 1949'.[75] The cuts were painful, and the Agenda 2010 reforms most decisively marked the farewell to social modernity.

The 'fourth law for modern labour-market services', better known as 'Hartz IV' after its progenitor, Volkswagen personnel director Peter Hartz, included the merger of unemployment and welfare into a single payment stream ('ALG II'), an active labour market policy, the reduction of the duration of unemployment pay ('ALG I') from thirty-six months to twelve months for unemployed persons under fifty-five, the extension of eligibility criteria and the lowering of the threshold for dismissal in small companies. Employees now had to fear a reduction in welfare after twelve months of unemployment, especially as a low means test threshold was applied. There had been downward mobility in the prior social modernity, but the steps on the ladder had been more manageable. Now the ladder was steeper: descent was much quicker and it was that much harder to rise again.

In the reformed welfare state, the paternalistic protection principle was supposedly modernized through deliberately introducing liberating notions of ability and participation. 'Demand and encourage', along with 'activation', were the mottos of welfare system reforms.[76] Yet these modernizations involved a

74 Elmar Rieger, 'Die sozialpolitische Gegenreformation. Eine kritische Analyse der Wirtschafts- und Sozialpolitik seit 1998', *Aus Politik und Zeitgeschichte* 52(46–47), 2002, 3–12.

75 Rüdiger Soldt, 'Hartz IV—Die größte Kürzung von Sozialleistungen seit 1949', *Frankfurter Allgemeine Zeitung*, 30 June 2004.

76 Irene Dingeldey, 'Wohlfahrtsstaatlicher Wandel zwischen "Arbeitszwang" und "Befähigung"', *Berliner Journal für Soziologie* 17(2), 2007, 189–209; Stephan Lessenich, *Die Neuerfindung des Sozialen. Der Sozialstaat im flexiblen Kapitalismus*, Bielefeld: transcript, 2008.

reduction in social citizenship rights. In social modernity, these had been far-reaching and were seen as inalienable; now they were tied to the fulfilment of obligations. The recipients of welfare benefits were no longer citizens with statutory rights, but became subaltern, second-class citizens, with whom the state made contracts in order to discipline and motivate them.[77]

The logic of liberalization privileged the market as a supplier, and welfare services were economized and partially transferred to it (under 'welfare markets'), while the state retreated to cover basic insurance.[78] Yet this regressive modernization should not be equated with a simple reduction in state activity on one hand and an extension of markets on the other. Even markets for welfare services, or private institutions, need the public hand of effective regulation.[79] This is not a question of market-correcting policy, but of market-preparing state activity.

For employees this has meant a fundamental change in the internal framework of the welfare state, as regressive moderniza-tion 'de-collectivized' social insurance.[80] Now each individual was required to act responsibly; this responsibility no longer meant the claim to an autonomous responsible life, but became essentially a byword for social discipline. Individual responsibility was now a civic duty.[81] By this standard, all those

77   Cf. Wolfgang Ludwig-Mayerhofer, Olaf Behrend and Ariadne Sondermann, 'Disziplinieren und Motivieren. Zur Praxis der neuen Arbeitsmarktpolitik', in Adalbert Evers and Rolf G. Heinze (eds), *Sozialpolitik. Ökonomisierung und Entgrenzung*, Wiesbaden: VS Verlag für Sozialwissenschaften, 2008.

78   Frank Nullmeier, 'Vermarktlichung des Sozialstaats', *WSI-Mitteilungen* 57(9), 2004, 495–500.

79   Cf. Berthold Vogel, *Die Staatsbedürftigkeit der Gesellschaft*, Hamburg: Hamburger Edition, 2007.

80   Castel, *La montée des incertitudes*, 30ff.

81   Cf. Stefan Lessenich, 'Der Arme in der Aktivgesellschaft. Zum sozialen Sinn des "Förderns und Forderns"', *WSI-Mitteilungen* 56(4), 2003, 214–19; idem, 'Soziale Subjektivität. Die neue Regierung der Gesellschaft', *Mittelweg 36* 12(4), 2003, 84–93; Aldo Legnaro, 'Moderne

who did not meet the liberal demand for responsibility were 'judged' and 'found guilty'.[82] In sum, this amounts to the transition to an authoritarian liberalism, which limits the rights of individuals if it supposedly benefits the community as a whole, the general welfare.[83] Only those individuals—particularly from the middle and upper strata—who conform in their behaviour and do not make demands on the welfare state (in other words, who successfully shoulder the challenge of individual responsibility) remain free from neo-paternalistic stimulus and experience a real gain in autonomy.

LABOUR MARKET AND ECONOMIC CITIZENSHIP RIGHTS

The transformation of work has been propelled from two sides: first, by the social regulation of work and the labour market as such (for example, by the welfare state), and second, by changes in production and business management.[84] As explained in the previous chapter, finance capitalism obtains direct influence on companies by way of 'shareholder value' management, and thereby also on work. It becomes the driving force of a new model of production, as companies are restructured along market-centred lines and production norms.[85] This is marked by a triad of

---

Dienstleistungen am Arbeitsmarkt—Zur politischen Ratio der Hartz-Gesetze', *Leviathan* 34(4), 2006, 514–32.

82   Castel, *La montée des incertitudes*, 45.

83   Cf. Alex Callinicos, *Bonfire of Illusions*, Cambridge: Polity Press, 2010, 58ff. This talk of general welfare, however, conceals definite interests that seek to provide themselves with moral legitimacy and have a disciplinary effect (cf. Claus Offe, 'Wessen Wohl ist das Gemeinwohl?', in Herfried Münkler and Karsten Fischer (eds), *Gemeinwohl und Gemeinsinn. Rhetoriken und Perspektiven sozial-moralischer Orientierung*, Berlin: Akademie Verlag, 2002.

84   Kevin Doogan, *New Capitalism? The Transformation of Work*, Cambridge: Polity Press, 2009.

85   Klaus Dörre and Ulrich Brinkmann, 'Finanzmarktkapitalismus. Triebkraft eines flexiblen Produktionsmodells?' in Paul Windolf

company policies: increasing flexibility, externalizing risks and reducing costs.

In the age of Fordism, companies were still relatively shielded from market fluctuations, but now production strategies are almost immediately linked to increasingly volatile markets. The time horizon of companies has been reduced, production has become specialized and flexible.[86] In order to obtain predefined profit margins in the context of 'shareholder value' orientation and at the same time deal with the volatility of market outlets, staff deployment in companies has been reorganized. Previously, strategies were directed to the cyclical average of planned production—the so-called 'personnel policy of the middle line'—whereas now they are oriented to the lower limit of capacity.[87] Management relies on ever fewer permanent staff, with an increasing share of flexible and precarious workers. In case of crisis, the latter can be 'switched off'—in the jargon used for dismissal by many German companies—at short notice or even immediately.[88] Under this policy, the permanent staff consists mainly of key skilled positions, and everything else is filled on a precarious basis using short-term agency contracts and subcontracted employees. And if this development has particularly affected large firms integrated into the world market, similar

---

(ed.), *Finanzmarkt-Kapitalismus. Analysen zum Wandel von Produktionsregimen. Sonderheft der Kölner Zeitschrift für Soziologie und Sozialpsychologie 45*, Opladen: VS, 2005.

86 Cf. Michael J. Piore and Charles F. Sabel, *The Second Industrial Divide: Prospects for Prosperity*, New York: Basic Books, 1984; Richard Sennett, *The Culture of the New Capitalism*, New Haven: Yale University Press, 2007.

87 Thomas Haipeter, 'Sozialpartnerschaft in und nach der Krise: Entwicklungen und Perspektiven', *Industrielle Beziehungen* 19(4), 387–411.

88 Cf. Hajo Holst, Oliver Nachtwey and Klaus Dörre, *Funktionswandel und Leiharbeit. Neue Nutzungsstrategien und ihre arbeits- und mitbestimmungspolitischen Folgen*, Arbeitsheft der Otto-Brenner-Stiftung 61, Frankfurt, 2009, p. 57.

tendencies are observable in many other branches. In the retail and service sectors, for example, agency and outsource staff are used to undermine settled wage rates and to externalize costs and risks. Under Fordism, there was to a certain point something like an integrated manufacturing process, in which skilled worker and canteen cook were part of a single firm with collectively agreed wage levels. Today, the model of the firm is increasingly that of a 'fragmented factory'. Its limits are no longer defined by the workshop walls; it is rather a network of differentiated systems of value creation,[89] made up of a number of semiautonomous profit centres, independent workplaces with differing wage and co-determination conditions, and above all, collaborators in heterogeneous and increasingly precarious situations.

With the 'modern labour market services' legislation ('Hartz I and II'), part-time employment and agency work were liberalized. The latter particularly abolished the ban on 'synchronization' and dismissal (it had previously been illegal for employment agencies to take on workers only for the duration of a particular job in a client company).[90] The boom in agency and low-paid work in the following years was a direct result of these measures. On top of this, precarious workers, particularly agency and subcontracted staff, are considered second-class citizens in terms of employment.[91] This is particularly clear in the case of agency

89 Cf. Jean-Pierre Durand, *The Invisible Chain. Constraints and Opportunities in the New World of Employment*, London: Macmillan, 2007; Ulrich Brinkmann, *Die unsichtbare Faust des Marktes. Betriebliche Kontrolle und Koordination im Finanzmarktkapitalismus*, Berlin: Edition Sigma, 2011; Manuel Castells, *The Rise of the Network Society*, Wiley-Blackwell, 2009.

90 Since then, however, some of these liberalizations have been repealed—for example, the restoration of the ban on 'synchronization'.

91 Ulrich Brinkmann and Oliver Nachtwey, 'Prekäre Demokratie? Zu den Auswirkungen atypischer Beschäftigung auf die betriebliche Mitbestimmung', *Industrielle Beziehungen* 21(1), 2014, 78–98; idem, 'Postdemokratie, Mitbestimmung und industrielle Bürgerrechte', *Politische Vierteljahresschrift* 54(3), 2013, 506–33.

workers. In formal legal terms, although the modernization of employment law in 2001 gave these workers additional rights of co-determination, in practice these were curtailed: within the agency they have the same rights as other employees, but in the firm where they actually work, possibly for several years, they have only very limited participation rights. Appearing on the balance sheet as 'material resources', they have no protection from dismissal, they often earn only half as much as permanent staff for the same work, and their position is inferior in terms of labour and health protection. As a result, they fall into a new dependency—for example, earning so little that their income does not cover their needs and they are forced to seek greater support from the state. Reducing state regulation of the labour market thus leads to an increase in social policy intervention. Agency workers also face a demeaning means test to certify that they cannot live reasonably on their income.

On top of everything else, works committees are weakened by the use of agency staff, while simultaneously being given more tasks. This generally erodes co-determination within the firm.[92] In the following chapter, we shall examine precarization more closely, focusing particularly on the erosion of economic citizenship rights—collective bargaining and rights at work. The system of collective bargaining has been perforated for several decades; it lost influence as a de-commodifying institution and has itself become a facilitator of market mechanisms.[93] Employees have partly abandoned traditional forms of social partnership and sought to circumvent wage agreements.[94] The representation of interests by works and enterprise committees has also been declining. In 2014, only 28 per cent of West German employees,

---

92 Ulrich Brinkmann and Oliver Nachtwey, 'Postdemokratie, Mitbestimmung und industrielle Bürgerrechte'.

93 Hajo Holst, 'Von der Branche zum Markt. Zur Regulierung überbetrieblicher Arbeitsbeziehungen nach dem organisierten Kapitalismus', *Berliner Journal für Soziologie* 21(3), 2011, 383–405.

94 Streeck, *Re-Forming Capitalism*.

and 15 per cent in the eastern half of the country, still worked in private firms with both an industry-wide wage scale and a works committee (as against 39 per cent and 25 per cent respectively in 1998).[95]

The example of a major German automobile manufacturer I have studied frequently since 2008 clearly demonstrates the developments described above.[96] The factory in question is one of the most modern in Europe—it opened in 2005 and already displayed the spirit of 'shareholder value' management. It is a so-called 'breathing factory', which can react quickly and flexibly to changes in demand.[97] The site offers sufficient space for integrated suppliers, and its workshops can be flexibly expanded. Of the normal staff, 30 per cent are agency workers, who can be 'switched off' immediately in case of crisis. At the time of my study, for example, only about half of the approximately 4,000 workers there were employees of the company itself, the rest being either agency workers or employed by other firms. The company's permanent staff have enjoyed comparatively good terms: their pay is collectively negotiated, their contract gives them certain extras, and they are represented by a strong works committee. On the other hand, the more than 1,000 agency workers then employed, after years of struggle by the trade union and works committees, had only recently received formally equal conditions to the core staff in terms of basic pay and working conditions, and still remained excluded from bonuses and other perks.[98]

95   Peter Ellguth and Susanne Kohaut, 'Tarifbindung und betriebliche Interessenvertretung: Aktuelle Ergebnisse aus dem IAB-Betriebspanel 2014', *WSI-Mitteilungen* 68(4), 2015, 290–97.

96   Cf. Brinkmann and Nachtwey, 'Postdemokratie', 523ff.

97   The developments described here refer to the time frame 2010–13.

98   The high proportion of agency and subcontracted staff also has an influence on the works committee, which is smaller than it would be if all workers on site had been employed by the company itself.

Even in the actual workplace, the world of the subcontractor staff is a parallel one, their boundary marked by a blue line drawn on the ground. This is the space that a logistics company uses for delivering new materials to the conveyor belts and workstations. This company is a subcontractor, and no cooperation is allowed between the employees of the automobile company and the staff of the outside firm, who are clearly in a worse position. In other cases, there is a kind of concealed contract. Accordingly, neither the employees of the logistics company on the one hand, nor those of the automobile company and agency workers on the other, are supposed to cross the blue line (though in reality this of course occurs frequently).

A few hundred metres away from this site is another assembly plant, rented from the main company by a separate supplier, where axles are produced. The supplying company itself employs only thirty-four workers on site, principally engineers and highly skilled workers, including ten staff from an agency that itself belongs to the company. The axles, however, are assembled by 470 temporary staff, who are provided by a total of seven agencies. In the main company, a leading automobile producer, working conditions are modern and even exemplary. There is no conveyor belt as such, but rather moving islands, on each of which an automobile body stands on a hydraulic platform. This is adjusted by computer to the body size of the assembler, and so meets the highest ergonomic standard, as does the sprung wooden floor. Two hundred metres away, where the axles are assembled, things are very different: assembly line work, no air conditioning, concrete floors, no ergonomic measures, less money and weaker social benefits.

In this particular case, one group of agency workers managed something that only rarely happens with precarious employees: setting up a works committee. This committee, however, only had co-determination rights for the agency staff. In other words, these individuals could influence working conditions in the office that managed their work, but not their own conditions in the company where they themselves actually worked; this was the responsibility of the works committee there. The committee, in turn, however, was made up of the aforementioned engineers and managers, who showed little interest in the needs of the line workers.

The overall situation is thus one of a distinct hierarchy, in which those employed in lower positions are at a clear disadvantage. The automobile manufacturer's permanent staff enjoy the highest level of job security, the best wages, and the greatest opportunities for democratic participation in the company. The agency workers in the main company have some share in the agreed wage conditions of the permanent staff, while those working for suppliers, and the agency workers these employ, no longer enjoy these standards.

The example described here is perhaps extreme, and such conditions are not the general rule. But it is certainly not unique. In many other branches—for example, in retail trade—the trend is in a similar direction. In the food industry, moreover, particularly in meat packaging, we often find a still more glaring state of affairs. There, sometimes only one worker in ten has a regular contract. In one factory that I studied, there were only 184 direct employees out of around 600 workers in total.[99] The majority of workers in this meat packaging facility were Romanian, officially employed by firms in their own country, and according to the regulations in force not entitled to any welfare rights in Germany. The works committees here were overburdened, and the Romanian workers had practically no one to represent their interests; even the foremen felt this gap. Regulations were frequently infringed, and communication was hardly possible in view of the language barrier. Initially the foreign workers were not even allowed to speak to the German workers or cooperate with them, as this would have amounted to a concealed contract.

99   Cf. Brinkmann and Nachtwey, 'Prekäre Demokratie?', 91ff.

It is deceptive to believe that such models only involve low-skilled activities. Besides the downward spiral under way in the individual factory, the flexibilization bound up with atypical forms of employment also influences the realm of highly skilled jobs. Both IT and engineering services are increasingly subject to agency work. 'Crowd-working', as practised in both the software and automobile industries, ever more frequently abolishes well-defined activities; this adds fuel to speculation about an 'end of fixed employment'.[100] What has grown particularly in the automobile industry in recent years are engineering services that contribute to the development of new models. Works committees repeatedly report many new and unknown faces that suddenly appear in the workplace canteen—and at the end of the product cycle disappear from the scene just as quickly. The contractor then moves on to another development project. At first engineers frequently find this nomadic existence satisfying and fulfilling; their activity is varied, and they are confronted with new challenges. Yet at some point their perspective changes. Travelling and rootlessness become problems, while the physical demands are ever harder to bear. Eventually, they often find themselves desperate for a regular job.

In social modernity, economic and social civil rights were universalized—in other words, extended to ever more groups. This improved the situation of workers in many sectors: unskilled workers generally had the same claim to co-determination and job security as white-collar staff.[101] Now this process has reversed.

---

100   Christoph Ruhkamp, 'Auslaufmodell Festanstellung?', *Frankfurter Allgemeine Zeitung*, 20 September 2014.

101   The last distinctions between workers and white-collar employees—for example, in wage scales and pensions—were abolished in Germany soon after the turn of the century.

DUAL INDIVIDUALIZATION

The free development of the individual—his or her ability to act as a responsible subject—is a key value of modern societies. In its present form this is the result of material, social and mental changes that have reciprocally influenced one another. Social modernity accelerated this process (see Chapter 2). Higher incomes and increased free time meant expanded room for action and made it possible for people to break out of their inherited social situation. Traditional social relations, family ties, and above all the marks of class membership lost their collective character, replaced by individualized values, behavioural dispositions and trajectories.[102] It is precisely these developmental tendencies that have been reinforced in regressive modernity, while increasing commercialization has led to a general individualization. A paradoxical situation arose. The welfare state made individualization possible for the first time, but the modern individual was likewise highly dependent on these social institutions (see Chapter 1).

Now the page has turned. The impulse to act as an individual comes not from citizens themselves, striving for emancipation from a rigid social order—instead, individuality is now a social imperative placed on citizens. French sociologist Robert Castel sees this as having a dual consequence for individuality.[103] Drawing on Norbert Elias's formulation, Castel sees us as living today in a pure 'society of individuals',[104] in which there is increasing pressure to behave according to the postulates of competitive

102   At the same time, many traditional class positions and modes of behaviour have continued in a modernized form—for example, in political preferences and partly also in social connections (Michael Vester, Peter von Oertzen, Heiko Geiling, Thomas Herman and Dagmar Müller, *Soziale Milieus im gesellschaftlichen Strukturwandel. Zwischen Integration und Ausgrenzung*, Frankfurt: Suhrkamp, 2001).

103   Castel, *La montée des incertitudes*, 26; cf. also Sennett, *The Culture of the New Capitalism*.

104   Norbert Elias, *The Society of Individuals*, New York: Continuum, 2001.

individuality. For many members of the middle class this is fine; they are able to take advantage of the opportunities arising and profit from this development, as for them liberation from collective arrangements actually does mean more autonomy and responsibility in the positive sense. They thus often develop an affirmative attitude toward liberalization, seeing themselves in solipsistic fashion as opportunity seekers,[105] and thereby threatening to become narcissistic 'excessive individuals' (*individus par excès*).[106] The large group of those who fail to keep up in the maelstrom of liberalization, who do not have the same resources at their disposal and often lack the basic preconditions for autonomy, become 'mere individuals' (*individus par défaut*). For them, liberalization and increased social uncertainty are actually threats. With the de-collectivization of the welfare state, there is also the growing danger of downward mobility and the stigmatization bound up with this. Unemployment, low pay, poverty, reduced prospects, and so forth were previously not considered personal deficiencies, but rather the shared collective fate of a class. Class milieus propagated and handed down 'sustaining counter-interpretations, forms of defence and support'.[107] Through individualization, this previously collective fate becomes the personal fate of the 'market individual'. The dependency of our society on education precisely reinforces this process. Education may be a universal value, but it also draws new barriers. At the end of the day, only very few manage to obtain and make use of a real opportunity: 'The result is the emergence of two worlds, one of a wide range of life chances and one of exclusion'.[108]

....

105   Many of the developments criticized here are also to be found in those milieus that identify with the predictions of Holm Friebe and Sascha Lobo, *Wir nennen es Arbeit: Die digitale Bohème oder Intelligentes Leben jenseits der Festanstellung*, Munich: Heyne, 2006.

106   Castel, *La montée des incertitudes*, p. 27

107   Beck, *Risikogesellschaft*, 144.

108   Ralf Dahrendorf, *The Global Class and the New Inequality*, Jerusalem: Israel Academy of Sciences and Humanities, 2000, 11; cf.

Other than was often expected, individualization did not give rise to a general increase in autonomy or greater diversity of life-styles. Genuine autonomy would mean that individuals were able to choose a style of life that ran against social norms; however, individualization has become twisted 'into an emotionally fossilized set of demands', while 'the ideal of a self-realization pursued throughout the course of a life has developed into an ideology and productive force'.[109] The impulse of liberalization, increased autonomy, takes the form of justifications and insecurities that undermine social solidarity. Greater dependence on the market tends to create an adaptability in which individuality shows itself only in what Freud called the 'narcissism of small differences'. In this way, individualization increasingly loses its emancipatory character to become a challenge, and for some people an unreasonable demand. It even threatens to become pathological, since sociality as such is negated.

JUSTICE: ONE STEP FORWARD, TWO STEPS BACK[110]

In social modernity, class compromise was institutionalized; social rights derived largely from work, while justice meant a reduction in social inequalities. This was not a question of equality of outcome, as critics of social justice frequently objected, but rather of an improvement in position, what François Dubet calls 'equality of position'.[111]

Herfried Münkler, *Mitte und Maß. Der Kampf um die richtige Ordnung*, Reinbek bei Hamburg: Rowohlt, 2010, 70ff.

109   Axel Honneth, 'Organized Self-Realization. Some Paradoxes of Individualization', in *European Journal of Social Theory* 7(4), 2004, 463–78, 474.

110   In this section I only deal with specific aspects of the discussion on justice—for example, its implications for questions of upward and downward social mobility. For key discussions of justice, cf. Callinicos, *Bonfire of Illusions*; Angelika Krebs (ed.), *Gleichheit oder Gerechtigkeit*, Frankfurt: Suhrkamp, 2000; David Miller, *Social Justice*, Oxford: Clarendon, 1976.

111   François Dubet, 'Die Grenzen der Chancengleichheit', *Nueva Sociedad* special issue, 2012, 165f.

Social justice in Dubet's sense refers to an unequal structure of social positions with respect to incomes, conditions of life, social security, access to social services, and so on. For people with lower incomes, for example, there is the question whether they can also afford to go on holiday. The impulse of social justice is vertical, directed to the class structure of society. Justice is to be produced by social ascent, which is 'an indirect consequence of relative social equality' and makes it possible to implement the merit principle and access to education.[112] At the same time, however, other inequalities found scant place in Dubet's conception of justice—for example, those between the sexes or ethnic groups.

In the wake of regressive modernization, there has been a revaluation of discourse on justice and equality. The prevailing model now is that of a radicalized equality of opportunity.[113]

Justice in this context means not so much the reduction of vertical inequalities as the abolition of horizontal discrimination defined by cultural characteristics.[114] The key concepts of this discourse are no longer social inequality and exploitation, but rather equal rights and identity. Equal opportunity, for example, now aims at the formally equal access of women to positions that were previously reserved for men. The vertical differences between occupational positions—between the female manager of a large corporation and a low-paid female employee of a cleaning company, scarcely play any role in this discourse. The problem with this shift is clearly not the impetus to improve women's position on the labour market. The problem is that equality policy is limited to this question, as radically equal opportunity reduces justice to the horizontal logic of inclusion and equal

---

112   Ibid, 165.

113   For a discussion of equal opportunity in the programme and policy of the SPD, cf. Oliver Nachtwey, *Marktsozialdemokratie. Die Transformation von SPD und Labour Party*, Wiesbaden: VS, 2009.

114   Cf. Nancy Fraser and Axel Honneth, *Redistribution or Recognition? A Political-Philosophical Exchange*, London: Verso, 2003.

treatment. The vertical logic of redistribution is increasingly blanked out.[115]

Radicalized equal opportunity also produces characteristic and paradoxical regressions. While everyone is supposed to have the same opportunities (for example, working-class children being able to rise to top positions), this policy has the side effect of increasing competition on the labour market, since the number of top positions is limited. Thus, actual equality of opportunity can even be reduced. Even in a formally equal system, prospects remain better for children of better-off and more educated parents. Privileges can be invisibly inherited by way of cliques and other discreet signals. This is particularly true for top positions. As Bourdieu showed in his theory of distinction, the better qualified, with their sovereign upper-class habitus, usually push out the less elegant members of the lower classes.[116] Often those who end up in top positions are themselves children of the elite.[117]

If all who participate in the market have the same access, then inherited social inequalities should no longer play a role, and in theory, only talent, achievement, energy and skill should decide. This is the meritocratic principle with its ideal of 'pure social mobility'.[118] Equality of opportunity is thus the justice principle of an individualized society, as it radicalizes autonomy, personal responsibility and self-realization, greater competition

115   Cf. Frank Nullmeier, 'Eigenverantwortung, Gerechtigkeit und Solidarität—Konkurrierende Prinzipien der Konstruktion moderner Wohlfahrtsstaaten?' *WSI-Mitteilungen* 59(4), 2006, 175–80.

116   Pierre Bourdieu, *Distinction: A Social Critique of the Judgement of Taste*, Cambridge, MA: Harvard University Press, [1979] 1996.

117   Michael Hartmann, *Der Mythos von den Leistungseliten*, Frankfurt: Campus, 2002.

118   Ralf Dahrendorf early on saw meritocracy as a 'global class consciousness' that primarily served to reproduce social inequalities: 'The Global Class and the New Inequality', *Lectures in Memory of Justice Lewis D. Brandeis*, Academy of Sciences and Humanities, Jerusalem, 12 March 1999.

between individuals and groups, and finally undermines ties of sociability and solidarity.

According to this model of 'fair competition', differences in position are conceived, at least in theory, as simply the result of performance. In this way an illusion is constructed: radical equal opportunity contains the paradox that while individuals are more than ever exposed to the market, the results of the market are distributed less than ever according to principles of performance.

Historically, the merit principle has been disputed both semantically and in practice; its implementation was characteristic of the rise of the bourgeoisie in a world that had long been marked by rigid social division and aristocratic privilege. Ownership, income and social position were now to be determined neither by geographic origin nor by ascriptive characteristics such as skin colour or sex, but rather as the result of a person's individual work and performance. The merit principle assumes a connection between individual effort and expected reward, and offers criteria as to how this reward should look in terms of income, social position, and so on. But the liberal merit principle has been hollowed out in recent years; instead of this we have a culture of success in which what counts is not effort but simply results. Economic and political elites are treated as high performers, who define performance by their very success. In a monstrous act of self-reference, the key measure of success is now success itself.[119] In this way, a manager is a high performer on the basis of his or her position in the social hierarchy, quite independent of their actual achievement. A hospital nurse, who works responsibly and with great personal attention for seven days a week, is not seen as a high performer—because she does not enjoy the same monetary success.

----

119 Sighard Neckel, *Flucht nach vorn. Die Erfolgskultur der Marktgesellschaft*, Frankfurt: Campus, 2008; Sighard Neckel and Kai Dröge, 'Die Verdienste und ihr Preis. Leistung in der Marktgesellschaft', in Honneth (ed.), *Befreiung aus der Mündigkeit*.

In short, the more a society is based on equality of opportunity, the more unequal it becomes, and the more legitimate its inequalities. Certainly, the validity of the performance principle is being steadily undermined, yet everyone is still supposed to enjoy the same chances: the losers are accordingly those who deserve to lose, and the winners those who deserve to win. Principles of modernity often continue to exist only as empty husks.

THE REGRESSION OF SOCIAL CITIZENSHIP

The phenomena of regressive modernity discussed above combine to produce a far-reaching change in citizenship rights. This affects democratic rights, the development of the market individual, as well as the de-collectivizing of the welfare state and social justice. The left-wing critique of bureaucracy and social modernity has in this way been fulfilled 'in a perverse form'.[120] The artistic critique of bureaucracy and standardization has ended up being used to dismantle the entire edifice of social modernity.[121]

Whereas in social modernity the extension of political, economic and social citizenship rights reached a high point, these are now being hollowed out by the forces of regressive modernization—and becoming an element of downward mobility. However, this has happened asymmetrically and unevenly in time. Today's political culture has become selectively more liberal. Political citizenship in the sense of individual equality has made advances. We could say that horizontally—between the sexes, between people with different sexual orientations, and in certain respects even between ethnic groups—society has become more equal and inclusive in terms of rights. At the same time, however, the illiberal treatment of beneficiaries of social

---

120   Sennett, *Culture of the New Capitalism*, 2.
121   Cf. Wagner, *A Sociology of Modernity*.

services has worsened.[122] Political equality goes together with greater vertical inequality and even increased discrimination. Social and economic rights have been constricted.

Though the retreat of social citizenship has not reached the pre-welfare state zero point of the nineteenth century, it is now back on a foundation of market liberalism. For while collective social rights have been undermined, new individual rights have been established—for example, strengthening the position of the individual as consumer or entrepreneur.[123] In this way, state citizenship rights are reconstituted as individual *market citizenship rights*.[124] In their extreme formulation, these need no comprehensive welfare state, or even extensive public services, to guarantee the existence of democracy.

The market citizen is a new social figure with specific rights: political equality, consumer protection, property rights, protection from discrimination. Ultimately, however, market citizenship rights are little more than an individual legal equality of consumers, an equality that produces greater inequalities in terms of distributing the gains of the market. The market citizen is basically no longer a citizen, but rather a client with

122 It is also an aspect of this unevenness that there are at the bottom end of society groups in which these dimensions intersect and reinforce one another: poor immigrants, who are also largely of Muslim confession, experience increased discrimination, whereas highly skilled IT specialists from abroad can expect a high degree of equality and integration.

123 Cf. Jörn Lamla, *Verbraucherdemokratie. Politische Soziologie der Konsumgesellschaft*, Berlin: Suhrkamp, 2013; Pierre Dardot and Christian Laval, *The New Way of the World: On Neoliberal Society*, London: Verso, 2013.

124 While social citizenship is based on the nation state, market citizenship has been established via the European Union as a legally secured norm (cf. Christian Joppke, 'Transformation of Citizenship: Status, Rights, Identity', *Citizenship Studies* 11(1), 2007, 37–48; Michael Faist, 'The Transnational Social Question: Social Rights and Citizenship in a Global Context', *International Sociology* 24(1), 2009, 7–35.

rights—the ideal subject of regressive modernization, facing the alien rule of total competition.[125]

The regression of social citizenship also has far-reaching implications for democratic life and its generic presumption of equality. In the past this was based on a relative 'relational equality': equal civic status, a certain similarity (if not equality) of life situation, equal autonomy and the absence of inherited status privileges.[126] It is precisely this relational equality that has now been abolished. The winners cut themselves off from the losers, in what has been called a process of re-feudalization.[127] At the top there is a 'secession of the wealthy',[128] which dissolves democratic intimacy and demands self-isolation. Correspondingly, a new paternalism is inflicted on the lower classes in the guise of liberation. The emancipatory surplus of the bourgeois epoch is increasingly dissolving. This rift in the fabric of democratic equality threatens democracy as such, particularly because it is sharpened by a social rift: collective downward mobility.

125   Cf. Hartmut Rosa, 'Capitalism as a Spiral of Dynamisation: Sociology as Social Critique', in Dörre, Lessenich and Rosa, Sociology, Capitalism, Critique; Rosanvallon, Society of Equals.

126   Ibid., 12ff. Individuals were not considered identical, but only as similar, and therefore could enjoy different levels of income.

127   Neckel, ' "Refeudalisierung" '.

128   Rosanvallon, Society of Equals, 279.

4

Downward Mobility

In the midst of the German economic miracle, Hannah Arendt formulated a prognosis that would become famous: the work-centred society would one day run out of work.[1] A quarter of a century later, in the 1980s, it seemed she might well have been correct. Traditional industrial society was changing at breakneck speed. Computers and robots were being introduced into production, unemployment had become a persistent mass phenomenon, and the service sector was steadily growing at the expense of traditional production. The work-centred society as we knew it seemed to be ending.[2] It seemed increasingly doubtful that labour was indeed a social condition 'that affects and penetrates all social forms and spheres of life, drawing them into its wake.'[3]

---

1   Hannah Arendt, *The Human Condition*, Chicago: University of Chicago Press, [1958] 1998.

2   André Gorz, *Farewell to the Working Class*, London: Pluto, 1987; Ralf Dahrendorf, *Die Chancen der Krise. Über die Zukunft des Liberalismus*, Stuttgart: DVA, 1987. In the 1990s this thesis was taken up again by Jeremy Rifkin, *The Zero Marginal Cost Society*, New York: Palgrave Macmillan, 2015.

3   Claus Offe and Karl Hinrichs, 'Sozialökonomie des Arbeitsmarktes. Primäres und sekundäres Machtgefälle', in Offe and Hinrichs (eds), 'Arbeitsgesellschaft'. *Strukturprobleme und Zukunftsperspektiven*, Frankfurt: Campus, 1984, 64.

Yet the mistake could scarcely have been greater. The importance of paid employment has since not declined but increased. The work-centred society has not ended; it is rather at a new beginning. This again puts wage labour at the centre of society—but under a very different manifestation than in social modernity.

The thesis of the end of the work-centred society never had a strong empirical foundation; in the 1970s and '80s this was more a prognosis mechanically derived from rising unemployment and increasing automation. Increased unemployment drew attention away from the fact that the number of economically active people had actually *risen* almost steadily in the 1970s.[4] The proportion of the total population who were economically active rose from 44.2 per cent in 1970 to 52.6 per cent in 2013.[5] The proportion of employees rose almost nine percentage points between 1970 and 2013, from 36.0 per cent to 45.4 per cent, while that of all economically active (including self-employed) people rose from 44 per cent to 50.9 per cent.[6]

This trend has continued almost without interruption. Never in the history of the Federal Republic were so many people in work as in 2018. In January of that year, 44.2 million people had paid employment,[7] while the number of officially unemployed

4   This was due above all to the increased participation of women and older people in the workforce (cf. Frank Schüller and Christian Wingerter, 'Arbeitsmarkt und Verdienste', Statistisches Bundesamt/ Wissenschaftszentrum Berlin für Sozialforschung (ed.), *Datenreport 2013. Ein Sozialbericht für die Bundesrepublik Deutschland*, Bonn: Bundeszentrale für politische Bildung, 2013, 117.

5   If only those people between ages fifteen and sixty-five are considered, the proportion in 2012 was 77 per cent (against 73 per cent ten years before).

6   Cf. Statistisches Bundesamt, 'Arbeitsmarkt. Bevölkerung und Erwerbstätigkeit', 2014, www.destatis.de (accessed February 2016); Schüller and Wingerter, 'Arbeitsmarkt und Verdienste'.

7   Statistisches Bundesamt, '44,2 Millionen Erwerbstätige im Januar 2018', press release, 28 February 2018, destatis.de (accessed May 2018). After the outset of the financial and economic crisis, which produced one of the greatest downturns in post-war German history, unemployment did not

was down to 2.56 million—a proportion of 5.9 per cent.[8] Unemployment had thus fallen back to the level of reunification, and an age of 'new full employment' is being celebrated.[9] As I shall show, however, this is a society of precarious full employment, geared to employment at any price.[10]

Quantitative and statistical perspectives on work, moreover, conceal the internal structural change in work-centred society. What is coming into being is a society of downward mobility, where the problem is not simply work but rather *integrative work*. Viewed in this way, the work-centred society characteristic of social modernity, in which work was still the precondition for social security, is indeed ending.[11] The 'brief dream of ever assured ascent' is over, and will in all likelihood not return.[12] With regressive modernization, the character of work is changing; what was formerly a source of ascent now brings the danger of downward mobility. Paid employment now guarantees ever fewer people

---

skyrocket but instead remained remarkably stable. Soon, people began speaking of a 'German employment miracle' (Paul Krugman, *Return of Depression Economics*, London: Allen Lane, 2008). Yet this 'miracle' was due primarily to government intervention (such as the extension of temporary subsidies and the 'scrapping premium'), renewed cooperation between unions and companies, as well as flexibility in collective bargaining (cf. Thomas Haipeter, 'Sozialpartnerschaft in und nach der Krise: Entwicklungen und Perspektiven', *Industrielle Beziehungen* 19(4), 2012, 387–411).

8   Bundesagentur für Arbeit, *Monatsbericht zum Arbeits- und Ausbildungsmarkt – Januar 2018*, Nuremburg.

9   Karl-Heinz Paqué, *Vollbeschäftigt. Das neue deutsche Jobwunder*, Munich: Carl Hanser, 2012. Cf. the website of the *Frankfurter Allgemeine Zeitung*, cited above.

10   Cf. Klaus Dörre, Karin Scherschel, Melanie Booth, Tine Haubner, Kai Marquardsen and Karen Schierhorn (eds), *Bewährungsproben für die Unterschicht? Soziale Folgen aktivierender Arbeitsmarktpolitik*, Frankfurt: Campus, 2013, 32ff.

11   Cf. Robert Castel, *La montée des incertitudes. Travail, protections, status de l'individu*, Paris: Éditions du Seuil, 2009, 12, 93ff.

12   Steffen Mau, *Lebenschancen. Wohin driftet die Mittelschicht?*, Berlin: Suhrkamp, 2012, 49; cf. Rainer Trinczek, 'Überlegungen zum Wandel der Arbeit', *WSI-Mitteilungen* 64/11, 2011, 606–14.

security, status and prestige, along with any possibility of planning their future. Processes of downward mobility have delivered repeated shocks to growing segments of society.

It is clear, however, that this diagnosis requires further differentiation. I shall therefore sketch the myths and realities of Germany's service society of downward mobility with a look at both precarious work and different social situations and mobilities. This is a multidimensional process, occurring at different levels simultaneously and marked by an internal polarization. Both middle and lower classes experience specific processes of downward mobility, which they cope with via different strategies. The society of downward mobility, as I shall assert at the end of this chapter, is leading to a renewed class society in Germany today.

INDUSTRIAL SERVICE SOCIETY

The desire to be free from work, or at least from its burdens, persistently fuels new myths. Over the past 150 years, work has become less heavy in physical terms, yet we are still light years away from being totally liberated from it.

The transformation of the work-centred society is particularly evident in the shift that has occurred between economic sectors. The share of the primary sector (agriculture, forestry and fishing) fell from 24.6 per cent of total employment in 1950 to 1.5 per cent in 2013. During this time, the secondary sector (classical productive industry) also declined in its share, from 42.9 to 24.7 per cent. There has been a corresponding rise in the tertiary sector (particularly in services) from 32.5 to 73.8 per cent.[13] There is no question about this change in economic structure; the modern economy has less agriculture and fewer factory smokestacks. But this

---

13   Statistisches Bundesamt, 'Arbeitsmarkt. Erwerbstätige im Inland nach Wirtschaftssektoren', 2014, www. destatis.de (accessed February 2016).

transformation, however impressive at first sight, is partly based on a statistical construct that conceals the continuing industrial character of value creation. Legal fragmentation and network patterns of organization within the firm have produced a statistical shift. If an automobile manufacturer outsources its canteen to a formally independent unit, then the latter is subsequently classed under services. Yet these remain industrial services that are directly linked to production and basically subordinate to it.[14]

The overall trends of increasing skill, a growing tertiary sector, and the feminization of the labour market have been substantial. But instead of the general upgrading of the occupational structure that was often expected, there has been a polarization. There are more jobs requiring higher skill and more requiring lower skill at the same time, leaving fewer in the middle.[15] The share of those whose activity is technical in character—the manual working class—has shrunk dramatically, from 44.8 to 33.3 per cent between 1990 and 2007. While the share of jobs with an organizational character—management and administrative tasks—has risen in the same time frame from 24.9 to 27.6 per cent, the number of self-employed persons has also escalated, from 9.7 to 11.3 per cent. In total, the share of those whose work is interpersonal has risen by 4.3 per cent to reach 27.9 per cent. The latter include not only teachers and nurses, but also sociocultural experts such as skilled salespeople, display, catering and care staff. More than half of all service

---

14   Ulrich Brinkmann, *Die unsichtbare Faust des Marktes. Betriebliche Kontrolle und Koordination im Finanzmarktkapitalismus*, Berlin: Edition Sigma, 2011. In my own studies, I came across one example where the entire axle production of an automobile manufacturer was outsourced to another company as an industrial service (cf. Ulrich Brinkmann, 'Postdemokratie, Mitbestimmung und industrielle Bürgerrechte, *Politische Vierteljahresschrift* 54(3), 2013, 506–33). The expansion of industrial service companies is likely to continue in the future.

15   Daniel Oesch and Jorge Rodriguez Menés, 'Upgrading or Polarization? Occupational Change in Britain, Germany, Spain and Switzerland, 1990–2008', *Socio-Economic Review* 9(3), 2011, 503–31.

jobs, however, are directly subordinate to industrial value creation.[16] In other words, this is not so much a service society liberated from industry as an industrial service society, in which the logic of industrial production and that of services are melded together.

The new branches of high technology, finance and creative industry are largely based on the social division of labour. Besides banking personnel, consultants of all kinds, engineers and IT specialists, along with administrative staff, there is a growing army of call-centre agents, personal trainers, couriers, burger flippers in fast-food chains, salespeople in discount stores, cleaners and care workers, as well as teachers.

What is still unclear is how digitalization and the advance of robotics will affect the occupational structure. When 'robots arrive', will future society still be based on work?[17] In the United States, employment has stagnated since the turn of the century, though labour productivity has risen.[18] There are further prognoses that more than half of all jobs could be automatized in the near future.[19] In particular, activities that are repetitive and demand little cognitive skill, along with work requiring only low qualification, could easily be replaced. Endangered jobs include not only lock-keepers but also bookkeepers, tax consultants and insurance brokers. These

16 Michael Vester, 'Postindustrielle oder industrielle Dienstleistungsgesellschaft. Wohin treibt die gesellschaftliche Arbeitsteilung?', *WSI-Mitteilungen* 64(12), 2011, 624, 638.

17 This is the message of several recent publications (cf. among others Martin Ford, *Rise of the Robots: Technology and the Threat of a Jobless Future*, New York: Basic Books, 2015; Erik Brynjolfsson and Andrew McAfee, *The Second Machine Age: Work, Progress, and Prosperity in a Time of Brilliant Technologies*, New York: W.W. Norton & Company, 2014).

18 Cf. ibid., 163ff.

19 Carl Benedict Frey and Michael Osborne, *The Future of Employment: How Susceptible are Jobs to Computerization?* Oxford: Oxford University Press, 2013; Holger Bonin, Terry Gregory and Ulrich Zierahn, *Übertragung der Studie von Frey/Osborne (2013) auf Deutschland, Kurzexpertise 57*, Mannheim: Zentrum für europäische Wirtschaftsforschung, 2015.

scenarios may well prove correct, but we have yet to see how digitalization will work out in practice. Historically, labour-saving innovations have been the rule rather than the exception. For example, in the early nineteenth century, mechanized looms in the factories threatened English weavers' domestic work. The result, however, was that new jobs were created precisely by technical progress. And after the Second World War, it was precisely those countries that invested most in robotics and automated production that had a particularly high level of employment: Germany, Japan and the United States. From this perspective, digitalization could also contribute to a co-evolution of new occupations and new jobs.

It is true, up to now, that for particular highly skilled occupations—consultants, engineers, knowledge producers—the vision of a service society based on social ascent and an increasing degree of freedom has been fulfilled. These individuals truly have achieved autonomy. This is because their fields of activity (specialized knowledge and expertise) acquire greater importance in modern production, which immediately gives them a higher degree of structural power[20] on the labour market.[21] The logic of the work process itself also offers them greater freedom. For the 'unskilled worker', however, the opposite is true.[22] At work they experience domination rather than autonomy. They have little choice in their actions, little freedom or creative room

20   On the power resources of groups of workers, cf. Stefan Schmalz and Klaus Dörre (eds), *Comeback der Gewerkschaften? Machtressourcen, innovative Praktiken, internationale Perspektiven*, Frankfurt: Campus, 2013; also Ulrich Brinkmann and Oliver Nachtwey, 'Krise und strategische Neuorientierung der Gewerkschaften', *Aus Politik und Zeitgeschichte* 60(13–14), 2010, 21–9.

21   This structural power, however, may undergo a dramatic change, as shown in connection with crowdsourcing in the previous chapter. It is precisely knowledge-intensive activities that will be increasingly performed in the global labour market in the future.

22   Hartmut Hirsch-Kreinsen, Peter Ittermann and Jörg Abel, 'Industrielle Einfacharbeit. Kern eines sektoralen Produktions- und Arbeitssystems', *Industrielle Beziehungen* 19(2), 2012, 187–210.

to manoeuvre. A combination of intensive 'social' rationalization strategies and direct forms of personal control makes them easily replaceable.[23] They accordingly possess only little structural power. In short, the reverse side of the highly skilled employee aristocracy in the service sector is the 'service proletariat'.[24]

THE DOWNWARD ESCALATOR

In the 1980s, West German society was still characterized by the 'elevator effect'.[25] As discussed in Chapter 1, this meant that, although inequalities certainly remained, rich and poor rode up together in the same social 'elevator', which reduced the significance of social distinctions. For the following analysis, however, the metaphor of an escalator[26] is more appropriate and insightful than that of an elevator, since upward and downward mobility exhibit both a collective and an individual dimension. In Ulrich Beck's elevator everyone travels upward together, but on the escalator the distances between individuals can change as the escalator moves up or down.

The image of the escalator also allows us to better understand the social structure of modern Germany. In spatial terms, we can imagine a situation like that of a department store. The escalator has already taken some well-to-do customers to the upper floor, where they look around or even continue to the floors above. For most of those who have not yet reached the upper floor, however, the direction of travel now shifts. It had been going up for a good while, but now begins going down. This process began insidiously.

23   Cf. Philipp Staab, *Macht und Herrschaft in der Servicewelt*, Hamburg: Hamburger Edition, 2014.

24   Friederike Bahl and Philipp Staab, 'Das Dienstleistungsproletariat. Theorie auf kaltem Entzug', *Mittelweg 36* 19(6), 2010, 66–93.

25   Beck, *Risikogesellschaft*.

26   Cf. on this Castel, *L'insécurité sociale*, 33, n22) and Stephan Voswinkel, *Was wird aus dem 'Fahrstuhleffekt'? Postwachstum und Sozialer Aufstieg*, Working Paper der DFG-Forschergruppe Postwachstumsgesellschaften, Friedrich-Schiller-Universität Jena, 2013.

Individual downward mobility or ruin has not yet become a mass phenomenon, and it is not impossible to ascend in some cases. *Collectively*, however, for the employed population the direction is downwards and the distances between levels above and below are increasing.[27] In particular, it is the younger age cohorts who are caught on the downward escalator. This escalator effect is especially visible in terms of real net incomes, which already began to fall again a few years after Beck's initial diagnosis.

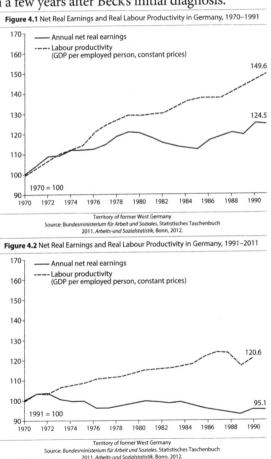

Figure 4.1 Net Real Earnings and Real Labour Productivity in Germany, 1970–1991

Territory of former West Germany
Source: *Bundesministerium für Arbeit und Soziales, Statistisches Taschenbuch 2011. Arbeits-und Sozialstatistik*, Bonn, 2012.

Figure 4.2 Net Real Earnings and Real Labour Productivity in Germany, 1991–2011

Territory of former West Germany
Source: *Bundesministerium für Arbeit und Soziales, Statistisches Taschenbuch 2011. Arbeits-und Sozialstatistik*, Bonn, 2012.

27   Beck isolates a number of dimensions: income, education, geographical mobility, law, knowledge, mass consumption. My focus here will be principally on income and social position.

The development of real net income is an important indicator of social position and opportunities for participation on the part of all employees. Until the early 1990s, the trend was upward (Diagram 4.1), a clear indication of the long-term action of the elevator effect. At the start of the 2000s, incomes reached a high point, before the trend reversed. Since 1993, real incomes have been falling (Diagram 4.2), despite some interruptions.[28] Only in the last nine years does this trend appear to have been stopped. Average real incomes have not fallen further, and since 2010 have even risen by almost 1 per cent per year on average.[29]

The relative decline of wages and salaries—the graph shows an average value that includes both high and low incomes—conceals the fact that at the same time the spread of earnings within firms and sectors has increased. At the sectoral level, basic earnings in finance and energy are twice as high as in catering or agency work. But within companies, too, the difference in pay between the simple case handler and managerial staff has grown. According to an OECD study, income inequality has risen particularly dramatically since the turn of the century.[30]

The fall in net real incomes is all the more significant given that in the same time frame productivity in Germany has risen continuously—with an interruption due to the economic crisis. Until the mid-1970s (cf. diagrams 4.1 and 4.2), real incomes and productivity rose in parallel. With the onset of the long downturn in the global economy, however, and as companies started investing heavily in labour-saving machinery, productivity and income

28   For the states of former East Germany, the escalator effect described here has looked rather different. Though there have been several downward movements, the period after reunification initially saw a high level of social ascent (cf. Rainer Geißler, *Die Sozialstruktur Deutschlands*, Wiesbaden: VS, 2014).

29   Statistisches Bundesamt, 'Tarifindex', 2015, www.destatis.de (accessed February 2016).

30   OECD, *Growing Unequal? Income Distribution and Poverty in OECD Countries*, Country Note Germany, Paris, 2008.

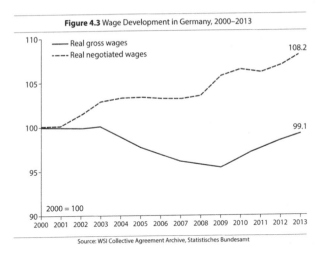

Figure 4.3 Wage Development in Germany, 2000–2013

Source: WSI Collective Agreement Archive, Statistisches Bundesamt

began to move apart. Since the 1990s, the linkage between the two curves has completely disappeared: while productivity and value creation have risen, real wages have dropped. A rather different picture is apparent, though, if wage rates and real earnings are distinguished.[31]

Despite some economically difficult years, nominal wage rates have actually risen, yet gross earnings have fallen at the same time (cf. Diagram 4.3).[32] Moreover, incomes fell particularly where there were no trade unions and collective bargaining. The weakening of economic citizenship rights and the erosion of collective bargaining have thus demonstrated immediate material effects.

The decomposition of data on the household level provided by the German Institute for Economic Research depicts the stratification of household incomes in the country. Most notably, the lower 40 per cent of German households—more than 30 million people— have experienced wage stagnation and losses since the 1990s.

31   A different image appears if negotiated wage rates and actual wages are distinguished. There are, however, no long-term time series for this. Cf. Diagram 4.2 and International Labour Organisation, *World of Work Report 2011: Making Markets Work for Jobs*, Geneva, 2011.

32   Gross earnings did not return to 2000 levels until 2014.

Figure 4.4 Development of the Wage Share (Unadjusted) in Germany, 1950–2010

Source: Markus M. Grabka and Jan Goebel, 'Realeinkommen sind von 1991 bis 2014 im Durchschnitt gestiegen—erste Anzeichen für wieder zunehmende Einkommensungleicheit', *DIW-Wochenbericht* (4), 2017

Until the early 1980s, it was not only real incomes that rose, but also the so-called wage ratio, the share of total national income made up of income from employment. This is the obverse of income from securities, rent, interest and the profits from entrepreneurial activity. The earned income ratio thus provides information on the social distribution of newly acquired prosperity.[33] For the duration of social modernity and the elevator effect, this ratio rose almost continuously in Germany. As far as income from employment goes, developments even rose above and beyond the elevator effect alone. Employees were able to

33 The wage ratio is not an uncontentious indicator, being distorted by a number of factors. For instance, it frequently rises at the start of an economic crisis, as profits collapse and earned income proportionally rises. If the salaries of directors and managers increase, this also raises the wage ratio, as managerial compensation is partly counted under earned income (cf. Claus Schäfer, 'Die Lohnquote—ein ambivalenter Indikator für soziale Gerechtigkeit und ökonomische Effizienz', *Sozialer Fortschritt* 53(2), 2004, 45–52; Thomas Weiß, 'Die Lohnquote nach dem Jahrtausendwechsel', *Sozialer Fortschritt* 53(2), 2004, 36–40.

increase their share of total created value substantially. Around 1982, however, when Helmut Kohl became chancellor and introduced the so-called 'moral turn', the rise in the wage ratio began to stagnate. And since the start of the 1990s, when regressive modernization accelerated, the wage ratio fell on average.

In short, since the 1990s German workers have received a decreasing share of the economic pie, while the portion going to members of the upper classes has grown. This trend is also apparent in several other dimensions of social inequality. In recent years, for example, the development of the so-called 'household equivalent income'[34] also shows a clear polarization. Studies of income differentials generally take equal-sized groups for the purpose of comparison. The result is clear enough: the rich are getting richer and the poor are getting poorer. The poorest fifth of households receive only 9.2 per cent of total social income, having lost almost 1 per cent from 1992 to 2011. Conversely, the richest fifth of households now receive 36.6 per cent. Altogether, the share of households with less than 50 per cent of average income has risen from 7.4 to 11.8 per cent in this time frame.[35]

As discussed previously, during the elevator effect, social inequality scarcely changed. The Gini coefficient for German household incomes in 1991 was almost identical to that in 1978.[36] Since 1991, however, this measure of inequality has risen, and in 2005 reached the same level as 1962, when it was

34 This 'equivalence income' is the weighted average income per individual household member. The weighting follows a Europe-wide standardized procedure. Below, household income is taken in relation to this weighting.

35 Jan Goebel, Peter Krause and Roland Habich, 'Einkommensentwicklung—Verteilung, Angleichung, Armut und Dynamik', *Statistisches Bundesamt/Wissenschaftszentrum Berlin für Sozialforschung 2013*.

36 The Gini coefficient is an internationally used measure of inequality. It can take values between 0 (completely equal distribution) and 1 (completely unequal).

calculated for the first time.[37] In other words, inequality between rich and poor has increased considerably in the last twenty years—a key characteristic of a downwardly mobile society.

Without redistribution by the welfare state, inequality would have grown more, as net household income inequality is attenuated by progressive taxation and state transfers in the form of both cash and services. We might have expected the transformation of the welfare state in recent years to reduce the extent of state redistribution. Yet precisely because market and wealth income inequality has increased, so too has redistribution. Without state compensation, the polarization of incomes today would be even greater.

The distribution of wealth basically follows the biblical 'Matthew effect': 'For unto everyone one that hath shall be given, and he shall have abundance'.[38] While the topmost 10 per cent of households already owned 44 per cent of net monetary wealth in 1970, by 2010 they controlled more than 66 per cent. The richest 1 per cent, the target of the Occupy movement (see the following chapter), possessed more than 35.8 per cent of net monetary wealth.[39] In 2008, by comparison, the poorer half of

37   Cf. Geißler, *Die Sozialstruktur Deutschlands*, 77. If only market incomes are taken into account, the Gini coefficient has risen. It stood at 0.485 in 2011, having increased significantly since 1991, whereas previously it had remained constant or even fallen. It reached its highest level in 2005, before falling back a little, and then increasing again; see Sachverständigenrat zur Begutachtung der gesamtwirtschaftlichen Entwicklung, *Jahresgutachten 2013/14. Gegen eine rückwärtsgewandte Wirtschaftspolitik*, Wiesbaden, 2013.

38   Cf. Robert K. Merton, 'The Matthew Effect in Science', *Science* 159(3810), 5 January 1968, 56–63. The Gini coefficient for wealth in Germany today is about 0.78, a particularly high level of concentration by international comparison (cf. Markus M. Grabka and Christian Westermeier, 'Anhaltend hohe Vermögensungleichheit in Deutschland', *DIW-Wochenbericht* 9, 2014, 151–64).

39   Cf. Hans-Ulrich Wehler, *Die neue Umverteilung. Soziale Ungerechtigkeit in Deutschland*, Munich: C. H. Beck, 2013, 73.

the population owned scarcely 1 per cent of all wealth in Germany.[40]

We should not assume that these developments will automatically reverse. As French economist Thomas Piketty analysed in a historically and internationally comparative study, the concentration of wealth rises if the return on capital is higher than the rate of economic growth. Piketty went on to show that in recent years the relationship between income from capital and other types of income has increasingly shifted in favour of the owners of capital.[41] In Germany, this inequality has not grown further since around 2005, yet in the context of post-growth capitalism (see Chapter 2) it will very likely rise again in the coming years—in the absence of any drastic redistribution policies.

Moreover, wealth no longer trickles down, as was frequently the case in the past. Society may well continue to get richer, but the poor no longer benefit from this. Since the turn of the century, poverty has not only increased, it has also solidified. Its rise in the last few years is characterized less by a marked increase in downward mobility than by a 'declining upward mobility'.[42] The society of downward mobility appears here in inverted form, so to speak:

40   Cf. Geißler, *Die Sozialstruktur Deutschlands*, 88. In 2012, the average German citizen had assets of more than €83,000. This is a considerable level of prosperity, giving a total of around €500 trillion. At the same time, the distribution of wealth has become increasingly unequal. The richest 1 per cent have increased their wealth to reach an average of €817,000, while the proportion of those with negative assets (i.e., debts) who particularly include the unemployed, has risen in ten years from 5.2 to 7.4 per cent (Grabka and Westermeier, 'Anhaltend hohe Vermögensungleichheit'). The authors of this study explicitly concede that the data collected very likely minimize the true degree of inequality.

41   Thomas Piketty, *Capital in the Twenty-First Century*, Cambridge, MA: Belknap, 2015.

42   Olaf Groh-Samberg and Florian F. Hertel, 'Ende der Aufstiegsgesellschaft?', *Aus Politik und Zeitgeschichte* 65(10), 2015, 25–32, 29.

as the absence of ascent. Those who are down find it hard to get on their feet again.

In Germany, however, poverty can be initially understood relatively, in relation to the average standard of living. Someone is defined as 'at risk of poverty'—in other words, relatively poor— if they receive less than 60 per cent of the average equivalent income.[43] In 2010, this meant 15.8 per cent of the population. These people generally possess consumer goods such as a washing machine, a refrigerator and a television. At the time of writing, it seems as if absolute poverty, the lack of essential material goods, will not necessarily rise, but the poor will continue to be left behind in the general rise of consumption possibilities. Even in a welfare state, however, poverty is not free of real material need: almost 17 per cent of these 'relatively poor' people say that they find it difficult to heat their homes, and 27 per cent to feed themselves adequately. Affording a computer is unfeasible for 16.2 per cent of them.[44] Yet the dangers of poverty reach even well into the middle class, where one in three people would find it difficult to deal with an unexpected expense of €1,000.[45]

PRECARIOUS WORK

A situation is precarious if it is unstable, insecure and revocable. In social modernity, work provided the foundation for societal integration and stability, and a secure job with protection from dismissal was the norm.[46] Yet the sphere of stability is visibly

----

43   Thus, poverty is not necessarily identical with hunger or a lack of essential goods.

44   Silvia Deckl, 'Einkommensungleichheit, Armut und materielle Entbehrung', in *Statistisches Bundesamt/Wissenschaftszentrum Berlin für Sozialforschung 2013.*

45   'Jeden Dritten werfen ungeplante Ausgaben von 1000 Euro aus der Bahn', *Frankfurter Allgemeine Zeitung*, 23 April 2018.

46   The concept of precarity is developed here with particular respect to employment. It goes without saying, however, that precarity has further

shrinking. In the wake of regressive modernization, we have the 'institutionalization of precarity'.[47] The main cause of the transition to a society of downward mobility does not lie simply in the growth of social inequality, but rather in the deterioration of labour relations.

At the height of social modernity, normal labour relations applied in almost 90 per cent of all jobs. This has since changed dramatically. In 1991, 79 per cent of all workers were employed under normal labour relations, but by 2014 the figure had fallen to 68.3 per cent. In certain years before this, the figure was as low as 67 per cent. In 2016, normal labour relations experienced a slight increase due to positive economic developments, reaching 69 per cent. Twenty-one per cent of workers were atypically employed, working either without job security, on inadequate terms, part-time or as agency workers.[48] Out of the 11 per cent who were self-employed, more than half were sole proprietors.[49]

dramatic social consequences: the boundary between work and free time crumbles, planning a family becomes harder, etc. (Kerstin Jürgens, 'Prekäres Leben', *WSI-Mitteilungen* 64(8), 2011, 379–85).

47   Castel, *La montée des incertitudes*, 159ff.

48   Between 1999 and 2013, agency work grew by 186 per cent (cf. Karin Scherschel and Melanie Booth, 'Aktivierung in die Prekarität: Folgen der Arbeitsmarktpolitik in Deutschland', in Karin Scherschel, Peter Streckeisen and Manfred Krenn (eds), *Neue Prekarität. Die Folgen aktivierender Arbeitsmarktpolitik—europäische Länder im Vergleich*, Frankfurt: Campus, 2013, 35).

49   Cf. Statistisches Bundesamt, *Statistisches Taschenbuch 2017*, 351. The classic self-employed (such as lawyers, shopkeepers or artisans) often themselves have employees. Solo freelancers, however, are frequently in a precarious work situation, as though they work in a similar way to employees (for example, under contract to a company), they lack any equivalent to trade unions, and have no rights of protection and codetermination. This is why the number of so-called 'top-ups', people who draw ALG-II payments despite paid work, has particularly risen in this category (cf. Lena Koller, Nadja Neder, Helmut Rudolph and Mark Trappmann, *Viel Arbeit für wenig Geld*, IAB-Kurzbericht 22/2012, Nuremberg).

After declining in importance over several decades, normal labour relations have stabilized again since 2007, and in some ways even gained ground, yet the underlying trend is impossible to ignore. There is no reason to sound the all-clear. This consolidation at a low level results above all from the relatively stable economic situation since 2005 and the demographic change that led to a certain shortage of specialist jobs and caused firms to instead bind their employees more tightly once again. Many jobs with normal labour relations, however, consist of indefinite part-time employment (defined as less than twenty-one hours per week), a sector that has more than doubled in size over the last fifteen years. Altogether, by 2016 the number of full-time jobs had fallen by more than a million since 2001, while part-time jobs had risen by 4 million.[50]

Within the group of atypical labour relations, it is temporary employment that has particularly increased; in 2009, almost every second new job was under a contract of limited duration.[51] Precarious conditions, moreover, are not found equally among all groups, but concentrated particularly among the low-skilled.[52] In a nutshell, the younger and less skilled you are, the greater your likelihood of atypical employment.

Age cohorts are also very differently affected by precarity. For older, professionally established workers, there is a lower risk of precarity, whereas it is greater for younger people. Among the latter, it particularly takes the form of instability in their first years of work; it is increasingly rare for them to be able to keep

50   Cf. Statistisches Bundesamt, *Statistisches Taschenbuch 2017*, 368, fn. 47.

51   Cf. Christian Hohendanner, *Unsichere Zeiten, unsichere Verträge?*, IAB-Kurzbericht 14/2010, Nuremberg. This leads to a situation in which atypical relations are most common at the start of a career (Petra Böhnke, Janina Zeh and Sebastian Link, 'Atypische Beschäftigung im Erwerbesverlauf: Verlaufstypen als Ausdruck sozialer Spaltung?', *Zeitschrift für Soziologie* 44(4), 2015, 234–52).

52   Cf. Schüller and Wingerter, 'Arbeitsmarkt und Verdienste', 120.

their first job. The average length of employment for young people has declined by 22 per cent since the mid 1970s, and the low-skilled in particular must frequently anticipate losing their job.[53] This does not necessarily mean that those starting out work feel particularly insecure. It is not unusual for even an insecure job to be subjectively experienced as progress by those who are at last participating in the labour market.

Working life, however, has completely lost its previous structure; careers and professional ladders have become discontinuous. The traditional career path—joining a firm when young and leaving it only at the end of working life, then going on to draw a pension—has become an infrequent relic of a previous age. On the other hand, ever more people experience breaks in their curriculum vitae, constituting a literal social injury. They fall into a widening 'twilight zone', oscillating between employment and unemployment. They may well work most of the time, but their jobs are seldom long-term.[54]

Occupation, income and prestige now all appear insecure. Like an abandoned ship on the high seas, many workers lurch through their working life exposed to external forces and unable to propel themselves forward. This toing and froing leads to a growing 'status inconsistency', in which the positions that a person occupies in various social dimensions appear to

---

53   Cf. Thomas Rhein and Heiko Stüber, *Bei Jüngeren ist die Stabilität der Beschäftigung gesunken*, IAB-Kurzbericht 3/2014, Nuremberg.

54   Natalie Grimm, Andreas Hirseland and Berthold Vogel, 'Die Ausweitung der Zwischenzone. Erwerbsarbeit in Zeiten der neuen Arbeitsmarktpolitik', *Soziale Welt* 64(3), 2013, 249–68. Cf. Julia Simonson, Laura Romeu Gordo and Nadiya Kelle, 'Separate Paths, Same Direction? De-standardization of Male Employment Biographies in East and West Germany', *Current Sociology* 63(3), 2015, 387–410. Another study, however, has shown that the number of direct individual deviations from normal labour relations into long-term precarious employment is relatively small (cf. Böhnke et al. 2015).

diverge.[55] Educational degrees and incomes no longer coincide—for example, when someone with a PhD in history works part-time in a kindergarten. This oscillation on the labour market, and work in occupations for which they are unqualified or over-qualified, often leads those affected to feel deprived, robbed of their dreams and socially disadvantaged.

Precarity, however, means much more than just the erosion of normal labour relations. Work gradually loses its function of social integration—for example, when even full-time employees in the lower wage groups are no longer protected from poverty.[56] It becomes notably harder to speak of 'normal' labour relations: if a third of all employees work in atypical and often precarious conditions, then normal labour relations are only nominally standard. The concept of atypical employment, moreover, does not correctly reflect the situation, as the forms of employment it embraces are no longer atypical, but actually par for the course.

The erosion of normal labour relations is closely bound up with the increasing employment of women. In social modernity, the role allotted to women was primarily that of housewife and mother. Today, paid employment for women is no longer uncommon, even when there is no economic pressure. This is particularly the case in households where one or both partners are highly skilled and more or less part of the middle class. Employment here is an act of emancipation and self-realization. But there are further reasons why ever more women go out to work. In households with low levels of skill and low incomes, the husband's salary is often no longer sufficient. This has led to the growth of atypical employment (under twenty-one hours per week),

55 Natalie Grimm, 'Statusinkonsistenz revisited! Prekarisie-rungsprozesse und soziale Positionierung', *WSI-Mitteilungen* 66(2), 2013, 89–97.

56 Cf. Hans-Jürgen Andreß and Till Seeck, 'Ist das Normalarbeitsverhältnis noch armutsvermeidend?', *Kölner Zeitschrift für Soziologie und Sozialpsychologie* 59(3), 2007, 459–92.

especially among female workers.[57] It also explains why, despite high levels of employment and only a minor decline in official working hours, the total volume of work in Germany has not risen, but actually fallen slightly on a per-capita basis.

Part-time employment also signifies another aspect of the situation. While for some people, as explained, it represents an entry to economic activity and a welcome or necessary additional wage, for others it is simply a particular form of precarity. Many employees on part-time contracts indeed wish for normal labour relations, seeing themselves as underemployed. For employers, on the other hand, part-time work is frequently cheaper.[58] It is often used to reduce the wages of lower-paid workers further, which is why they also receive a lower hourly rate than full-time employees.[59] This relative underemployment also serves business managers as a lever for greater flexibility and overtime. In the retail sector, for example, employees who work only a few hours per week are often used as stand-ins. They have very little control over their own working time, and must be perpetually ready to fill gaps or work overtime.

Precarious employment has a different guise at the level of the firm and that of the so-called labour market sector. Here it is clear that despite all changes, dramatic diagnoses of a 'precarization society' have (so far) not materialized.[60] Precarity is not (yet) universal or omnipresent, and there are still areas of the labour market that are relatively stable. If employees are taken

57   Cf. Schüller and Wingerter, 'Arbeitsmarkt und Verdienste', 116.

58   Christian Woitschig, Hanna Brenzel, Alexander Eglmair, Alexander Kubis, Andreas Moczall and Susanne Wagner, *Betriebe wie Beschäftigte können profitieren*, IAB-Kurzbericht, Nuremberg, 2013.

59   Cf. Mirjam Bick, 'Verdienste und Arbeitskosten', in *Statistisches Bundesamt/Wissenschaftszentrum Berlin für Sozialforschung 2013*, 132.

60   Cf. Oliver Marchart, *Die Prekarisierungsgesellschaft. Prekäre Proteste—Politik und Ökonomie im Zeichen der Prekarisierung*, Bielefeld: transcript, 2013; Stefanie Hürtgen, 'Prekarität als Normalität', *Blätter für deutsche und internationale Politik* 53(4), 2008, 113–19.

on as permanent staff under normal labour relations, they have as a rule achieved this in their firm's *internal* labour market. Here, they can count on a high degree of job security and good prospects of promotion, as well as a good income if they are highly qualified. The company structure also gives them relative freedom from external developments like rising unemployment. On the same firm's *external* labour market, however, the situation is exactly the opposite: in the case of marginal and low-skilled employees, both security and income are low.[61] Stability for permanent staff in Germany has hardly eroded; in recent years it has actually risen in formal terms due to a small increase in employment duration.[62] This does not, however, contradict the findings presented here: increasing flexibility also brings a growing need for workers with key skills in the core areas of a firm. These workers are tied to the company for the long term, in order to protect its knowledge and weather changes to work processes.

In the shadow of this stability, however, increased forms of market orientation have appeared, and even well-established employees have seen their status weaken. Workers in large organizations could traditionally count on regular advancement during their time of employment, but internal promotion has become harder, less direct and predictable. Now both expectation and status security are conditional, as employees are constantly subjected to competency tests.[63] Security becomes a kind of

61   Cf. Alexandre Krause and Christoph Köhler, 'Von der Vorherrschaft interner Arbeitsmärkte zur dynamischen Koexistenz von Arbeitsmarktsegmenten', *WSI-Mitteilungen* 64(11), 2011, 588–96; idem, *Arbeit als Ware. Zur Theorie flexibler Arbeitsmärkte*, Bielefeld: transcript, 2012.

62   Kevin Doogan, *New Capitalism? The Transformation of Work*, Cambridge: Polity, 2009.

63   Cf. Berthold Vogel, *Wohlstandskonflikte. Soziale Fragen, die aus der Mitte kommen*, Hamburg: Hamburger Edition, 2009; Luc Boltanski and Eve Chiapello, *The New Spirit of Capitalism*, London: Verso, 2005.

bonus, which workers have to pay for with increased performance. This process is in turn guided by benchmarks and other numerical targets, leading to constant competitive pressure among workers, again linked to the threat of downward mobility.[64] Despite deliberately quantifiable criteria, the transparency of these tests is reduced, and it becomes ever less clear exactly which benchmark now counts.[65]

Internal labour markets have also lost their previous dominance in firms. It is true that over half of all workers are still employed on this basis, yet external markets are steadily increasing in importance. This often has a psychological effect on the permanent staff, as they can see the growing uncertainty in these external markets.[66] They too feel threatened, despite their formal security.

The rise of precarity within firms as well as in the general labour market thus has far-reaching consequences for labour policy. Besides subjective insecurity, employees are split into two groups, with a 'secondary' imbalance of power between them with respect to their position in the firm and in the general labour market:[67] the permanent staff, who experience their relative security as a privilege; and, on the other side, the precariat, who, as Pierre Bourdieu aptly analysed, are almost 'ready to do anything' in order to escape insecurity.[68] During my own

64   Cf. Stephan Voswinkel, *Was wird aus dem 'Fahrstuhleffekt'? Postwachstum und Sozialer Aufstieg*, Working-Paper der DFG-Forschergruppe. Postwachstumsgesellschaften, Friedrich-Schiller-Universität Jena, 2013, 22.

65   Stephan Voswinkel, 'Arbeit und Subjektivität', in Klaus Dörre, Dieter Sauer and Volker Wittke (eds), *Kapitalismustheorie und Arbeit*, Frankfurt: Campus, 2012.

66   Cf. Peter Bartelheimer and René Lehweß-Litzmann, 'Externe Arbeitsmärkte. Gesellschaftliche Voraussetzungen und prekäres Potential', in Krause and Köhler (eds), *Arbeit als Ware*.

67   Offe and Hinrichs, 'Sozialökonomie des Arbeitsmarktes', 70.

68   Pierre Bourdieu, *Algeria 1960*, Cambridge: Cambridge University Press, [1963] 1979, 66.

research, I frequently came across the phenomenon of workers in precarious situations over-fulfilling company norms, as they had to compete anew practically every day. They work more, longer, and more intensively. They face enormous physical and mental stress. There are of course also employees who actually value this freer working life, with its 'here today, gone tomorrow' attitude, but these are a minority. More common in reality is a different type of agency worker.[69] These individuals repeatedly tell of their fear of being suddenly left with nothing, and no longer being able to manage a stable career. The worry is always with them, tormenting them at night and preventing them from sleeping. They dream of a better future, but often lack the energy to work for this. Some of them seethe inside; they are disillusioned or angry with society, often a mixture of the two. For example, they report long journeys to work each day, with the pay hardly enough for the petrol. Most often, they exhibit shoulder-shrugging resignation. The straw that many cling to is the hope of making the jump at some point to permanent employment, which would be to them like winning at bingo or the football pools. Yet it very often leads to conformist behaviour, as the agency workers themselves are well aware:

> There's a system to it. The more flexible or insecure the situation, the simpler it is to manipulate people. If they don't know what they might be doing tomorrow, they can easily be strung along ... Because you want to be taken on you don't say anything, otherwise you'd often say that it's not right. You hold your tongue.[70]

69   Cf. among others Hajo Holst, Oliver Nachtwey and Klaus Dörre, *Funktionswandel und Leiharbeit. Neue Nutzungsstrategien und ihre arbeits- und mitbestimmungspolitischen Folgen*, Arbeitsheft der Otto-Brenner-Stiftung 61, Frankfurt, 2009.

70   Interview at a leading German car producer with an agency worker who had previously worked for a subcontractor.

The attitude of the permanent staff toward those precariously employed ranges from negativity to empathy and solidarity. While many seek a better position for agency workers and their integration into the firm's social community, I came across cases—for instance, in an energy technology company, where the most unpleasant tasks (with negative health effects) were deliberately given exclusively to agency workers. Many permanent staff see agency workers as a buffer that protects their own employment in case of a crisis or threat of dismissal.

By their readiness to do more than their colleagues, agency workers can be used by management to reduce the 'comfort zones' of permanent employees, as a personnel manager explained in an interview. In the average firm, moreover, the permanent staff experience precarious employment as a means of social discipline that bridges the internal and external labour markets; this has altered the 'reserve army' mechanism on the labour market.[71] In the past, it was the unemployed who filled

71   Hajo Holst and Oliver Nachtwey (2010), 'Die Internalisierung des Reservearmeemechanismus. Grenztransformationen am Beispiel der strategischen Nutzung von Leiharbeit', in Karina Becker, Lars Gertenbach, Henning Laux and Tilmann Reitz (eds), *Grenzverschiebungen des Kapitalismus*, Frankfurt: Campus, 2010. This concept of an industrial reserve army was developed by Karl Marx, who described the temporarily surplus workers as a 'relative surplus population' and distinguished three forms, 'the floating, the latent, and the stagnant' (*Capital* Volume One, Harmondsworth: Penguin, 1976, 794); cf. Oliver Nachtwey, 'Arbeit, Lohnarbeit und Industriearbeit', in Ingrid Artus, Alexandra Krause, Gisela Notz, Tilman Reitz, Claudius Vella and Jan Weyand (eds), *Marx für Sozialwissenschaftlerinnen. Eine Einführung*, Wiesbaden: VS, 2014. The 'floating' or 'fluid' surplus population consists above all of those sections of the working class in the centres of industrial production. The category closest to the modern concept of the precariat is Marx's third form, the 'stagnant' part of this relative surplus population: 'This forms a part of the active labour army, but with extremely irregular employment . . . Its conditions of life sink below the average normal level of the working class, and it is precisely this which makes it a broad foundation for special branches of capitalist exploitation' (*Capital* Volume One, 796).

the ranks of the capitalist reserve army, exerting an external structural pressure on wages and working conditions. Precarious employment now internalizes this function within the firm. The agency workers may be inside the firm, but they have one foot outside of it in unemployment, so their mere presence reminds the permanent staff that their future might also become less secure.

To sum up, in modern Germany's society of precarious full employment, the persistent division between employed and unemployed is supplemented by a dualized labour market with two interpenetrating worlds—one of shrunken stability and one of expanded precarity.[72] Forms of agency, subcontracting and temporary work, moreover, combined with an active social policy, have made firms more prepared to take on new workers, as in these cases they now face hardly any dismissal costs. The unemployed industrial reserve army is reduced at the price of an increased reserve army, made up of the underemployed (part-time workers) and over-employed (workers on low wages who have to take on several jobs at once). In the past, economists still assumed that developed capitalist economies had to grow by at least 3 per cent annually in order to keep down unemployment.[73] Since then, this threshold of activity has been set lower, and assumes that even under post-growth conditions—in other words, with an average growth of less than 3 per cent—there can be an increase in jobs. Yet this is an extremely risky, and literally precarious estimation.[74]

....

72   Cf. Markus Promberger, 'Eine Strategie oder viele Strategien? Zur Polyvalenz flexibler Beschäftigungsformen im betrieblichen Einsatz am Beispiel der Leiharbeit', in Krause and Köhler (eds), *Arbeit als Ware*.

73   This is what economists call 'Okun's law' (cf. Paul A. Samuelson and William D. Nordhaus, *Economics*, New York; McGraw-Hill, 1995).

74   The demographic shift may prove a countervailing tendency. An extrapolation of present-day society, other things being equal, will lead in a few years to a greater shortage of specialist skills, which could again strengthen the position of workers.

DOWNWARD MOBILITY, STATUS ANXIETY
AND THE PRECARIOUS MIDDLE

In recent years Germany has seen a lively discussion on the middle class, provoked by the discovery of its shrinkage. In postwar Germany, this middle class was always more than a social datum. It was (and still is) seen in public debate as an anchor of stability, a reference point of social normality, an element of integration and, not least, a sign of social permeability and ascent. It is thus not surprising that German society views itself as a society of the middle.[75]

However, what exactly makes up this middle is also contested—apart from its simple place between the upper and lower classes. Taking the Weberian distinction between ownership and earnings, we could approximate that its members are dependent on their income; property may well play a certain role, but other wealth is generally absent. Members of this class include artisans and shopkeepers, businessmen and farmers—in other words, the old middle class—as well as officials, the liberal professions, and more recently increased numbers of skilled employees and workers. Their professional profile generally includes a high level of education, a skilled occupation, prestige, a secure status and a good income. Dominant in their view of themselves are cultural values such as responsibility and motivation.[76] Contrary to this self-image of deserving their prosperity simply by their achievement, however, members of the middle class are highly dependent on institutional protection, on the 'formative power' of the welfare state.[77] Many of them are

---

75   Herfried Münkler, *Mitte und Maß. Der Kampf um die richtige Ordnung*, Reinbek bei Hamburg: Rowohlt, 2010.

76   Cf. Mau, *Lebenschancen*; Münkler, *Mitte und Maß*; Rolf G. Heinze, *Die erschöpfte Mitte. Zwischen marktbestimmten Soziallagen, politischer Stagnation und der Chance auf Gestaltung*, Weinheim: Juventa, 2011.

77   Vogel, *Wohlstandskonflikte*.

employed in public service; child allowances, health provisions and progressive income taxes support their way of life. On the other hand, however, it is also the middle class that pays for the welfare state more than any other group.[78]

In the last few years, however, with the growing shadow of precarious employment, the middle class has been seen as endangered. Precisely because its members generally cannot rely on the security of property or wealth, they are threatened with downward mobility. In his historical analysis of French labour, Robert Castel proposed a model for classifying new social insecurities.[79] For him it is not so much a question of measuring whether the middle class, as defined by income, is shrinking, and by how much; instead, Castel's typology expands the material conditions of income, professional position, job security, social welfare and growing savings to also include subjective factors and perspective on life. Along with the present status of an employee, there is also an increased probability and worry of experiencing downward mobility.[80] Precarity ultimately results in the erosion of social networks, in worse prospects of participation and the reduced possibility of a planned, future-oriented way of life. Those affected experience these phenomena as a crisis of meaning and a loss of their social reputation. Castel distinguishes three zones: one of 'integration', another of 'vulnerability' and a third of 'uncoupling'. In the zone of integration, normal labour relations are the rule and social networks remain intact. This also includes, however, certain groups with an 'atypical' occupational

78   Cf. Münkler, *Mitte und Maß*, 49.

79   Cf. Robert Castel, *From Manual Workers to Wage Laborers: Transformation of the Social Question*, New Brunswick, NJ: Transaction Publishers, 367ff.

80   The feeling of social vulnerability and precarity more or less assumes that security is something within people's experience (cf. Berthold Vogel, 'Soziale Verwundbarkeit und prekärer Wohlstand', in Heinz Bude and Andreas Willisch (eds), *Das Problem der Exklusion. Ausgegrenzte, Entbehrliche, Überflüssige*, Hamburg: Hamburger Edition, 2006, 346.

situation—for example, highly qualified freelance engineers—who are socially integrated by virtue of their market position and do not feel subjectively insecure. In the zone of vulnerability, insecure employment is the rule, and both subjective security and social networks are eroded. In the zone of uncoupling, finally, are those groups who are excluded from social involvement at most levels (especially regarding security, participation and culture).

Similar conclusions have been reached for the situation in Germany. Here the zones of vulnerability and uncoupling have likewise expanded in recent years.[81] Transitional areas especially— those that Berthold Vogel classifies as 'social vulnerability' and 'precarious prosperity'—have seen mobility both up and down, processes of destabilization and growing insecurity.[82]

The middle-class convergence characteristic of social modernity resulted 'from a continuing stream of ascent from the low strata. This dynamic of absolute upward mobility seems to have been significantly curtailed, despite the continued expansion of education. This means that the middle class no longer grows by a stream of upward mobility.'[83] But not only is this upward dynamic stagnating, downward mobility is also increasing. In 1997, according to the current classification (70 to 150 per cent of average equivalent income), 52.8 million Germans, or 65 per cent of the population, still belonged to the middle class. Since then this proportion has declined, if more sharply in the east than in the west. In Germany as a whole, 47.3 million people belonged to the

81   Robert Castel and Klaus Dörre (eds), *Prekarität, Abstieg, Ausgrenzung. Die soziale Frage am Beginn des 21. Jahrhunderts*, Frankfurt: Campus, 2009; Klaus Dörre, 'Prekarität—eine arbeitspolitische Herausforderung', *WSI-Mitteilungen* 5, 2005.

82   Vogel, 'Soziale Verwundbarkeit'.

83   Bertelsmann Stiftung (ed.), *Mittelschicht unter Druck?*, Gütersloh, 2012, 7ff. Cf. also Gerhard Bosch and Thorsten Kalina, *Die Mittelschicht in Deutschland unter Druck*, IAQ-Report 2004–15, Duisburg/Essen.

middle class in 2010, a decline of 6.5 percent. Significant here is not just the proportion of the middle class in quantitative terms, but also its internal stability and coherence. Thus, the upper segments of the middle class, particularly the large areas of 'secure prosperity', remain almost completely shielded from social turbulence and downward mobility.[84] It is therefore not 'the middle class' as a whole that is on the downward escalator. And yet, 'that the middle class is shrinking at all is a completely new phenomenon, representing a break with the long prevailing model of growth and prosperity'.[85] We can even speak of a polarization of the middle. At its lower end, downward mobility is more frequent, and previously stable margins are caught in the maelstrom of regressive modernity. The lower middle class[86] has declined most, its share falling by 15 per cent since 1997.[87]

Despite the greater resilience of the upper middle class, disquiet is rising, and dreams of uninterrupted ascent, independence and security are no longer necessarily fulfilled. A 'normal working insecurity' has arisen.[88] It is true that there is still the demand for (highly) skilled labour, yet these groups of workers face competition from one another. Previously, their qualifications guaranteed them something of a privileged status, but now the population with their skills is rising, along with the level of standardization in the work they perform. Skilling and relative de-skilling are simultaneous processes. Those who adapt successfully to the transformation of the work-centred society thus also

84   Groh-Samberg and Hertel, 'Ende der Aufstiegsgesellschaft?'; idem, 'Abstieg der Mitte? Zur langfristigen Mobilität von Armut und Wohlstand', in Nicole Burzan and A. Berger (eds), *Dynamiken (in) der gesellschaftlichen Mitte*, Wiesbaden: VS, 2010.

85   Mau, *Lebenschancen*, 61; cf. Münkler, *Mitte und Maß*, 56ff.

86   This describes households with equivalent incomes of between 70 and 90 per cent of the median.

87   Cf. Bertelsmann Stiftung (ed.), *Mittelschicht unter Druck?*, 20ff.

88   Michael Vester and Christel Teiwes-Kügler, 'Unruhe in der Mitte: Die geprellten Leistungsträger des Aufschwungs', *WSI-Mitteilungen* 60(5), 2007, 231–38.

have to live with greater insecurity.[89] This is something I have frequently encountered in my research: an engineer or IT expert working for a car manufacturer enjoys a senior professional position, a good income and a high level of security. But alongside the plant where he works there are now other research and development service companies, where engineers and IT experts work for the same car manufacturer, but on a subcontract basis. They also earn well, but not quite as well as their colleagues employed directly by the main firm, nor do they enjoy the same participation rights. For many highly qualified staff, activity of this kind is quite attractive, up to a certain point. As long as they are young and flexible, they value working for a good salary in different places for a different firm each time. Even a master craftsman, employed by an agency, opined in an interview: 'When you're young, you think: never mind, I have two good hands.' But this generally changes over the years. Then the need for greater security makes itself felt even among engineers, especially if they want to start a family.

For large sections of the German middle class, as mentioned, it is not the actual threat of disaster that has increased, so much as the worry of disaster.[90] The 'status-worried middle'[91] has in particular been struck by a kind of panic. It seems to many people that their own stability is at an end, that 'collapse . . . is completely possible'.[92] Among the cited reasons for this is that the downward escalator has become significantly steeper.

89   Cf. Vogel, *Wohlstandskonflikte*, 220.

90   Cf. Holger Lengfeld and Jochen Hirschle, 'Die Angst der Mittelschicht vor dem sozialen Abstieg. Eine Längsschnittanalyse 1984–2007', in Burzan and Berger (eds), *Dynamiken (in) der gesellschaftlichen Mitte*; Petra Böhnke, 'Hoher Flug, tiefer Fall? Abstiege aus der gesellschaftlichen Mitte und ihre Folgen für das subjektive Wohlbefinden', in Nicole Burzan and Peter A. Berger (eds), *Dynamiken (in) der gesellschaftlichen Mitte*, Wiesbaden: VS, 2010, 231–48.

91   Vogel, *Wohlstandskonflikte*, 185.

92   Bude and Willisch (eds), *Exklusion*, 13.

Even in the secure middle, pressure waves can be traced pushing from the points of impact to the marginal zones. Almost everyone counts people with precarious jobs among their friends or acquaintances, or knows people who have suffered a change for the worse. By comparing with 'social neighbours', fear of downward mobility creeps up the office blocks and into the houses of the comfortable suburbs.[93] As mentioned, employees in firms where colleagues have been dismissed and replaced by precarious workers experience a particular vulnerability. Above all, they feel a growing sense of precariousness for their children, as it is clear that even with the best qualifications, foreign language skills and experience abroad, they will often have to face the treadmill of internships or temporary work, and frequently have to prove themselves before obtaining employment on regular terms. The previously quoted agency worker also reported:

> When I look at my children, I immediately feel afraid. Perhaps I convey this to them . . . The elder girl has studied biology, and the younger one is still finishing school. But she naturally wants to do well in order to get a job. I never had this way of thinking.

Among the younger generations, the typical employment biography has completely changed. Children of academics are often still unable to secure a 'stable career path' in their late thirties.[94] This does not necessarily affect their standard of living directly, as frequently their relatively prosperous parents are in a position to assist them for a time.[95] At some point, most of them do reach the secure middle—only a few fall by the wayside completely—but they certainly do so later than earlier generations did.

---

93   Klaus Kraemer, 'Abstiegsängste in Wohlstandslagen'.
94   Mau, *Lebenchancen*, 71.
95   This of course involves a certain social selection. Not all parents are able to finance their children's internships.

The lubricant of education is supposed to re-energize the motor of social ascent, yet this is a dangerous process, as it is also possible to slip downward in the educational competition. The expansion of higher education, from which the middle classes particularly benefited over several decades, has been increasingly accompanied by a devaluation of degrees and more intense competition.[96] A higher education no longer automatically guarantees a rise in status. If everyone stands on tiptoe, no one sees any better.

Education has become a paradoxical medium of ascent; ultimately it is still a means of selection.[97] It is principally those already better placed who profit from the increased opportunities. Children from the lower classes often see education as an unreasonable demand, a struggle in which they are going to lose. Middle-class children are in a stronger competitive situation, precisely on account of their qualifications. Children from the upper class, on the other hand, have it easier, as their parents transmit to them greater social and cultural capital, and they can often plug directly into their parents' networks. They have habitually internalized what matters for the elite—taste, behaviour, culture—and so either rise in a relatively frictionless fashion, or simply remain at the top.[98]

It is not just education that has become an ambivalent force for social ascent. Choice of profession also no longer guarantees a high social status. This is bound up, among other things, with fragmented processes of downward mobility within occupational groups. A senior teacher earns a relatively comfortable income and need not worry about the future; they may even be able to retire early. In the same school and in the same class, however, there is possibly also a younger teacher on a temporary contract

96   Cf. Heinz Bude, *Bildungspanik. Was unsere Gesellschaft spaltet*, Munich: Carl Hanser, 2011.

97   Cf. Geißler, *Die Sozialstruktur Deutschlands*, 348ff.

98   Cf. Michael Hartmann, *Eliten und Macht in Europa. Ein internationaler Vergleich*, Frankfurt: Campus, 2007; idem, *Der Mythos von den Leistungseliten*, Frankfurt: Campus, 2002.

who has to claim unemployment benefit during the summer vacation and has no prospects for permanent employment. (Many German states now rely on a growing number of flexible teachers who are no longer guaranteed permanent positions.) In the postal service, too, although there are still many permanent employees, newly hired staff generally are not offered any job security (cf. Chapter 5). Among certain occupational groups the differences can be tremendous, as with journalists, for example. Those who began working at major German publications like *Stern*, *Spiegel* or *Die Zeit* ten or twenty years ago could expect a secure future. In the big publishing houses today, on the other hand, not only have precarious jobs and poorly paid groups of online writers proliferated, but not even the established staff can feel secure any more. A growing share belong to the 'media precariat' and earn less than €30,000 per year.[99] Another example is that of lawyers, formerly the very model of status and prosperity. This professional group now divides into those who continue to earn good money and enjoy a high social prestige while employed in large offices or working for corporations, and a growing flock of precarious self-employed legal professionals, who fail to gain a steady footing in an over-filled market.

Similar phenomena occur in many branches. Frequently, employees with different levels of job security and economic citizenship rights work side by side, and it is even not uncommon for them to perform the same activities. It is above all the younger age groups who encounter worse employment conditions, and manage only very slowly, if at all, to work their way up to the level of their parents' generation.

IMMOBILE DOWNWARD MOBILITY

Modern societies see themselves as having left behind the class structure of the past and broken up social divisions of status.

---

99   Mau, *Lebenschancen*, 61, 89.

Everyone is supposed to be able to move up, even if it is clear that this is not in fact possible for all. Even ignoring the classic American tale of the wonderful rise from dishwasher to millionaire, from the very bottom to the very top, the degree of vertical mobility and social permeability is an important indicator of modern capitalism's ability to make good on its own claims. As long as mobility is assured, the popular argument runs, inequalities are legitimate, as in theory each individual is able to move up.[100]

The metaphor of the upward escalator links collective ascent (of classes) with individual ascent (between classes). The concept of social mobility, however, is generally used to study and aggregate individual advances from an initial class position (or that of one's parents).[101] Children from farming or working-class parents, for example, might become middle-rank employees or academics. Agricultural labour and unskilled jobs, however, have declined with the growth of the tertiary sector. Industrial change is therefore the only permanent motor of ascent.

The following fundamental question therefore arises: what is the importance of occupational upward mobility today? The last section discussed the difficulties of analysing occupational groups in relation to social stability. If the son of a skilled worker finishes secondary education and becomes a journalist, or the daughter of a commercial employee becomes a lawyer, then both have risen in relation to their parents, according to the

100 Studies of the middle class, and of social strata in general, habitually analyse their stability and coherence. Social mobility, however, shows the extent to which it is possible to change one's class for a higher one. In other words, it is a question of connection between social origin and social position. This is ultimately mediated by education and qualifications, as social origin influences people's aspirations.

101 Mobility studies also use the concept of absolute mobility, which takes into account movement between groups and classes. As a rule, however, ascent and descent are analysed as *relative* mobility; in other words, individual change of position between strata and class positions.

traditional model. Their jobs bring greater social prestige—however, they may no longer automatically earn more money than their parents. Likewise, whether they are precariously employed and under constant threat of unemployment is generally not taken into account. In analyses of mobility, too, occupations are highlighted rather than labour relations. Yet, as shown by the findings on precarity, current social insecurities particularly accumulate in the realm of labour relations. Today, professional ascent no longer necessarily leads to social ascent. On the other hand, anyone who goes downhill in occupational terms is also more likely to experience downward social mobility.

Despite these reservations, studies of changes in social mobility are highly instructive. In total, ascent is substantially more common than descent, which is above all due to the aforementioned continual change in occupational structure. Across all occupational classes, the connection between social origin and final position has grown weaker in West Germany since the 1970s, though in the states of former East Germany it has again grown stronger.[102]

Analyses of mobility become more instructive with further differentiation. Among western German men, the ratio of upward to downward movements has slightly deteriorated. The decisive developments are to be found at the very top and very bottom of the occupational hierarchy—in both cases, social mobility has again declined, and inheritance of social origin become more common. For women in western Germany, however, upward mobility has increased, reflecting their greater equality of opportunity in society. In the west, women from the upper classes have also managed to transmit their social position to their daughters, while women from the working class

102 Cf. Reinhard Pollack, 'Soziale Mobilität', *Statistisches Bundesamt/Wissenschaftszentrum Berlin für Sozialforschung 2013*, 189–97.

often rise disproportionately. As a percentage, their ratio of ascent is closer to that of men, who had already enjoyed greater mobility.

The situation is different in the eastern states. Here, downward mobility has increased among both men and women, and movements up and down are almost equal in number. Accounting for the inherent trend toward a more highly skilled occupational structure, this is a critical development, pointing to a downward trend in eastern Germany and a persistent gap between the new and old federal states.

In the past, social ascent was a family project, and it was generally the husband who managed this for himself and his kin. Today, women and men seek to rise equally, which ultimately leads to a 'heightened competition for mobility' between men and women.[103] The fact that women can achieve social ascent by their own efforts far more strongly than in the past is also reflected on the marriage market. Surgeons no longer pursue nurses, but rather anaesthetists or other surgeons. Academic women marry men with similar qualifications and status.[104] This educational homogamy is a side effect of women's increased qualification levels and their improved status on the labour market. It also constitutes an emancipatory gain when women rise by avenues other than a socially asymmetrical marriage, yet it means at the same time that a social closure takes place on the marriage market.

As a whole, despite continuing ascents, the character of upward mobility in Germany today has changed. It no longer brings with it optimistic expectations for the future.[105] If all areas

---

103   Voswinkel, *Was wird aus dem 'Fahrstuhleffekt'?*, 21.

104   Cf. Mau, *Lebenschancen*, 131.

105   This is not least because the channel of ascent in public service has been immensely constricted. It had already been blocked for a long time, as a whole generation of young qualified employees entered public service in the period of its expansion and prevented new cohorts from following (cf. Vogel, *Wohlstandskonflikte).*

are taken together, it turns out that 'income groups are less permeable'.[106] Against the background of a 'general trend to greater downward mobility', the vector of social mobility has turned in the opposite direction.[107]

This has very different effects depending on the particular stratum. At the upper levels of society, there is basically no escalator leading down, and only a few ladders lead up to these. Those who reach the top practically attain a sealed-off plateau. On top of this is the 'Matthew effect' of prosperity. Looked at from below, the plateau is for most of the population an impenetrable barrier—the ladders at the edges have been removed.

The majority of descents affect groups who do not come from the uppermost levels of the occupational hierarchy. In both western and eastern Germany, for example, the unemployed are generally and increasingly located among skilled and unskilled manual workers.[108] Workers in the lower occupational groups are strengthened with the impression that they can spare themselves the trouble of trying to rise into the middle class, as it is no longer worth the effort.[109] Ulrich Beck assumed that risks continue to be democratized across social boundaries. The 'social risk', however, has risen asymmetrically, and not at all democratically.[110] The lower someone stands in the social hierarchy, the greater their risk of slipping further or at best remaining in position.

But are the results presented here sufficient for us to speak of an entire *society* of downward mobility? More people are still

---

106   Goebel, Krause and Habich, 'Einkommensentwicklung', 6.

107   Pollack, 'Soziale Mobilität', 196; cf. also Groh-Samberg and Hertel, 'Ende der Aufstiegsgesellschaft?'

108   Cf. Pollack, 'Soziale Mobilität'.

109   Cf. Stefan Hradil, 'Der deutsche Armutsdiskurs', *Aus Politik und Zeitgeschichte* 60(51–52), 2010, 3–8. Despite Stephan Voswinkel's assumption in his otherwise excellent study of social advance (*Was wird aus dem 'Fahrstuhleffekt'?*), this orientation is still socially desired—it is just that the promise it makes is no longer kept.

110   Castel, *La montée des incertitudes*, p. 31.

moving upward than down, and at the upper levels there is little cause for concern; here people can still count on social mobility. What supports the notion of Germany as a downwardly mobile society, however, is that the *normality* of upward mobility in social modernity has been broken, and a collective economic and social descent on the part of the employed population has become part of the overall picture. They are on an escalator leading down.

There is also a normative argument for this diagnosis. German society is falling from a level of social development already reached—that of pronounced social integration, relative equality and social citizenship rights (though not necessarily material equality), and this despite a continuing rise in prosperity. The additional wealth is landing in pockets that are already well-filled. Such a society is also then no longer fair in the sense of the liberal principle of difference, according to which advantages for the better off are legitimate to the extent that the less well-off also profit from them.[111] We could say that downward social mobility and increasing inequality are expressions of decline in a society that had previously attained a higher degree of equality. This is a form of *decadence*, which etymologically derives from the Latin verb for falling or sinking.

A NOTE ON THE RELATIVE STRENGTH OF THE GERMAN ECONOMY

In public debate over the robust economic conjuncture through to 2018, a particularly positive role was ascribed to the labour market reforms of Agenda 2010. Thus far, there have been no reliable studies indicating a strong connection between these measures and economic trends. However, there has indeed been a rise in the global competitiveness of German corporations. This development calls for an explanation. Since 1995, German relative unit labour costs, which are a good indicator of

---

111   Cf. John Rawls, *A Theory of Justice*, Cambridge, MA: Harvard University Press, 2005.

competitiveness, improved compared to their major rivals in the
industrialized world.

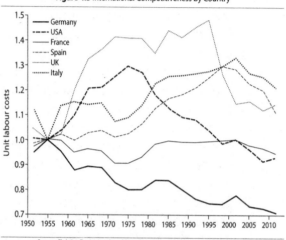

Figure 4.5 International Competitiveness by Country

Source: Christian Dustmann, Bernd Fitzenberger, Uta Schönberg and Alexandra Spitz-
Oener, 'From Sick Man of Europe to Economic Superstar: Germany's Resurgent Economy',
Journal of Economic Perspectives, 28 (1), 2014, 167–88

Of course, historically speaking the German economy has
been strongly export-oriented. Since the Second World War, state
economic policy, business associations and trade unions have
cooperated to enhance international competitiveness (described
as 'neo-corporatism' in the academic literature). German monetary policy has always been an instrument to keep the price of
German products stable on the world market, while trade unions
have repeatedly exercised wage restraint.[112] Another factor not to
be underestimated was the institutional orientation of the German
export model. So-called 'diversified quality production' emerged
from the combination of a strong engineering tradition, a highly

---

112   Cf. Robert Brenner, *The Economics of Global Turbulence*,
London: Verso, 2006; Fritz Scharpf, 'International Monetary Regimes and
the German Model', *MPIFG Discussion Paper* 18/1, Cologne: Max Planck
Institute for the Study of Societies, 2018.

qualified workforce, cooperative and decentralized labour relations and a relevant share of medium-sized companies which
could flexibly adapt to the demands of the world market. Under
these conditions, German firms were able to specialize in less
price-sensitive product lines, in investment goods and high-qual-
ity consumer durables.[113]

However, unemployment has risen considerably since the
1980s. This was due in particular to the restrictive monetary
policy pursued by the Bundesbank and fiscal restraint on the part
of successive governments. German reunification not only caused
unemployment to rise even further, but also placed an enormous
strain on the state budget. The disintegration of the Eastern bloc
put further pressure on German capitalism, for it meant not only
new markets for German products, but also new geographical
opportunities to relocate production. This proved extremely
attractive for German companies, which were able to find enough
qualified workers at significantly lower wages without modifying
their training systems significantly. The introduction of the euro
provided Germany with the medium-term advantage that other
European countries could no longer counter German wage pressure by devaluating their own currencies. In the end, Germany's
export orientation produced large export surpluses at home, but
also caused growing international trade imbalances.

A study looking into the development of the German economy titled 'From Sick Man of Europe to Economic Superstar'
rejected the narrative of Agenda 2010 as a capitalist success story,
instead highlighting a wider combination of factors in which
Agenda 2010 was only a minor player.[114] The main reason for
German economic success appears to be rooted in the long-term

---

113   Cf. Andt Sorge and Wolfgang Streeck, 'Diversified Quality
Production Revisited: The Transformation of Production Systems and
Regulatory Regimes in Germany', *MPIfG Discussion Paper* 16/13, Cologne:
Max Planck Institute for the Study of Societies, 2016.

114   The following argument owes a lot to Dustmann, Fitzenberger,
Schönberg and Spietz-Oener, 'Sick Man of Europe'.

changes in the system of industrial relations. The authors demonstrated that the rise in wage inequality in Germany was indeed dramatic, but much less so in the export-oriented manufacturing sector where real wages remained relatively stable or even grew. The manufacturing sector, however, benefitted from declining wages and prices in other sectors making important contributions to the end product, as the amount of value creation performed by the manufacturing sector in relation to the end product is roughly only one third.

Nevertheless, the fact remains that the unit labour costs of end products had fallen sharply. How did this happen? First of all, although productivity gains in manufacturing have been relatively high, other factors were also involved. Since the mid-1990s, real wages had fallen in sectors supplying inputs and services to the export sector. Moreover, the value chain shifted. Eastern expansion proved to be a double advantage for German companies: German industry outsourced more primary products and services to Eastern Europe than its rivals, which brought with it the possibility of outsourcing (or the threat thereof) while also opening up an effective transnational value chain. Although the depth of the value chain was reduced, it gave German industry a cost advantage in global competition. Above all, however, it was true for manufacturing (as for all other sectors) that the lower wage groups in particular suffered heavy losses, thereby driving down unit labour costs. This was made possible by the strong decentralization of German industrial relations from the sector to the company level beginning in the 1990s—in contrast to many European competitors, where not only is the legal minimum wage higher, but industry wage standards apply uniformly across the country.

In Germany, the decentralization of wage regulations occurred on several levels. The first was the reduced coverage of sectoral collective bargaining agreements, which included a growing number of companies and employees (cf. Chapter 3). An important factor here was the institutionalized class struggle, as many companies left the employers' associations and with them the scope of wage regulations. This resulted in another important development, namely the flexibilization of collective bargaining agreements. In order to prevent further erosion of the collective bargaining system as a whole, the trade unions cleared the way for company-level deviations from sectoral wage agreements in the mid-1990s. In the resulting agreements, entrepreneurs were permitted to implement massive wage reductions, particularly in the lower wage groups.

The increase in German competitiveness therefore began long before the introduction of Agenda 2010, which would only take effect later as German capitalism continued to struggle with the costs of reunification. Agenda 2010 has not directly led to more employment but did increase pressure on wages, which had already been falling for nearly a decade. This then contributed to the current and even improved global market position of the German economy after the financial crisis in 2008. However, it should be kept in mind that the rise of the Global South has played a special role here, as the German economy with its 'diversified quality production' enjoys strong comparative advantages in the international division of labour, such as in mechanical engineering.

What can be taken as almost certain, however, is that the Agenda's reforms have contributed to the formation of a new underclass in Germany. This underclass consists of the recipients of state transfer payments, casually referred to as 'Hartz-IVers', and the growing army of low-paid workers.

NEW STRATIFICATIONS

The change of paradigm from 'active' to 'activating' labour market policy establishes a regime of 'strict stimulus' among those receiving benefits.[115] This regime compels those on benefits to constantly meet stressful requirements (proof of job applications and so on). The

---

115   Cf. Dörre et al. (eds), *Bewährungsproben*; Scherschel and Booth, 'Aktivierung in die Prekarität'.

tendency is for them to be pressed down to or below the threshold of social respectability, which marks the social yardstick for measuring lower levels of earnings.[116] The recipients of unemployment pay are involved in this inasmuch as the 'poverty gap', the difference between this regime and the average net wage, grows.[117] The relatively favourable labour market situation has led to a decline in those receiving unemployment pay,[118] though this started at a very high level. Since the 1960s, the 'welfare classes'[119]—in other words, the groups receiving state transfer payments—have steadily grown.[120]

The relative uncoupling of the welfare class of unemployment pay recipients is particularly apparent in relation to those of average or higher incomes. Their disposable income has scarcely changed in relation to that of the low paid. Under precarious full employment, the labour market has bifurcated; in the lower segment, wages are often below the aforementioned threshold of respectability. According to a study by the University of Duisburg-Essen, in 2012 almost one out of every four employees in Germany received a wage below the low-wage threshold of €9.30 per hour. Since 1995, the number of workers in the low-paid sector has risen from 5.9 to 8.4 million. Five per cent of all employees (1.71 million) actually earned less than €5 per hour before the introduction of the general minimum wage in 2015.[121]

116   Cf. Klaus Dörre, Anja Happ and Ingo Matuschek, *Das Gesellschaftsbild der LohnarbeiterInnen. Soziologische Untersuchungen in ost- und westdeutschen Industriebetrieben*, Hamburg: VSA, 2013, 36, 43.

117   Geißler, *Die Sozialstruktur Deutschlands*, 239ff.

118   At the same time, and particularly with the upturn in the labour market, the number of beneficiaries has not fallen to the same extent as that of the unemployed (Scherschel and Booth, 'Aktivierung in die Prekarität').

119   Mario Rainer Lepsius, 'Soziale Ungleichheit und Klassenstrukturen in der Bundesrepublik Deutschland', in Hans-Ulrich Wehler (ed.), *Klassen in der europäischen Sozialgeschichte*, Göttingen: Vandenhoeck & Ruprecht, 1979.

120   Cf. Geißler, *Die Sozialstruktur Deutschlands*, 232ff.

121   Cf. Thorsten Kalina and Claudia Weinkopf, *Niedriglohnbeschäftigung 2012 und was ein gesetzlicher Mindestlohn von €8.50 verändern könnte*, IAQ-Report 2014–02, Duisburg/Essen.

The low paid are particularly concentrated in the service sector: call centres, unskilled work in the food industry, cleaning and care work, as well as the retail trade.[122] Those most affected are women and immigrants. For many low-paid workers, the wage received is scarcely enough for living expenses. More than 1.3 million persons were so-called 'top-ups' in 2012, working in 'mini jobs' or under conditions in which they needed welfare benefits.[123] Since 2004, the working poor have nearly doubled. In 2014, 9.6 per cent of all employees suffered from poverty—in other words, they lived on less than 60 per cent of the average adjusted net income.[124] In Germany, Europe's richest industrial country, the number of working poor has risen more sharply than in any other EU state.[125] The farther down people stand in the occupational hierarchy, the greater their danger of slipping into consolidated poverty.[126]

ANOMIE IN A SOCIETY OF DOWNWARD MOBILITY

Particularly in a society that continues to view itself as one of ascent, normative insecurity grows when there actually is no longer any upward movement. Many people are probably familiar with the childhood experience of trying to run up an escalator going down. In a society of downward mobility, many people find themselves

---

122   Cf. Gerhard Bosch and Claudia Weinkopf (eds), *Arbeiten für wenig Geld. Niedriglohnbeschäftigung in Deutschland*, Frankfurt: Campus, 2007.

123   Bundesagentur für Arbeit, *Hintergrundinformation. Neue Ergebnisse zu sozialversicherungspflichtig beschäftigten Arbeitslosengeld-II-Beziehern in Vollzeit und Teilzeit*, Collection Hintergrundinformation, Nuremberg, 2014.

124   For the unemployed, the proportion in poverty is 29 per cent. The data presented here, moreover, refer to the situation before the financial crisis.

125   Dorothee Spannagel, *Aktivierungspolitik und Erwerbsarmut in Europa und Deutschland*, WSI Report 36, Düsseldorf: Hans-Böckler-Stiftung, 2017.

126   Groh-Samberg and Hertel, 'Ende der Aufstiegsgesellschaft?'

permanently in this situation. They have to run upward just to keep their position. This leads to constant worry, and 'status struggles over the entitlement to prosperity'.[127] It is increasingly common for what Robert K. Merton called 'anomic' constellations to arise, in which established social norms that form a precondition for social integration are successively eroded and lose their validity.[128] If ascent no longer seems possible, and possibilities of solidarity action—for example, in a trade-union context—are either almost non-existent or ineffective, people cling more firmly to self-optimizing strategies. These lead to a more intense and almost total surrender to competition. Many people boost their individual performance and work with increasingly less restraint,[129] trying to be productive at all times. They give up claims to a good life or a balance between life and work; they accept stress and loss of meaning, and run ever faster. Their expectations of autonomy and self-development are 'counteracted by a stronger sacrifice for the sake of ascent'.[130] They indulge less in cultural individualism, and increasingly renounce a hedonism removed from the market (for example, leisurely study). Their life conduct is dominated by many of the same claims that the older generation perceived of as petty and conformist—a 'return of conformity' has arisen.[131] Many people have a strong impression that they are constantly stepping on the gas pedal, yet the wheels just keep spinning because the handbrake is jammed—a feeling of a 'frenetic standstill'.[132] This angry

127 Berthold Vogel, 'Soziale Verwundbarkeit und prekärer Wohlstand', in Bude and Willisch (eds) *Das Problem der Exklusion*, 354.

128 Cf. Robert K. Merton, *Social Theory and Social Structure*, New York: Macmillan, [1949] 1968.

129 I often encountered in my research the expression that 'work norms are no longer heeded'.

130 Voswinkel, *Was wird aus dem 'Fahrstuhleffekt'?*, 30.

131 Cornelia Koppetsch, *Die Wiederkehr der Konformität. Streifzüge durch die gefährdete Mitte*, Frankfurt: Campus, 2013.

132 Hartmut Rosa, 'Capitalism as a Spiral of Dynamisation: Sociology as Social Critique', in Dörre, Lessenich and Rosa, *Sociology, Capitalism, Critique*, 85.

productivism is symptomatic of a competitive self, which clearly sees no possibility of finding paths of sociability and solidarity in a context of insecurity, fear of downward mobility and intensified marketization. Social norms such as the performance principle become pathological means of self-assertion, perverted into unruly coping strategies.[133] This frequently ends in burnout and exhaustion.[134]

In parallel with this, we are experiencing a real renaissance of bourgeois zeal. People radicalize the desire for education and social ascent, while secondary virtues such as conscientiousness and discipline have made a return even in liberal milieus. The whole conduct of life serves the project of retaining status.[135]

In what is left of free time, people invest in education—either further education for themselves or that of their children, who start learning Chinese at an early age and practise the violin or are sent to private schools. There they are supposed to learn to become modern, cultivated people, the better to withstand the intensified pressure of competition. Individualized coping strategies of this kind, however, function immediately as 'refined closure mechanisms' vis-à-vis the inflationary educational degrees of other groups.[136] This leads to sharper battles for distinction, of the kind that Bourdieu investigated in his eponymous book.[137] Social superiority is articulated in terms of

133   Cf. Alex Honneth, 'Brutalization of the Social Conflict: Struggles for Recognition in the Early Twenty-first Century', *Distinktion: Journal of Social Theory* 13(1), 2012, 5–19; Sighard Neckel, 'Die Verwilderung der Selbstbehauptung. Adornos Soziologie: Veralten der Theorie—Erneuerung der Zeitdiagnose', in Axel Honneth (ed.), *Dialektik der Freiheit. Frankfurter Adorno-Konferenz 2003*, Frankfurt: Suhrkamp, 2005.

134   Cf. Sighard Neckel, Anna Katharina Schaffner and Greta Wagner (eds), *Burnout, Fatigue Exhaustion: An Interdisciplinary Perspective on a Modern Affliction*, London: Palgrave Macmillan, 2017; Voswinkel, 'Arbeit und Subjektivität'.

135   Groh-Samberg and Hertel, 'Ende der Aufstiegsgesellschaft?'

136   Cf. Münkler, *Mitte und Maß*, 71.

137   Bourdieu, *Distinction*.

better education, elevated manners, refined taste, artistic sense, liberal values and consumption patterns. Consumption in particular is a two-edged sword here, as it is seen as the prerogative of those who can afford it. Its demonstrative character threatens the practice of solid housekeeping among the lower middle classes. The supposedly unjustifiable consumption style of the lower class is therefore often sharply criticized, in a gesture of social and cultural superiority.[138] The new underclass, so the customary reproach runs, shuns education, is work-shy and has lost its orientation to upward social mobility.[139] The status anxiety of the middle class leads among other things to the economic interpretation, negative classification and devaluation of weaker groups, as shown in Wilhelm Heitmeyer's long-term study on xenophobic attitudes among the German population *Deutsche Zustände*.[140] To a certain degree the middle class has abandoned solidarity with the weak; it has built security by shutting itself off. Where there was previously a certain liberality, more rigorous ideas of morality, culture and behaviour have now returned. With increased fears of 'contamination' and 'infection', people seek the greatest possible distance and strict isolation from the 'parallel society' of the lower class.[141] They are generally less inclined to accept society's 'encouragements to diversity'.[142]

138   Cf., for example, Paul Nolte, *Generation Reform. Jenseits der blockierten Republik*, Munich: C. H. Beck, 2004; Thilo Sarrazin, *Deutschland schafft sich ab. Wie wir unser Land aufs Spiel setzen*, Munich: DVA, 2010.

139   Cf. Klaus Dörre et al. (eds), *Bewährungsproben*, 18ff.

140   Wilhelm Heitmeyer, *Deutsche Zustände. Folge 1–10*, Frankfurt: Suhrkamp, 2002–12.

141   Bude and Willisch (eds), *Exklusion*, 113ff. By this policy of exclusion, the middle class avoid certain competitive situations. And as they frequently prefer not to reveal the mechanisms of competition and social exclusion from which they often profit, Herfried Münkler even notes a 'notorious tendency to bigotry' (*Mitte und Maß*, 171ff.).

142   Mau, *Lebenschancen*, 162.

The precarious middle classes, who actually experience relative downward mobility, count this as personal failure. Here individualistic and fatalistic interpretations of their own work prevail. They seek at almost any price to integrate into society by competition at work. This also has the consequence of resentment towards the weaker, the supposedly lazy or those considered less motivated.[143]

As a result of this, those threatened with downward mobility cling all the more fiercely to their past or imaginary status as part of the middle class. Some of them ritually maintain their upward orientation, even if they have inwardly long since abandoned this perspective. The social figure of the worker is no longer a sufficiently positive self-description. It has been a long time since workers built seven-gated Thebes, and in practice no one still sees them as the universal subject of social emancipation. The worker is rather seen as dependent, as someone who has not succeeded as an individual. The collective identity of the working class has been replaced by a general striving for middle-class status.[144] All in all, in recent years a subjective sense of belonging to the working class has been abandoned, while inclusion of oneself in the middle class has grown—even despite downward mobility.[145]

Nothing much remains for those who have suffered downward mobility, or who occupy the lower segments of the labour market. Previously, workers had still internalized a highly positive image of their own future, a striving for ascent and self-responsibility. Today they feel themselves excluded, declassed, discriminated against and without hope. They hardly still believe

143 Cf. Grimm, Hirseland and Vogel, 'Die Ausweitung der Zwischenzone'; Dörre et al., *Bewährungsproben*.

144 Cf. Göran Therborn, 'Class in the Twenty-first Century', *New Left Review* II(78), 6.

145 Cf. Roland Habich, 'Soziale Lagen und soziale Schichtung', *Statistisches Bundesamt/Wissenschaftszentrum Berlin für Sozialforschung 2013*, 191–88.

in a better future for themselves.[146] Ascent into a higher class has vanished from their mental horizon; they have become phlegmatic and fatalistic about their status.[147]

THE NEW CLASS SOCIETY

In Germany, downward mobility is producing a new class society. The upper class inhabits a socially sealed-off, stable world. The middle class reproduces itself by the increasing practice of social closure and cultural distinction. The mixture of social-status control and discipline, precarious jobs and welfare benefits, is constructing a new underclass,[148] fixed in a social situation from which only a few manage to climb out and up. They are not excluded from paid employment, but integrated either indirectly (as recipients of transfer payments) or directly (as low-paid workers).[149] Class matters, and its relevance is growing,

146   Cf. Bahl and Staab, 'Das Dienstleistungsproletariat'; Stéphane Béaud and Michel Pialoux, *Die verlorene Zukunft der Arbeiter. Die Peugeot-Werke von Sochaux-Montbéliard*, Konstanz: UVK, 2009; Dörre et al., *Bewährungsproben*.

147   Cf. Dörre et al., *Bewährungsproben*; Franz Walter, 'Die starken Arme legen keine Räder mehr still. Der "Malocher" trat ab und ein Prekariat entstand', in Johanna Klatt and Franz Walter (eds), *Entbehrliche der Bürgergesellschaft. Sozial Benachteiligte und Engagement*, Bielefeld: transcript, 2011.

148   In the debate on the 'new underclass', this is presented with a deliberate intent to demean a group on the basis of culture, their deviant behaviour supposedly bearing the main responsibility for their own fate (cf. Nolte, *Generation Reform*).

149   The various social-science debates around exclusion and the underclass have many points of contact. The concept of exclusion is applicable to the underclass as this is analysed here, but with the qualification that it is marked by an inside/outside distinction in the context of high unemployment. At the same time, the debate on exclusion has brought striking diagnoses of new questions of inequality, prefiguring many of the phenomena analysed here. Cf. Heinz Bude, *Die Ausgeschlossenen. Das Ende vom Traum einer gerechten Gesellschaft*, Munich: Carl Hanser, 2008; idem, 'Die Überflüssigen als transversale Kategorie', in Peter A. Berger

particularly in terms of life expectancy. The difference in life expectancy between men from the top 10 per cent and men from the bottom 10 per cent has grown from four to seven years since the end of the Second World War.[150]

It is not surprising, then, that the concept of class has returned to social debate, its renaissance driven by social realities.[151] The previously 'invisible class society' has been brought into the light of day.[152] Chapter 1 outlined how often thinkers in post-war Germany proclaimed the end of class society.[153] The

and Michael Vester (eds), *Alte Ungleichheiten. Neue Spaltungen*, Opladen: Leske+Budrich, 1998; Heinz Bude and Andreas Willisch (eds), *Exklusion. Die Debatte über die 'Überflüssigen'*, Frankfurt: Suhrkamp, 2008; idem (eds), *Das Problem der Exklusion*, Hamburg: Hamburger Edition, 2006; Martin Kronauer, *Exklusion. Die Gefährdung des Sozialen im hoch entwickelten Kapitalismus*, Frankfurt: Campus, 2002.

150 Cf. Peter Haan, Daniel Kemptner, Holger Lüthen, 'The Rising Longevity Gap by Lifetime Earnings: Distributional Implications for the Pension System', *DIW-Discussion Papers* 1698, 2017.

151 In the present book, the concepts of class and stratum are used synonymously for empirical description, since despite analytic distinctions that may well be substantial, they both comprise people in similar socio-economic situations, with similar life experiences and personal characteristics (attitudes and value orientations, needs and interests, mentalities and lifestyles), as well as similar life chances and risks (cf. on this, Geißler, *Die Sozialstruktur Deutschlands*, 93ff.). In analysis by stratum, these are seen as forming a hierarchical order, in which their members have better or worse conditions than others. In class analysis it is assumed that one class is better off because another is worse off. This involves questions of systematic exploitation, privilege and disadvantage (cf. Martin Groß, *Klassen, Schichten, Mobilität. Eine Einführung*, Wiesbaden: VS, 2008). In what follows, the class concept is used primarily with respect to behavioural characteristics.

152 Karl-Siegbert Rehberg, ' "Klassengesellschaftlichkeit" nach dem Ende der Klassengesellschaft?', *Berliner Journal für Soziologie* 21(1), 2011, 7–21. Cf. Groß, *Klassen, Schichten, Mobilität*.

153 Rainer Geißler, 'Das mehrfache Ende der Klassengesellschaft', in Jürgen Friedrichs, M. Rainer Lepsius and Karl Ulrich Mayer (eds), *Die Diagnosefähigkeit der Soziologie. Sonderheft Kölner Zeitschrift für Soziologie und Sozialpsychologie 38*, Opladen: Westdeutscher Verlag, 1998. Even so, structures of vertical inequality persist (cf. Geißler, *Die*

social ascent of the working class left considerable doubt about the concept of class.

The class concept is still contested on the grounds of its political implications. Particularly among those who counted themselves as belonging to the working class, the idea of class was less and less a guide to action over the course of the twentieth century; a proletariat conscious of itself—the 'class for itself'—appeared only rarely and in homoeopathic doses.

Consequently, German sociology also turned its back on the concept of class. Instead of classes and strata, investigation turned to individual conditions of life and milieu, to questions of horizontal differentiation such as ethnicity and gender, and to the significance of lifestyle (for example, free-time behaviour).[154]

Today, however, we could say that in a certain contradictory fashion, at least, the refutation of Marx has itself been refuted. In a broad sense, class society in the Marxian sense has re-established itself. For Marx, class was a relational concept: the exclusion from ownership of the means of production implied a fundamental asymmetry of power and distinguished workers from capitalists.[155] Viewed in this way, Marx's concept of class is

---

Sozialstruktur Deutschlands; Groß, *Klassen, Schichten, Mobilität*). Modern sociological approaches have also displayed stronger horizontal differentiations (cf. Michael Vester, Peter von Oertzen, Heiko Geiling, Thomas Herman and Dagmar Müller, *Soziale Milieus im gesellschaftlichen Strukturwandel. Zwischen Integration und Ausgrenzung*, Frankfurt: Suhrkamp, 2001; Daniel Oesch, *Redrawing the Class Map. Stratification and Institutions in Britain, Germany, Sweden and Switzerland*, Houndmills: Palgrave, 2006.

154   Cf. Nicole Burzan, 'Zur Gültigkeit der Individualisierungsthese. Eine kritische Systematisierung empirischer Prüfkriterien', *Zeitschrift für Soziologie* 40(6), 2011, 418–35; Stefan Hradil, *Soziale Ungleichheit in Deutschland*, Wiesbaden: VS, 2005.

155   Cf. Christoph Deutschmann, *Postindustrielle Industriesoziologie. Theoretische Grundlagen, Arbeitsverhältnisse und soziale Identitäten*, Weinheim: Juventa, 2002; Irene Dingeldey, 'Wohlfahrtsstaatlicher Wandel zwischen "Arbeitszwang" und 'Befähigung"', *Berliner Journal für Soziologie* 17(2), 2007, 189–209, 95ff.

completely relevant again today, as never before have more people been dependent on wages, above all because they do not possess any means of production.[156] The (working) class-in-itself—as Marx called it—has grown both nationally and globally. At the international level, social distinctions between nations may well have lessened in the recent past, but within states they have increased immensely.[157] Nevertheless, we cannot speak of a dichotomous class society as Marx and Engels prophesied in *The Communist Manifesto*.[158] Despite downward mobility, the middle class continues to be important.

For a modern class analysis, then, the most appropriate approach is a 'pragmatic realism' that embraces the dimensions of power, exploitation, closure and life chances.[159]

156 Moreover, operative power of disposal over the means of production needs to be considered, which makes the picture more complicated (cf. Eric Olin Wright, *Classes*, London: Verso, 1985).

157 Cf. Therborn, 'Class in the 21st century'. There has been a relative decline of Western societies in the international system, which reasons of space prevent me from discussing here. They may well continue to produce prosperity on the whole, but on the global level relations have been transformed in many respects. The importance of Western capitalisms in the world economy is declining in relative terms, while developing countries are becoming industrial nations. In countries such as China, Brazil or India, extreme poverty has been reduced, and there are for the first time significant middle strata. In the Western world, however, the trend is again in the other direction, for the first time since the Great Depression of the 1930s.

158 It is also unfair to Marx to take the words of *The Communist Manifesto*, a political text par excellence, as his only theory of class. The dichotomous concept was an 'abstract' model; in later writings Marx very clearly made differentiations with respect to position in production, the social division of labour, and the interests bound up with this. Yet he did not develop a specific theory of classes: 'Here the manuscript breaks off', as Engels noted at the end of Marx's uncompleted chapter (Karl Marx, *Capital* Volume Three, Harmondsworth: Penguin, [1894] 1981, 970).

159 Eric Olin Wright, 'Understanding Class: Towards an Integrated Analytical Approach', *New Left Review* II(60), 2009, 101–16; cf. Reinhard Kreckel, *Politische Soziologie der sozialen Ungleichheit*, Frankfurt: Campus, 2004.

Such an approach would draw on both Weber and Marx. German sociology has interpreted class situations principally as market situations, which depend on property and employment opportunities.[160] The perspectives of Marx and Weber should be seen not as conflicting but as supplementing one another.[161] Besides Marx's relational notion of class, Weber's working and property classes have again gained relevance. We can understand with Marx the general rise of dependence on wage labour, and analyse with Weber the life and market opportunities and resources of particular groups—from bankers to call-centre workers. As explained, the status principle that Weber emphasized has also made a return, as upper and middle classes once again assert their status through their way of life, and use various classifications—such as diet, culture and educational qualifications—to strengthen their membership of a particular group. These processes reinforce the social closure of class boundaries,[162] as wealth and poverty increasingly tend to be socially inherited. Positions of social power are ultimately expressed in monopoly rents and surplus profits. If social ascent is no longer attainable, this reinforces the 'internal image' of a class-structured society, in which social permeability continues to dwindle.[163]

What arises from downward mobility is not immediately specific classes in the sense of homogeneous living conditions, from which a parallelism of interests can be articulated. We rather observe new class structurations. These are characterized, according to Giddens, by market position and prospects of mobility, division of labour within the firm, and relations of domination in which systematic disadvantages condense.[164] For

---

160   Max Weber, *Economy and Society*, Berkeley, CA: University of California Press, [1921/1922] 1978, 302ff., 927.

161   Wright, 'Understanding Class'.

162   Kreckel, *Politische Soziologie*, 52ff.

163   Sighard Neckel, *Flucht nach vorn. Die Erfolgskultur der Marktgesellschaft*, Frankfurt: Campus, 2008, 37.

164   Anthony Giddens, *The Class Structure of the Advanced Societies*, 287ff.

temporary employees, agency workers, part-time and subcontracted staff, the low paid, those on 'mini jobs', 'clickworkers', the self-employed and people on benefits, forms of underprivilege are combined with deficits in terms of social and economic citizenship rights. These form the nucleus of a new underclass; they have basically no assets, and hardly any resources of political influence. Agency workers, for example, cannot become members of a works council in the company where they work, even if they have been there for years.

But the new class relations are fragmented and complicated, so that a common interest hardly gets articulated. A teaching assistant who is out of work during the summer break has in some respects more in common with the skilled agency worker than with the tenured senior teacher. Both find themselves in highly insecure labour relations, and both are disadvantaged in terms of pay and rights in relation to their colleagues who are permanent staff. The differences are even more considerable in the activity demanded of them and in their conduct of life.

Below the class of wealth owners and top managers, there is a growing highly skilled service class, who do not enjoy the same job security as their superiors. Between the permanent staff with normal labour relations, negotiated wage rates and works council representation, and the workers in a cleaning company or the sales staff in retail, there are countless distinctions of class structuration.

Modern class relations are more complex than the simple oppositions of rich/poor or above/below. Vertical social inequalities are interwoven with horizontal disparities.[165] Gender and ethnicity each form autonomous and irreducible structures of

165   Cf. Joachim Bergmann, Gerhardt Brandt, Klaus Körber, Ernst Theodor Mohl and Claus Offe (1969), 'Herrschaft, Klassenverhältnis und Schichtung', in Theodor W. Adorno (ed.), *Spätkapitalismus oder Industriegesellschaft? Verhandlungen des 16. Deutschen Soziologentages vom 8. bis 11. April 1968 in Frankfurt am Main*, Stuttgart: Enke, 1969; Offe, *Strukturprobleme*; Kreckel, *Politische Soziologie*.

discrimination. These horizontal disparities are again combined with specific forms of 'secondary exploitation'.[166] This involves a specific production of class relations that goes beyond 'normal' capitalist exploitation: those affected are first and foremost the precariously employed, whose low degree of social and economic citizenship rights is linked with horizontal disparities. Women and immigrants face particular discrimination on the basis of supposedly ascriptive characteristics (for example, women are 'more suitable' for care work). In such cases, class relations combine with forms of (horizontal) oppression to produce class disparities. To elaborate on this using women's employment: while the position of women in the labour market has considerably improved in recent years, women with the same qualifications continue to be paid less; they are also underrepresented in leading positions.[167] The gender pay gap in Germany was between 40 and 50 per cent in 1950.[168] It has since fallen significantly, but is still 21 per cent.[169] Gender-specific inequalities in the labour

166   Klaus Dörre, 'Landnahme und soziale Klassen. Zur Relevanz sekundärer Ausbeutung', in Hans-Günter Thien (ed.), *Klassen im Postfordismus*, Münster: Westfälisches Dampfboot, 2010; idem, 'Krise des Shareholder Value? Kapitalmarktorientierte Steuerung als Wettkampfsystem', in Klaus Kraemer and Sebastian Nessel (eds), *Entfesselte Finanzmärkte. Soziologische Analysen des modernen Kapitalismus*, Bielefeld: transcript, 2012.

167   On top of this is the persistence of gender-specific activities on the labour market. Cf. Jutta Allmendinger and Thomas Hinz, 'Geschlechtersegregation im Erwerbsbereich. Berufsfelder, Organisationen und Arbeitsgruppen', in Wolfgang Glatzer and Ilona Ostner (eds), *Deutschland im Wandel. Sozialstrukturelle Analysen*, Opladen: Leske+Budrich, 1999; Karin Gottschall, 'Geschlechterverhältnis und Arbeitsmarktsegregation', in Regina Becker-Schmidt and Gudrun-Axeli Knapp (eds), *Das Geschlechterverhältnis als Gegenstand der Sozialwissenschaften*, Frankfurt: Campus, 1995.

168   Cf. Geißler, *Die Sozialstruktur Deutschlands*, 384.

169   Cf. Statistisches Bundesamt, 'Gender Pay Gap 2016: Deutschland weiterhin eines der EU-Schlusslichter', www.destatis.de (accessed February 2018).

market remain striking in almost all dimensions.[170] At the same time, the debate over discrimination against women focuses mainly on the question of equal opportunity (see Chapter 3). Just as significant, yet paid far less attention, are social inequalities among women. Not all face equal discrimination. The 'winners' of recent equality policies are particularly women from the middle class.[171] On the other hand, out of all women in full-time employment, one in three earns only the minimum wage. So, while German women are indeed more equal in terms of rights, inequality among women has never been as great as it is today. The rise in women's employment has thus involved an extremely contradictory form of regressive modernization, as their increased participation in the labour market has precisely been a 'precursor of precarity'.[172] The horizontal equalization of women has proceeded in such a way as to heighten vertical inequalities among both women and men.

While women, men and immigrants in the upper reaches of the social hierarchy have experienced greater equality of opportunity and a reduction in horizontal disparities, at the other end of the scale the various dimensions of class disparity accumulate. Women in lower social positions are also as a rule those who face the greatest discrimination and the strongest horizontal disparities. A woman manager has a completely different chance of being treated equally than does an immigrant cleaning woman. In short, class,

170   Cf. Scherschel and Booth, 'Aktivierung in die Prekarität'; Brigitte Aulenbacher, and Angelika Wetterer (eds), *Arbeit. Perspektiven und Diagnosen der Geschlechterforschung*, Münster: Westfälisches Dampfboot, 2009.

171   Brigitte Aulenbacher, 'Frauen, Männer, Prekarität. Vom fordistischen Versprechen auf Wohlstand zur postfordistischen Reproduktionskrise', in Peter Hammerschmidt and Juliane Sagebie (eds), *Die Soziale Frage zu Beginn des 21. Jahrhunderts*, Neu-Ulm: AG SPAK Verlag, 2011, 126.

172   Nicole Mayer-Ahuja, *Wieder dienen lernen? Vom westdeutschen 'Normalarbeitsverhältnis' zu prekärer Beschäftigung seit 1973*, Berlin: Edition Sigma, 2003, 89ff.

gender and ethnicity fuse at the lower end of downward mobility into a conglomerate of oppressive and exploitative mechanisms.

In social modernity, the tendency was for class positions to be levelled upward, especially by the guarantee of equal social citizenship; but regressive modernization, the society of downward mobility, establishes a plurality of downward class structurations. The majority of freelance or agency workers lead a precarious life, but for a minority—for example, the aforementioned young and well-paid IT specialists—this actually means a gain in autonomy. There has not been the formation of a 'precariat' as a new social class.[173] Up to now, neither an action potential nor a class consciousness has arisen that grips the masses.[174] There is not a single precariat, but rather 'many precariats'.[175] Their characteristics depend not only on qualifications and the contextual conditions of the labour market, but also on their subjective positions. Precarious creative workers of both genders frequently make a virtue of necessity ('I can't imagine having a boss; I need my freedom'). This untroubled freedom, however, ultimately often relies on the cushion of parental prosperity. In branches of former public service, on the other hand, consciousness of a devaluation of the career path is much stronger. The 'service proletariat' of unskilled work also remains fragmented in terms of its interests.[176]

173   As against the argument of Guy Standing, *The Precariat: The New Dangerous Class*, London: Bloomsbury, 2011.

174   Traditional Marxist class theories have always argued from class position to a corresponding quasi-objective class consciousness.

175   Bude, *Das Problem der Exklusion*, 117.

176   Cf. Philipp Staab, *Macht und Herrschaft in der Servicewelt*, Hamburg: Hamburger Edition, 2014; Bahl and Staab, 'Das Dienstleistungsproletariat'. As against *The Communist Manifesto*, Marx maintained in *The Eighteenth Brumaire of Louis Bonaparte* that a bad social situation does not automatically lead to a corresponding consciousness. He famously wrote about the small peasants that 'the small peasant proprietors form an immense mass, the members of which live in the same situation but do not enter into manifold relationships with each other. Their mode of operations isolates them instead of bringing them into mutual

Contemporary studies show clearly the prejudice and contradiction in the consciousness of industrial workers in Germany today.[177] Only in the milieu of welfare recipients is it possible to observe a certain homogenization of way of life and attitude that might indicate the future formation of a social class. They are often unable to afford the same style of material or cultural consumption as the permanently employed. The shame of those on benefits, the fear of social infection or misunderstanding in relation to the lives of friends and colleagues in the zone of integration or vulnerability, leads to mutual estrangement. In the end, they remain largely among themselves.[178]

The new class structurations thus initially have led only to 'quasi-groups',[179] even though these face common problems and have potentially common interests. The outcome remains uncertain, as even if vertical class relations return, society has been pluralized.[180] Precarious or proletarian conditions have now arisen, but no political commonality is yet detectable. We have a 'class society without class tension', in which classes do not constitute themselves through collective action.[181] However, precarity and downward mobility are leading to acts of revolt, as will be shown in the next chapter.

---

intercourse . . . They are therefore incapable of asserting their class interest in their own name' (*Surveys from Exile*, London: Verso, 2012, 238–9).

177   Cf. Klaus Dörre, 'Schluss: Strukturierende Effekte selektiver Arbeitsmarktpolitik', in Dörre et al., *Bewährungsproben*.

178   Ibid.

179   Cf. Ralf Dahrendorf, *Class and Class Conflict in an Industrial Society*, London: Routledge, 1959.

180   Moreover, the concrete extent and effects of individualization are still contested. Cf. Nicole Burzan, 'Zur Gültigkeit der Individualisierungsthese. Eine kritische Systematisierung empirischer Prüfkriterien', *Zeitschrift für Soziologie* 40(6), 2011, 418–35; Thomas Lux, 'Jenseits sozialer Klassen? Eine empirische Überprüfung der Individualisierungsthese am Beispiel von Ungleichheitseinstellungen und Wahlverhalten', *Zeitschrift für Soziologie* 40(6), 2011, 436–57.

181   Heinz Bude, 'Klassengesellschaft ohne Klassenentspannung. Leben in der fragmentierten Gesellschaft', *Neue Gesellschaft, Frankfurter Hefte* 59(3), 2012.

5
Revolt

Mass rallies and Monday demonstrations against Hartz IV; the Occupy movement; protests against nuclear power, surveillance and major construction projects; angry progressive citizens in Stuttgart and their right-wing counterparts in Dresden—since the turn of the century, we have witnessed a veritable renaissance of revolt across German society.[1] Nevertheless, the country has remained relatively peaceful compared to many countries in western and southern Europe that have been truly rocked by mass protests, especially since the financial crisis that began in 2007. European capitals have been the scene of riots, while new social movements such as the Spanish *Indignados* have emerged, leading to the establishment of new protest parties such as Podemos.

The overall picture of this revolt, however, is hard to decipher, and even highly contradictory. Many protests flare up only for a moment and remain episodic. They also exhibit a normative

---

1 In the big German cities, especially Berlin, several small demonstrations or actions take place most days. As far back as 1997, Wilhelm Heitmeyer (*Bundesrepublik Deutschland. Auf dem Weg von der Konsens- zur Konfliktgesellschaft*, Frankfurt: Suhrkamp, 1977) saw Germany as on the path from 'a consensus to a conflict society', though with a focus on controversies over social or ethnic issues.

confusion, as many of their protagonists see themselves as transcending the traditional divisions of left and right. What unites them is the perception that certain social promises that held modern societies together for a long time are no longer being kept.

Social conflicts generally arise when large numbers of people share the feeling that they are being treated unfairly, or that their rights are being abused. The workers' movement emerged in response to the exploitation of industrial capitalism, and the upsurge of the women's movement was fuelled by massive and widespread experiences of discrimination. Urban riots frequently erupt after certain social groups have been humiliated for years. These protests pursue specific ideas of justice that are generally dependent on context: demands for redistribution, for intervention in the economy or even property organization, express an underlying 'moral economy'.[2]

Conflicts of this kind need not necessarily be economic or related to distribution in a narrow sense; they may also raise questions of domination, of social status or legitimacy. Every society allots its members ranks and positions. As a rule, this hierarchical status order is accepted even by those who do not inhabit the upper echelons, yet they involve an 'implicit social contract'[3] by which even the subordinate groups enjoy specific rights, while the groups at the top have particular duties they are obliged to fulfil. An unemployed person is protected from arbitrary treatment to a certain extent by the authorities, and even a chief executive officer is expected to obey the law. Axel Honneth added a further dimension to this idea: in his view, conflicts arise when injury is done to normative expectations of (legal) equality and treatment, autonomy and social valuation. If members of a

2   E. P. Thompson, 'The Moral Economy of the English Crowd in the 18th Century', *Past and Present* 50, 1971, 76–136.

3   Barrington Moore, *Injustice: The Social Bases of Obedience and Revolt*, London: Routledge, 1978.

social group experience their expectations being systematically disappointed, this can become the starting point of a 'struggle for recognition'.[4]

It is quite normal, then, for protest movements to arise if the existing social order no longer works and its institutions no longer function.[5] This was the case, for example, in Spain and Portugal when financial and economic crises resulted in a further sharp rise in the high unemployment level, while the mechanisms of social security failed to deliver. For the younger generation, unemployment was above 30 per cent. Social reality no longer matched the norm of upward mobility.

Has the 'social question' and the (class) conflict bound up with it made a return with the society of downward mobility? To anticipate a partial answer to this: yes, but not in the form in which it was previously known. There will be no return of the class struggle of the nineteenth and early twentieth centuries, or of the traditional proletariat. The wheel of social differentiation and pluralization can no longer turn back; the social question on conditions of individualization structured by the welfare state is now raised in a fundamentally different way. New collective actors arise only in the process of major conflicts with several episodes, in which common practice and meanings develop.

Before proceeding to sketch the new social conflict within conditions of downward mobility, it is necessary to analyse earlier conflicts and protest movements. By way of summary, we can say that particular eras are marked by specific kinds of conflict. In early capitalism, social struggles revolved predominantly around political emancipation from the old feudal order, individual (economic) freedom and establishing a state of law, along with

---

4 Axel Honneth, *Struggle for Recognition: The Moral Grammar of Conflicts*, Cambridge: Polity, 1996.

5 Cf. Frances Fox Piven and Richard A. Cloward, *Poor People's Movements: Why They Succeed, How They Fail*, New York: Random House, 1971.

democratically representative institutions such as parliaments. At the head of these progressive movements stood the enlightened bourgeoisie, who led the workers and peasants.

In the mid-nineteenth century, as capitalism was more or less firmly established, the organized workers' movement first appeared on the historical stage in Germany. The Allgemeine Deutsche Arbeiterverein (ADAV) founded by Ferdinand Lassalle in 1863 inscribed on its banner the French Revolution's demand for 'liberty, equality, fraternity'. In the liberal capitalism of these years, as well as the organized capitalism of the first half of the twentieth century, the political landscape was determined by 'wild' and unregulated class struggles.

The early German workers' movement fought generalized battles for legal, political and social recognition. It also laid the foundation for the establishment of a specific identity for wage earners, and developed a dense network of trade unions, and cultural and leisure organizations.[6] A classic slogan of this phase ran: 'A fair day's wage for a fair day's work'.[7] This formula, apparently simple at first glance, expressed a key issue of that age. The working class suffered from massive impoverishment, lived in atrocious conditions and was squeezed between the domination

---

6   Cf. Thomas Welskopp, *Das Banner der Brüderlichkeit*, Bonn: Dietz, 2000. With a politics oriented around identity and lifestyle, the early workers' movement thus displayed many features that are attributed to today's new social movements (cf. Craig Calhoun, ' "New Social Movements" of the Early Nineteenth Century', *Social Science History* 17(3), 1993, 385–427).

7   On the Christian roots of this demand for a 'just wage', cf. Michael Kittner, *Arbeitskampf. Geschichte—Recht—Gegenwart*, Munich: C. H. Beck, 2005, 33ff and 228ff. Marx and Engels initially supported this 'natural' slogan of the workers' movement. Only later did they argue against it, on account, among other things, of its immanently reformist character. Cf. Karl Marx, *Value, Price and Profit* (*Marx-Engels Collected Works*, vol. 20, London: Lawrence and Wishart, [1865] 1985), and Frederick Engels, 'A Fair Day's Wages for a Fair Day's Work' (idem, vol. 24, [1881] 1989).

of the capitalists and the privileges of the guild masters. Accordingly, the slogan did not refer primarily to redistribution, but rather to human 'dignity' and 'recognition of labour as the foundation for maintaining oneself and one's family'.[8] The socialist workers' movement that developed in the second half of the nineteenth century did not just struggle for the socialization of the means of production, but equally for universal citizenship rights: unrestricted universal suffrage and political equality for women.

But the political modus operandi of the workers' movement changed in the latter half of the twentieth century. Its practice of conflict, precisely because of its successes, had adapted to the institutional arrangements of social modernity. By way of collective bargaining, co-determination and the welfare state, the 'wild' conflicts of the past were curtailed. With the institutionalization of class conflict, the German workers' movement largely abandoned its perspective of social transformation. Socialism became an abstract term, more or less ashamedly tucked away in the party programme. Class struggle was now largely reduced to strictly regulated wage negotiations. The trade unions particularly sought to tread the already beaten path of collective bargaining: higher wages, improved social security, lower working hours. Variations on the expression 'a fair whack' were the typical rhetoric. This meant focusing demands on little more than questions of distribution. Basic questions of recognition were largely excluded, and the workers' movement thus lost its moral sting.[9]

---

8   Dietmar Suß, ' "Ein gerechter Lohn für ein gerechtes Tagewerk"? Überlegungen zu einer Geschichte des Mindestlohns', *Archiv für Sozialgeschichte* 54, 2014, 125–45.

9   Cf. Stephan Voswinkel, *Anerkennung und Reputation. Die Dramaturgie industrieller Beziehungen*, Konstanz: UVK, 2011, 16; Walther Müller-Jentsch, *Soziologie der industriellen Beziehungen. Eine Einführung*, Frankfurt: Campus, 1997, 202; Axel Honneth, 'Moral Consciousness and Class Domination: Some Problems in the Analysis of Hidden Morality',

The precondition for this diminution of conflict in Germany was a society of social ascent. The apogee of social modernity, occurring around 1968, was the starting point for waves of protest.[10] This was an anti-authoritarian revolt against conventions, hierarchies and the side effects of capitalism, such as ecological problems. These actions were followed by the 'new social movements', the social and particularly ideological basis for which was provided by the younger, post-materialist generations.[11] These and the members of the 'new middle class' strove for greater autonomy and participation within the existing order.[12] They focused less on aspects of distribution, and more on questions of identity and recognition.[13] Viewed historically, the prevailing structures of social conflict were also expressed in Germany's party system:[14] the class struggle or the conflict

in *Disrespect: The Normative Foundations of Critical Theory*, London: Polity 2007, 91. This does not mean, however, that all trade-union conflicts took place within the institutional framework (cf. Kittner, *Arbeitskampf*); for example, the campaign 'On Saturdays My Dad Belongs to Me', the struggle for the 35-hour week, or the strike that successfully defended existing sick-pay entitlement. The Kohl government was defeated by trade-union resistance when it tried to abolish this in 1996 (Wolfgang Streeck, *No Longer the Century of Corporatism. Das Ende des 'Bündnisses für Arbeit'*, MPIfG Working Paper 03/4, Cologne, 2003).

10   Other factors involved in this were the protest against the Vietnam War, the colonial liberation movements, and others. Cf. Chris Harman, *The Fire Last Time: 1968 and After*, London: Bookmarks, 1988.

11   Roland Inglehart, 'Changing Values among Western Publics from 1970 to 2006', *West European Politics* 31(1–2), 2008, 130–46.

12   Cf. Dieter Rucht, *Modernisierung und neue soziale Bewegungen. Deutschland, Frankreich und USA im Vergleich*, Frankfurt: Campus, 1994; Joachim Raschke, *Soziale Bewegungen. Ein historisch-systematischer Grundriss*, Frankfurt: Campus, 1987.

13   Nancy Fraser and Axel Honneth, *Redistribution or Recognition? A Political-Philosophical Exchange*, London: Verso, 2003.

14   Cf. Seymour M. Lipset and Stein Rokkan (eds), *Party Systems and Voter Alignments. Cross-National Perspectives*, New York: The Free Press, 1967.

between labour and capital was institutionalized with the establishment of the Social Democratic Party (SPD), while post-materialist demands were anchored in the parliamentary system by the Greens.

As shown in previous chapters, the recent past has been marked by a change in social direction. The downward mobility that has arisen can be characterized by growing inequality, a frequently downward social escalation, the demolition of social and economic citizenship rights, and new class structurations.

We have already shown how only 29 per cent of employees in western Germany and less than 15 per cent in the east work for firms with both a works council and negotiated wages. For many groups, unemployment increasingly erodes social integration: social security, prestige and esteem are no longer sufficiently provided. Large groups face a deficit of collective recognition.[15] The latent class division in social modernity has regained its significance, while class conflict is being 'de-institutionalized'.[16] But this does not automatically mean the return of class struggle, which has lost its former social foundation—the traditional working class, ready for action, with a shared horizon of meaning.

The new conflicts arise in a situation marked by a lack of transparency and growing instability. Traditional class allegiances and identities—indeed, institutional and organizational ties in general—have weakened. The differentiation of the social structure and the individualization of lifestyles have melted the glaciers of the old collective organizations like parties and trade unions. Whereas in the late 1970s, one in three German workers still belonged to a trade union affiliated with the major

---

15 Honneth, *Freedom's Right*, 223ff.

16 Oliver Nachtwey, 'Zur Remoralisierung des sozialen Konflikts', *Westend. Neue Zeitschrift für Sozialforschung* 10(2), 2013, 69–80.

nationwide confederation, the DGB,[17] the proportion had fallen to 18 per cent by 2013. Both the SPD and the Christian Democrats have lost around half of their members since the 1990s.

Though this does not mean a decline in political or social commitment as such, instead political activity has become more situational, selective and uncommitted while institutionalized representative democratic involvement has shrunk. Even trade unions and left-wing parties no longer seek to maintain the traditional structures of conflict—where this is still possible. A politics oriented around class questions is viewed by most large organizations as an anachronistic relic of a bygone age, no longer relevant in the social market society.

Consequently, the social question is hardly taken up at all in politics, or only very selectively. In post-democracy, a consensus of material constraints blocks the channels by which interests are articulated. This, however, leads to a 'crisis of representation', and basically also a crisis of parliamentary democracy.[18]

In the 1970s, it was still the 'late capitalist' interventionist state that produced a legitimacy deficit to be taken up by social movements;[19] in the present constellation, however, problems of legitimation are produced by new social and democratic inequalities, which the 'old' late-capitalist state had kept in check.[20]

----

17   Translator's note: the Deutsche Gewerkschaftsbund ('German Trade Union Confederation', or DGB) unites the eight major unions, organized by industrial sector, and has an influence on social policy well beyond immediate trade-union questions.

18   Danny Michelsen and Franz Walter, *Unpolitische Demokratie. Zur Krise der Repräsentation*, Berlin: Suhrkamp, 2013; Markus Linden and Winfried Thaa (eds), *Krise und Reform politischer Repräsentation*, Baden-Baden: Nomos, 2011.

19   Jürgen Habermas, *Legitimation Crisis*, London: Heinemann, 1976; Claus Offe, *Strukturprobleme des kapitalistischen Staates*, New York: Campus, 2006.

20   Oliver Nachtwey, 'Legitimationsprobleme im Spätkapitalismus revisited', in Karina Becker, Lars Gertenbach, Henning Laux and

NEW CONFLICTS AROUND WORK AND SOCIAL DEMANDS

It is significant that two of the greatest social protests in the post-war history of West Germany did not arise directly from questions of inequality or justice, but in both cases involved social and economic citizenship rights, albeit under different banners: in one case against their inadequacy, and in the other against their demolition.

In 1952, hundreds of thousands of trade unionists protested against the passage of the enterprise law. This law was supposed to guarantee them a greater say in the management of their firm, yet the draft law remained far below expectations, even below existing state regulations. The 1951 mining industry co-determination law guaranteed equal representation of workers and employers on the supervisory boards of large companies. For the trade unions, co-determination was a key element of an economic democracy in which employees determined policy on an equal basis with the representatives of capital. The draft for the new enterprise law, however, while conceding a greater say for workers in many ways, did not succeed in extending parity-based co-determination to all branches. Further, trade union representatives feared they would lose influence through the legally prescribed autonomy of works councils. In the unions' view, which would be confirmed by the subsequent course of events, the new enterprise law did not achieve the aim of economic democracy.[21]

Tilmann Reitz (eds), *Grenzverschiebungen des Kapitalismus*, Frankfurt: Campus, 2010.

21   Cf. Alex Demirovic, *Demokratie in der Wirtschaft. Positionen—Probleme—Perspektiven*, Münster: Westfälisches Dampfboot, 2007. The enterprise laws of 1972 and 2011 extended co-determination rights. Some critical points for the trade unions, such as the dual character of co-determination in Germany (the trade unions have relatively little possibilities of influence in the firm), remained unchanged.

The second major wave of social protest arose as a reaction to the Agenda 2010 legislation.[22] Several left-wing groups and associations of the unemployed, the alter-globalization network ATTAC and some union members had called for a demonstration 'against sweeping social cuts' in Berlin on 1 November 2003. Instead of the expected 25,000 demonstrators, conservative observers estimated more than 100,000 in the streets—a surprisingly high number in recent protest history, especially considering that no major organization was involved. Discontent and anger was widespread throughout the entire population at the time, and many bystanders who stumbled upon the protest march joined spontaneously. In early 2004, the DGB unions, which had initially hesitated to denounce the new measures given their traditionally close ties to the SPD, mobilized more than half a million demonstrators in four cities. This was a larger number than had taken to the streets for social demands in more than half a century. Autumn of the same year saw a better-known type of protest, but a surprising one in this context—the 'Monday demonstrations', which were designed to ritually assert a firm determination and recur ideally until their demands were met. In the course of the East German revolution, Monday demonstrations were an important instrument of opposition. At that time, the demand was for political freedom; these rallies were now against the demolition of social citizenship rights by the so-called 'Hartz' legislation. Throughout the Federal Republic, and especially in eastern Germany, it was the unemployed who handled the overall organization of the Monday rallies—a

---

22 Some 350,000 people had already demonstrated in the Bonn Hofgarten in 1996 against benefits cuts and particularly against the proposed change to sick-pay regulations. This successful mobilization, however, was due above all to the efforts of the DGB trade union federation (Gérard Bökenkamp, *Das Ende des Wirtschaftswunders. Geschichte der Sozial-, Wirtschafts- und Finanzpolitik in der Bundesrepublik 1969–1998*, Stuttgart: Lucius, 2010).

remarkable development in view of the well-known problems of mobilizing the precariat.[23] Some of the groups that arose at this time still exist and demonstrate today.

This wave of protest was the foundation for the new party Die Linke, which united the ex-Communist Party of Democratic Socialism (PDS) with a split from the West German SPD known as the Wahlalternative Arbeit und Soziale Gerechtigkeit ('Electoral Alternative for Labour and Social Justice', WASG); Die Linke primarily organized and represented those populations threatened by downward mobility.[24] Here, the renewal of the social question found expression in party politics.

While social protests in the political arena increased as a result of Agenda 2010, workplaces initially remained largely calm. In fact, never in German post-war history had there been so few strikes as during this phase, even if the German inclination to strike is not very strong. This has much to do with the country's industrial relations. Before a strike, many institutional filters and levels of compromise are involved, trade-union centralization is relatively great and the inherited tradition of social partnership continues to be influential.[25] In post-war

23 Dieter Rucht and Mundo Yang, 'Wer protestierte gegen Hartz IV', *Forschungsjournal Neue Soziale Bewegungen* 17(4), 2004, 21–7; Christian Lahusen and Britta Baumgarten, *Das Ende des sozialen Friedens? Politik und Protest in Zeiten der Hartz-Reformen*, Frankfurt: Campus, 2010. It is especially among the lower classes that there is no automatic connection between underprivilege and revolt. In these zones there is even greater competition for positional goods. Cf. Klaus Dörre, Karin Scherschel, Melanie Booth, Tine Haubner, Kai Marquardsen and Karen Schierhorn (eds), *Bewährungsproben für die Unterschicht? Soziale Folgen aktivierender Arbeitsmarktpolitik*, Frankfurt: Campus, 2013.

24 Oliver Nachtwey and Tim Spier, 'Günstige Gelegenheit? Die sozialen und politischen Entstehungshintergründe der Linkspartei', in Tim Spier, Felix Butzlaff, Matthias Micus and Franz Walter (eds), *Die Linkspartei. Zeitgemäße Idee oder Bündnis ohne Zukunft?*, Wiesbaden: VS, 2007.

25 Ulrich Brinkmann and Oliver Nachtwey, 'Industrial Relations,

society, trade unions and employers' associations transformed their formerly antagonistic relationship into one of cooperation. Their aim was to combine economic dynamism with social equilibrium. The trade unions have tended to consider strikes as a 'sword on the wall', only to be taken up as a last resort.[26]

Until the 1990s, unions' weakness caused them to focus primarily on defending existing institutional resources;[27] this resulted in many branches where collective bargaining still held, and the number of strikes fell almost to zero. In the 1960s and '70s, disputes were largely confined to the engineering, electrical and chemical industries. Then for more than a decade, and still longer in the chemical industry, there were no strikes at all. The social-partnership orientation of the unions in these branches became even stronger after the financial crisis, as this stance seemed to promise stability.[28]

In other sectors of the economy, however, the erosion of collective bargaining was so pronounced that a minimum wage

Trade Unions and Social Conflict in German Capitalism', *La Nouvelle Revue du Travail* 2/3, 2013, nrt.revues.org (accessed February 2016).

26   Müller-Jentsch, *Soziologie der industriellen Beziehungen*, 22; Heiner Dribbusch (ed.), 'Streik-Bewegungen. Neue Entwicklungen im Arbeitskampf', *Forschungsjournal Neue Soziale Bewegungen* 22(4), 2009, 56–66.

27   Ulrich Brinkmann, Hae-Lin Choi, Richard Detje, Klaus Dörre, Hajo Holst, Serhat Karakayali and Catharina Schmalstieg (eds), *Strategic Unionism. Aus der Krise zur Erneuerung?*, Wiesbaden: VS, 2008.

28   Thomas Haipeter, 'Sozialpartnerschaft in und nach der Krise: Entwicklungen und Perspektiven', *Industrielle Beziehungen* 19(4), 2012, 387–411; Heiner Dribbusch, 'Sozialpartnerschaft und Konflikt: Gewerkschaftliche Krisenpolitik am Beispiel der Automobilindustrie', *Zeitschrift für Politik* 59(2), 2012, 123–43; Klaus Dörre, 'Funktionswandel der Gewerkschaften. Von der intermediären zur fraktalen Organisation', in Klaus Dörre and Thomas Haipeter (eds), *Gewerkschaftliche Modernisierung*, Wiesbaden: VS, 2011; idem, 'Überbetriebliche Regulierung von Arbeitsbeziehungen', in Fritz Böhle, G. Günther Voß and Günther Wachtler (eds), *Handbuch Arbeitssoziologie*, Wiesbaden: VS, 2010.

became necessary for the first time to guarantee the slightest social security. The unions, especially those in the service sector, could see the implementation of the minimum wage as a success in their lengthy campaign—though they also had to admit that it was likewise a sign of their weak bargaining position.

Since around 2008, however, there has been a slow but steady upturn in strikes.[29] The union Verdi indicated an increase from thirty-six cases of industrial action in 2004 to more than 200 in 2012. The catering and hospitality union NGG (Nahrung-Genuss-Gaststätten) also recorded a rising number of strikes.[30] The range of striking occupational groups runs from motorway service station staff to lock operators, bus drivers, airport security guards, and even employees of cash-in-transit companies. A wave of strikes began in 2015 that would previously have been almost unthinkable in Germany,[31] with militant stoppages lasting for weeks in the public services, among social workers and primary teachers, in the postal service, the railways, in hospitals and at Amazon.

These new struggles have been almost completely in the service sector. This is where the tendency toward the de-institutionalization of social conflict has advanced furthest, where the system of wage agreements is most eroded, and above all where the number of local struggles is steadily on the rise.[32] Because

29   Heiner Dribbusch and Peter Birke, *Die DGB-Gewerkschaften seit der Krise. Entwicklungen, Herausforderungen, Strategien*, Friedrich-Ebert-Stiftung, Berlin, 2014.

30   Cf. ibid., 13ff.

31   Wolfgang Streeck, 'The strikes sweeping Germany are here to stay', *The Guardian*, 22 May 2015, www.theguardian.com (accessed February 2016).

32   At company level, the frequency of conflict is rising in those areas no longer subject to sectoral wage agreements (cf. Axel Hauser-Ditz, Markus Hertwig and Ludger Pries, 'Verbetrieblichung und betrieblicher Konflikt', *Kölner Zeitschrift für Soziologie und Sozialpsychologie* 64(2), 2012, 329–59).

employers in this sector are particularly aggressive in their actions, there is now 'hardly a day without a strike'.[33]

Some of these recent strikes were initiated by small unions with a specific 'trade' basis—such as the pilots' union Vereinigung Cockpit, the Marburger Bund (doctors' association), or the train-drivers' union GDL (Gewerkschaft Deutscher Lokomotivführer). Since these unions' members enjoy a particularly strong structural position on the labour market, their strikes are often depicted in the media as scandalous and egoistic. This interpretation, however, disguises the social basis of these conflicts, which often result from the paradoxical consequences of regressive modernization. When railways, air traffic and hospitals were previously in the public sector, their employees were civil servants or enjoyed good wage agreements. Today, though, these companies have been privatized, or at least operate according to principles of private ownership. For many of their employees this has meant a loss of status, social security and guaranteed wages. The major trade unions are generally powerless in the face of this deterioration, and in some cases—for example, the railway union Transnet—they have even contributed to attempts at quasi-privatization.[34]

In the end, the former trade union strongholds were razed, and traditional ties of solidarity between weaker and stronger occupational groups more or less destroyed. This has led to an uncomfortable situation for the major unions of the DGB, as they continue to organize those groups of workers with the least power, while groups with a strong structural position—pilots, train drivers and doctors—unite on an occupational basis and return to collective bargaining. It was particularly these

33   Torsten Bewernitz and Heiner Dribbusch, 'Kein Tag ohne Streik: Arbeitskampfentwicklung im Dienstleistungssektor', *WSI-Mitteilungen* 67(5), 2014, 393–401.

34   Norbert Hansen, the union's former president, was later co-opted onto the board of Deutsche Bahn AG for his valuable services.

organizations that came out on strike in reaction to the reduction of salaries.

Particularly significant are the service sector strikes that marked the renewal of the workers' movement, as the forms of conflict have changed. Since routine collective bargaining now often fails to succeed, if it indeed takes place at all, conflicts no longer run along familiar lines and are less ritually orchestrated. Symbolic actions such as slogans printed on clothing, flash mobs, online campaigns and other instruments from the repertoire of social movements are now deployed more frequently in industrial struggles.

The new strikes are also more democratic in their organization. Traditionally, members would vote at the start and the end of a conflict, but the union leadership managed the running of the strike. With the strikes of 2009 and 2015 in the social and educational services (kindergartens, and facilities for young people and those with disabilities), delegate conferences were held frequently, so that workers could play a more direct role in the strike. This was highly successful: far more workers were mobilized than originally anticipated.

These strikes are typical of the recent past, in which recognition is a key issue at stake. These morally charged social conflicts are not waged for a small pay increase, but rather for dignity, status and respect.[35] The stoppages that Verdi organized in the social and educational services in 2015 are good examples of this development. The key issue there was official recognition of the demands made on educators—Verdi spoke of a 'revaluation' of their labour. According to the trade union, this should be reflected in a higher classification, greater status and higher pay. Kindergarten teachers often felt themselves treated as mere childminders while their work demanded skilled educational tasks. Another example is that of the mainly women workers in cleaning companies, who are not only badly paid but also feel

35   Nachtwey, 'Zur Remoralisierung des sozialen Konflikts'.

that their work and presence are ignored by their clients and the public. Germany's first nationwide strike in the cleaning sector in 2009 was therefore described as a 'revolt of the invisible'. Women workers, often precarious and in many cases immigrants, who in the past had rarely appeared as a 'vanguard of the proletariat' (a role that had almost always fallen to skilled workers), now took centre stage. In the struggles at online retailer Amazon, in the postal service and in the retail trade (strikes that were often waged under the slogan of 'greater respect in retail'), or in the growing conflicts in the health sector, workers in recent years have increasingly struggled for recognition of their social and economic rights and dignity. At Amazon and in the postal service, key issues were workers' status and (connected with this) whether they would be guaranteed a wage contract, and if so, at what rate. Amazon, one of the leading firms in the digital economy, initially refused to offer its workers any collective agreement; it was only prepared to apply the agreement of the logistics sector, which was based on very low pay. The Verdi union, on the other hand, demanded a wage agreement along the lines of the retail trade and mail order sales, which offered significantly better conditions. The postal service decided, despite rising profits, to outsource a part of its business and employees to forty-nine new companies, which would no longer be bound by the relatively generous previous wage agreement, but would orient themselves around the lower wages of competitors like the private parcel delivery company Hermes. This meant an enormous loss of status in relation to the old wage agreement. According to Verdi's estimates, workers in the new subsidiaries earned around 20 per cent less.[36]

A different dynamic developed in the hospital disputes. While nursing staff have traditionally been disinclined to conflict

---

36 The post office added a sting to their offer: workers in the subsidiary companies would not only receive lower wages, but also be hired on temporary contracts.

given their professional ethic, they are in many cases now moti-vated to resistance precisely on account of the demands of this ethic being unachievable due to underfinancing and staff short-age.[37] All these disputes involve new conflicts of morality, but in the end the issue is one of a re-institutionalization of contractual norms, or, in the case of sectors without agreed wages and works councils, an application of economic citizenship at the firm level for the first time.

This change in social conflict has also affected the organiza-tional practice of the DGB unions beyond the field of industrial struggles.[38] Alongside the general attitude of cooperation and social partnership, conflict-oriented sub-strategies have arisen. The IG Metall union is a good example of this: it has not under-gone any disruptive strategic change, and in its core branches—particularly big companies in the electrical, steel and automobile industries—it has continued to pursue social partnership. Yet at sectoral and local levels, it has changed, as activists have rejected traditional behavioural models and everyday routines, and devised innovative practices.[39] In North Rhine-Westphalia, for example, IG Metall developed projects that, besides improving the integration of its membership, envisaged further strategies involving an aggressive campaign that energized the workforce and especially its own members. The campaign 'Better, Not

37 Cf. Oliver Nachtwey and Luigi Wolf, 'Legitimationsprobleme im Spätkapitalismus revisited', in Becker et al., *Grenzverschiebungen des Kapitalismus*; Oliver Nachtwey and Marcel Thiel, 'Chancen und Probleme pfadabhängiger Revitalisierung. Gewerkschaftliches Organizing im Krankenhauswesen', *Industrielle Beziehungen* 21(3), 2014, 257–76.

38 Brinkmann and Nachtwey, 'Industrial Relations'.

39 Graham Turner, *No Way to Run an Economy: Why the System Failed and How to Put It Right*, London: Pluto, 2009. The service union Verdi has also frequently embarked on a stronger conflict orientation. There have been similar campaigns in security companies, telecommunication, distribution, the health sector and retail trade.

Cheaper' combined participatory and pay-oriented practices. The union's 'TarifAktiv' approach sought to pressure firms that departed from wage agreements. Wage commissions were set up at company level to sit at the negotiating table. IG Metall also opened a central organizing department in 2008, with national resources at its disposal. Companies that, in the union's eyes, are not on a path of cooperation are pressed into doing so by either gentle or firmer pressure. In this way, the union has succeeded, over years of struggle, in achieving (relative) equality in wage agreements between agency workers and permanent staff. To this end, it deliberately organized agency workers and invented new forms of participation, but also mobilized the power of the permanent staff. In innovative branches such as wind energy, which had previously been a blind spot on the union organization map, it has also launched systematic campaigns. Groups of organizers are deployed at particular companies to, for example, visit workers at home in order to engage them by direct discussion. Groups go leafleting together, plan actions or address the press. The goal is basically to empower the workers to start a movement of their own within their company. In certain wind energy firms this has met with success; IG Metall has not only recruited hundreds of new members, it also established works councils and used strike action to win a wage agreement.[40]

The developments described in this chapter show that labour conflicts have again increased. But this increase is only one factor. In many struggles, there has also been an expansion in the issues contested. In 2015, Verdi's strikes in the social care and education sectors related to the sphere of social reproduction and linked up with the issues that couples face concerning the social division of labour in the household and around childcare.[41]

------

40 Cf. Detlef Wetzel, *Organizing. Die Veränderung der gewerkschaftliche Praxis durch das Prinzip Beteilung*, Hamburg: VSA, 2013.
41 This theme also links up with important questions of gender justice; cf. Kerstin Jürgens, 'Deutschland in der Reproduktionskrise',

Conflicts over living space and the quality of urban life have also recently joined the fray. In the industrial services sector, production has shifted more toward city centres, and while rents have risen, incomes have fallen or stagnated. In nineteen of twenty large German cities, the minimum wage is not enough to cover the cost of living.[42] Urban space was always an arena of social conflict, and this tendency has sharpened.[43] The low interest rates of the European Central Bank have caused a particular form of spatial inequality, as a massive rise in housing prices and rents combined with gentrification pushes sections of the population with inadequate incomes out of entire city districts, a process that has given rise to an increasing number of local protests across Germany in recent years. Elsewhere, there are shortages of kindergartens or transport connections, as well as public spaces. In Hamburg, for example, there were protest movements in support of artists who were being driven out of the run-down alternative cultural district. In Berlin a referendum succeeded in blocking construction on the former Tempelhof airport site, which remains a freely accessible public space.

EUROPE-WIDE CONFLICTS OVER DOWNWARD MOBILITY

A look at southern and western Europe makes it clear how calm things are in Germany. The conflicts in our country have largely remained latent, which is no doubt due to the present economic and institutional stability. In southern Europe, there have been several major waves of protest, culminating in a series of mass

---

Leviathan 38(4), 2010, 559–87, and Gabriele Winker, *Care Revolution. Schritte in eine solidarische Gesellschaft*, Bielefeld: transcript, 2015.

42   Alexander Herzog-Stein, Malte Lübker, Toralf Pusch, Thorsten Schulten and Andrew Watt, *Der Mindestlohn: Bisherige Auswirkungen und Zukünftige Anpassung*, WSI Policy Brief 24/04/20018.

43   David Harvey, *Rebel Cities: From the Right to the City to the Urban Revolution*, London: Verso, 2013.

and general strikes.[44] The trigger for these was often the exclusion of trade unions from political negotiations.[45] The militancy in these conflicts has also increased. In France, but also in other European countries, there have been several instances of 'boss-napping'.[46]

The dynamic of conflict in Europe requires a detailed study of its own, and can only be sketched briefly here. But these conflicts also have to be seen in the context of the breakdown of European social modernity. The liberalization of the labour market that is currently taking place in the countries of southern Europe was introduced in Germany in the wake of Agenda 2010.

The basic lines of social development since the Second World War are similar across most European countries. In northern and western Europe, a new social consensus formed after 1945, and in the countries of southern Europe after the fall of the dictatorships.[47] This led to comprehensive welfare states, a marked rise in social expenditure, and successive advances of nationalization to

----

44   Alexander Gallas and Jörg Nowak, 'Agieren aus der Defensive. Ein Überblick zu politischen Streiks in Europa mit Fallstudien zu Frankreich und Großbritannien', in Alexander Gallas, Jörg Nowak and Florian Wilde (eds), *Politische Streiks im Europa der Krise*, Hamburg: VSA, 2012.

45   Cf. Kerstin Hamann, Alison Johnston and John Kelly, *Striking Concessions from Governments: The Success of General Strikes in Western Europe, 1980–2009*, 2013, ssrn.com/abstract=2313413 (accessed February 2016).

46   Stefan Schmalz and Nico Weinmann, 'Zwei Krisen, zwei Kampfzyklen. Gewerkschaftsproteste in Westeuropa im Vergleich', in Stefan Schmalz and Klaus Dörre (eds), *Comeback der Gewerkschaften? Machtressourcen, innovative Praktiken, internationale Perspektiven*, Frankfurt: Campus, 2013.

47   Cf. Tony Judt, *Postwar: A History of Europe Since 1945*, New York: Vintage, 2010. In speaking here of Europe, I refer in particular to the original European Union countries, prior to the accession of Eastern European states that were previously part of the Soviet bloc during the epoch of social modernity.

create a mixed economy.[48] Social mobility likewise increased.[49] However, in the late 1970s, the heyday of the European welfare state came to an end, capitalism entered an era of post-growth, and the pendulum began to swing back. In the two following decades, the attenuation of income inequality slowed and ultimately went into reverse. Wealth inequalities grew from the 1970s onward, while upward mobility stagnated.[50] These developments were a result of liberalization and the wholesale unchaining of market forces, in Germany as elsewhere.[51]

The countries of southern Europe faced financial collapse after the crisis of 2007–08. Various European rescue packages were put together, and the European Central Bank was forced to intervene on several occasions. In the context of these programmes, the countries affected by the crisis were forced to adopt drastic austerity programmes, only receiving new credits on the condition that they committed themselves to a massive reduction in their state debts, which had been inflated by the bank rescue operation.[52] The welfare state was trimmed back, and achievements in the health and education sectors reversed.

48 Harmut Kaelble, *A Social History of Europe, 1945–2000: Recovery and Transformation After Two World Wars*, New York: Berghahn, 2013; Göran Therborn, *European Modernity and Beyond: The Trajectory of European Societies 1945–2000*, Thousand Oaks, CA: Sage Publications, 1995. This was certainly not a uniform process; rather, various types of social modernity emerged, with different forms of social security and welfare state. Cf. Gøsta Esping-Andersen, *The Three Worlds of Welfare Capitalism*, Chapter 1.

49 Cf. Steffen Mau and Roland Verwiebe, *European Societies: Mapping Structure and Change*, Bristol: Policy Press, 2010.

50 Cf. Kaelble, *Social History of Europe*; Therborn, *European Modernity*.

51 Cf. Armin Schäfer, 'Liberalization, inequality and democracy's dis-content', in Armin Schäfer und Wolfgang Streeck (eds), *Politics in the Age of Austerity*, Cambridge: Polity Press, 2013.

52 Before the crisis, Spain had a lower proportionate level of debt than Germany.

In 2010, Greece saw the largest protest movements since the fall of the dictatorship in 1974. In Athens, Thessaloniki and other cities, half a million people came out in the streets. In Portugal, Great Britain, France and Italy there were also massive protests.[53] Portugal, where trade unions and left-wing parties were still relatively well anchored in society, is also a good example of the change in the agents of conflict. The number of participants in a demonstration organized by left-wing forces was much lower than one initiated by four Facebook activists, at which well over 100,000 mainly young people—out of a population of only 10 million—came into the streets against the spread of precarity.

As well as these mass protests, the last decade has seen the rise on a European level of another type of revolt, fundamentally different in form, that is not a direct reaction to austerity policy: urban insurrections. The fact that riots have shaken the capital cities of countries as diverse as Great Britain, France and even Sweden is an indication that they are a general expression of European social conflict. In all of these cases, the riots particularly affect poor, multi-ethnic districts with high levels of unemployment, and in all cases the inhabitants not only felt stigmatized both socially and in public discourse, but experienced constant discrimination by so-called preventive policing strategies in which people of colour are regularly stopped and searched without material grounds.[54] For the inhabitants of stigmatized districts, it is literally their postcode that prevents upward mobility. Anyone coming from these disadvantaged quarters, such as

53   Cf. Isabel Ortiz, Sara Burke, Mohamed Berrada and Hernán Cortés, *World Protests 2006–2013*, New York: Initiative for Policy Dialogue and Friedrich-Ebert-Stiftung, 2013.

54   Cf. Oliver Nachtwey, 'Großbritannien: Riot oder Revolte', *Blätter für deutsche und internationale Politik* 56(9), 2011, 13–16; Carl-Ulrik Schierup, Aleksandra Alund and Lisa Kings, 'Reading the Stockholm Riots—A Moment for Social Justice?', *Race and Class* 55(3), 2014, 1–21.

the *banlieues* of Paris, has job applications rejected simply on account of their address.[55] The riots express marginalization, stigmatization and the failed promise of civil equality; they are a form of 'moral escalation' on the part of the socially excluded.[56] Nothing less, but also nothing more. The riots had no programme, rarely made any concrete demands, and did not follow any collectively determined action models. They represented an emotional discharge of anger over the failure to meet minimal democratic and social standards, which the primarily immigrant inhabitants of these districts suffered from.

POST-CONVENTIONAL PROTESTS

As a consequence of the financial crisis, a new type of post-conventional protest emerged: the Occupy camps and the actions of the *Indignados* in Spain. Organized via social media, participants occupied public spaces and erected camps. The new European and North American protest movements saw themselves as laboratories of democracy, as a reaction to disappointed expectations of upward mobility, as conflicts over social citizenship rights and participation. They were generally urban movements that tended to involve young and relatively highly skilled people, for whom modern capitalism's promise of equal opportunity, upward mobility and security by way of education had not been fulfilled. These movements were both a result of the de-institutionalization of social conflict and an expression of a protest

55 Cf. Robert Castel, *La Discrimination négative*, Paris: Seuil, 2007.

56 Ferdinand Sutterlüty, 'Riots—Moralische Eskalationen?' *Westend. Neue Zeitschrift für Sozialforschung* 10(2), 2013, 3–23. In Britain, the riots were also inspired by a 'moral economy' that expressed the moral deficit of the elites. Shortly before young people made off with flat-screen televisions from plundered shops, it had been reported that British politicians had illegally appropriated perks—including flat-screen TVs—at the cost of taxpayers (Nachtwey, 'Großbritannien').

that is itself largely de-institutionalized. Despite finishing a course of study, young people can only expect to start with precarious and underqualified jobs, frequently even spells of unemployment. Wolfgang Kraushaar sees these recent protests as a 'revolt of the educated'.[57] The Occupy movement in Germany, according to the results of his investigation, was actually a protest movement of mainly skilled but also precarious employees, and only some 40 per cent of Occupy activists enjoyed normal labour relations.[58] Two-thirds of the activists had at least started higher education, but only a few had a job that matched their training. A third of all employees reported being over-qualified for their present employment. The younger generation of activists in Spain also have a historically unmatched level of qualification, mastering foreign languages and accumulating experience abroad. But instead of being able to start their own families, they have to continue living with their parents, as they have scarcely any right to unemployment benefits and cannot afford a home of their own.

The Spanish *Indignados*, who attracted great attention for months on end, were the starting point of the new movement. Their protests began on 15 May 2011, when rallies in fifty-eight cities were called over the Internet. A month later, there were demonstrations in eighty cities, with over a million people taking part. Tens of thousands participated in camps and assemblies.[59]

57   Wolfgang Kraushaar, *Die Aufruhr der Ausgebildeten. Vom arabischen Frühling zur Occupy-Bewegung*, Hamburg: Hamburger Edition, 2012.

58   On these and the following figures for the Occupy movement in Germany, see the empirical studies by the author and colleagues (Ulrich Brinkmann, Oliver Nachtwey and Fabienne Décieux, *Wer sind die 99%? Eine empirische Untersuchung der Occupy-Proteste*, Arbeitspapier der Otto-Brenner-Stiftung 06, Frankfurt, 2013; Fabienne Décieux and Oliver Nachtwey, 'Postdemokratie und Occupy', *Forschungsjournal Soziale Bewegungen* 27(1), 2014, 75–89).

59   Cf. Andy Durgan and Joel Sans, ' "No One Represents Us": The 15 May Movement in the Spanish State', *International Socialism* 132, 2011, 23–34.

Their demand *¡Democracia real ya!* ('real democracy now') became known far beyond the country's borders.

The *Indignados* were inspired by the uprisings of the Arab Spring, especially the protests in Cairo's Tahrir Square. Soon they themselves inspired a new wave of activists. In September 2011 some 2,000 people occupied Zuccotti Park in Manhattan, and one of the most significant protest movements of recent years was born: Occupy Wall Street.[60] Occupy began with a tweet that directly referred to the Arab Spring ('Are you ready for a Tahrir moment?'), and its particular aim, to establish assembly democracies in the public spaces of big cities, was influenced by the movement of the *Indignados*.[61]

This small park close to the New York Stock Exchange became both the spatial and the symbolic starting point of a new wave of protest that in only a month spread across the world. On 15 October 2011, Occupy's first international day of action, 40,000 people demonstrated in Germany alone. A few hundred set up camps in public spaces.

The protests' international symbol was the slogan of the '99 per cent', whom the '1 per cent' super-rich had increasingly excluded from social prosperity and political influence. This slogan expressed both the dimension of economic distribution (downward mobility) and that of political rule (post-democracy). And it staked the claim to represent at least symbolically the majority of the population.

In many respects, Occupy shared the values of the 'new social movements'. Most of its activists adopted a post-materialist attitude: autonomy, participation and self-determination were important to them, along with creativity and freedom. But

60 Cf. Ruth Milkman, Stephanie Luce and Penny Lewis, *Changing the Subject: A Bottom-Up Account of Occupy Wall Street in New York City*, New York: The Murphy Institute, 2012.

61 The same holds for the occupation of the Syntagma square in Athens.

Occupy also went beyond this. Many movements after 1968 were inspired by the artistic critique of the norms of social modernity, while gradually abandoning questions of political economy. The Occupy activists joined both forms of criticism together, also standing for social justice and redistribution.[62]

In this way, Occupy hit on something fundamental. The new social movements had chiefly pursued 'projects in society' rather than 'society as a project', as had still been the case with the workers' movement.[63] With Occupy there suddenly reappeared on the stage of protest a systemic movement that understood the restructuring of society as a whole as its project.[64] The systemic aspect was almost in its very nature: first, the movement singled out the role of the banks in the financial crisis, banks that had been singled out by politicians as 'system-relevant', for particular criticsm. Second, they established that capitalism had undergone a veritable 'systemic change' in the past.[65] And third, the question of democracy pointed to the political order as a whole.

The new movements in Europe and North America responded in an unconventional way. One particular aspect was their

---

62   A striking fact, however, was the lack of clarity of world outlook, shown, for example, in a relative indifference to models of political order. A majority of participants may well have seen 'socialism' as a good idea, yet just as many were for a renewal of the 'social market economy'. Occupy was good in being *against*, but far less sure in what it was *for*.

63   Dieter Rucht, 'Gesellschaft als Projekt—Projekt in der Gesellschaft', in Ansgar Klein, Hans-Josef Legrand and Thomas Leif (eds), *Neue Soziale Bewegungen—Impulse, Bilanzen und Perspektiven*, Opladen: Westdeutscher Verlag, 1999.

64   This was evident both in the diagnosis of the crises and in what Occupy activists particularly criticized. They prioritized systemic causes (for example, on the question of the reasons for the financial crisis) over sub-systemic—let alone personal—ones.

65   Wolfgang Streeck, *Re-Forming Capitalism: Institutional Change in the German Political Economy*, Oxford: Oxford University Press, 2009, 93–105. This change took place in the specific institutional system of German capitalism, but was similar in principle in most European countries.

democratic populism, enlivened by a sharp distancing from the 'establishment'. A clear demarcation was made from political elites and traditional forms of interest articulation (such as trade unions and parties), linking the social conflict with a call for 'real' democracy for the majority, and with their own practice of the permanent assembly democracy of the camps.

Occupy displayed in exemplary fashion its distance from traditional politics: around half of its activists distrusted all political parties. Even the left parties were seen by many not as part of the solution but as part of the problem. In the federal elections of 2012, the majority of Occupy supporters in Germany did vote for Die Linke, but a quarter of them abstained or cast a blank vote.[66] The major political parties failed to attract 5 per cent support. And while a relative majority of activists classed themselves as on the left, almost half of them rejected any left-right schema.

The radical-democratic impulse represented a strikingly anti-institutional form of politics. With the exception of their permanent assembly democracy, these activists largely rejected traditional forms of organization, including the principle of representation and delegation. The principle of political horizontality—refusal of structures and leading personalities—was thereby radicalized to a 'first-person politics'. All forms of hierarchy, fixed identities and political norms were rejected. In horizontal politics, the actors may well be together and act simultaneously, but there is no orchestrating body.[67]

This political approach, however, has its inherent problems. There was clearly more involved than an 'acting crowd',[68] yet the

66 The majority of core activists who spent the night in the camp voted for the Pirate Party.

67 Cf. Isabell Lorey, Jens Kastner, Gerald Raunig and Tom Waibel (eds), *Occupy! Die aktuellen Kämpfe um die Besetzung des Politischen*, Vienna: Turia+Kant, 2012.

68 Herbert Blumer, 'Collective Behavior', in Robert Park (ed.), *An Outline of the Principles of Sociology*, New York: Barnes & Noble, [1939] 1951.

soft identity meant at the same time a rather low degree of connectedness. For employees and citizens with family obligations and a limited time budget, the radical-democratic 'inclusion' of the permanent assembly democracy actually had an excluding effect. Only those who participated in it full-time could effectively contribute. This had the paradoxical result that while the movement expressed the tension that had developed between capitalism and democracy, in practice people were excluded 'post-democratically'.

After this initial moment, the movements took very different paths. Occupy itself largely vanished, not least because it had no organizational structures or leading figures. In Spain, the process eventually produced a performative paradox. First, the movement refocused itself, and many activists began to involve themselves in struggles against housing eviction, or in building a local infrastructure of solidarity—collective kitchens, advice services, health care—where government provision had in many cases fallen victim to austerity policy. Spain's traditional left-wing parties of the Izquierda Unida (United Left) did not succeed in building organic connections with these voluntary associations, and the protest party Podemos was ultimately founded in 2014. Its anti-austerity message was directed against the whole establishment, what Podemos called the ruling 'caste' of Spanish politics.[69] Podemos saw itself as a new kind of party, populist in the literal sense, remote from both traditional left rhetoric and from established forms of politics.[70] Instead of subordinate groups

---

69   The extent of corruption in Spain is generally known to be enormous, and almost none of the traditional actors were unaffected by it, from the conservative Partido Popular through to the trade unions.

70   A central intellectual reference point for the strategy of Podemos was the work of the Argentinian-British political scientist Ernesto Laclau, who sketched out what he viewed as a progressive populism. This abandoned the traditional distinction between 'left' and 'right', instead tracing a line of conflict between 'above' and 'below', and between 'elite' and 'people' (not in an ethnic sense, but meaning the subaltern majority

constricted by rules, programmes or protocols, its rank and file were so-called 'circles', meetings that were as participative as possible. As a party, however, Podemos is itself subject to the mechanisms of parliamentarianism. Above all, it marks a departure from the relative lack of leadership of the *Indignados*; the orientation is now rather to a model of charismatic populism, embodied by the media-friendly figure of its leading candidate Pablo Iglesias, who has ended up curtailing many elements of rank-and-file democracy.[71]

CITIZENS ON THE BARRICADES

Citizens' protests of recent years represent yet another type of conflict that has played a particularly important role in Germany. In many places, there have been objections to the erection of new power lines and big construction projects, against Internet surveillance and censorship, for and against wind turbines, against nuclear power and educational reforms.[72] A good example of these protestors are those who demonstrated against plans for the urban renewal of central Stuttgart, described rather deprecatingly in the media as *Wutbürger* ('angry citizens'). The protests against the redevelopment of the old Stuttgart railway station, which was to cost billions and was questionable in architectural, transport, economic and ecological terms, became a prototype of a revival of political engagement in civil society, throwing established politics into disarray.

Such protests in Germany are certainly no new phenomenon. In the 1960s and early '70s, there were already a series of

of the population). Cf. Ernesto Laclau, *On Populist Reason*, London: Verso, 2007.

71   Cf. Raul Zelik, *Mit Podemos zur demokratischen Revolution? Krise und Aufbruch in Spanien*, Berlin: Bertz+Fischer, 2015.

72   Franz Walter, Stine Marg, Lars Geiges and Felix Butzlaff (eds), *Die neue Macht der Bürger. Was motiviert die Protestbewegungen?* Reinbek bei Hamburg: Rowohlt, 2013.

initiatives and civil society protest movements, in some respects far larger than those of today.[73] Despite their importance in terms of democratic politics, and the legitimate concerns of their participants, these citizens' movements were paradoxically themselves part of a post-democratic constellation.

The citizens' movements of the late 1970s and '80s were more focused on single issues, and in no way so revolutionary and anti-capitalist as those of the original 1968ers. On the whole, however, they were still pervaded by a demand to change society. The struggles against nuclear power plants and construction projects were linked with ideas of post-industrial sustainability, solidarity with the Third World, and the quest for new ways of living. The women's liberation movement did not just want equal access to leading positions, but also demanded the abolition of patriarchy. Today, the demands made on society are quite timid by comparison. In some cases, these protests follow the logic of 'not in my backyard'. The occasion for conflict lies in the protestors' immediate vicinity, and they are only opposed to new development on that basis.

Almost all of the new citizens' movements display resentment toward actually existing democracy, with its representatives, politicians and experts, and its parliamentary institutions.[74] The criticism of democracy, however, does not keep their supporters from going to the polls en masse or even joining political parties. In this respect, they are akin to the social movements of the 1970s, when people often spoke of purely formal democracy. Today's protest movements criticize the lack of transparency in decision-making, which follows economic interests above all or is presented as without alternative due to material

73   Cf. Kraushaar, *Die Aufruhr der Ausgebildeten*. We still lack a proper historical comparison, particularly with respect to numbers.

74   Cf. Walter et al., *Die neue Macht der Bürger*, 321ff.; Thymian Bussemer, *Die erregte Republik. Wutbürger und die Macht der Medien*, Stuttgart: Klett-Cotta, 2011.

constraints, as in the case of the 'Stuttgart 21' development or the expansion of the Frankfurt airport. They argue for greater participation at all levels—from the development of new projects through to plebiscites. Participation itself, however, frequently turns out to be a question of class membership.

Some of the citizens' protests, as in the case of Stuttgart 21, are 'quite literally a citizens' [*Bürger*] protest in the sociological sense'. Those involved here were above all people with high levels of education and sufficient material resources, and 'the more demanding the desire to participate, the stronger educational attainment presses through and asserts itself'.[75] The extension of democratic participation by way of citizens' initiatives or plebiscites can even end up deepening social inequality. A referendum in Hamburg in 2010, for example, overturned an educational reform that had been agreed by the city parliament on a cross-party basis. The reform as originally planned sought to keep pupils learning in the same classroom for a longer period of time, which would in turn narrow the perceived advantage of attending a traditional *Gymnasium*. It was above all citizens from the more prosperous districts of the city with low unemployment who took part in the referendum and voted against the reform.[76]

Looked at in this way, participation is on the whole an ambivalent factor in democracy. True, a higher average level of education, along with wider voting options, have massively broadened the experience of autonomy, yet the gain in individual input into decision-making can go together with a growing mistrust for compromises that respect the interests of diverse groups. As a rule, the modern individual is no longer integrated into collective moral milieus, but partly takes on the expectations of the market-citizen consumer who is quickly plagued by frustration if

75   Walter et al., *Die neue Macht der Bürger*, 307, 309.
76   Armin Schäfer and Harald Schoen, 'Mehr Demokratie, aber nur für wenige? Der Zielkonflikt zwischen mehr Beteiligung und politischer Gleichheit', *Leviathan* 41(1), 2013, 94–120.

they do not get what they want. The individualization of citizen-ship rights is echoed by individuals in their normative expecta-tions.[77] This development, however, has consequences for the effectiveness of contemporary protests. These are an important element in the modernization of modern societies, almost akin to their 'immune system'.[78] But they can also become an auto-immune disease that ultimately destroys the system, if the exer-cise of rights turns into uncompromising self-assertion and fails to recognize the necessity of representation, the majority princi-ple and balance in democratic systems. Some protests of the 'angry citizens', in particular, tend in this direction. More than a few former 1968ers who have landed successfully in the bour-geois milieu fall into this group. They are engaged sporadically here less as citizens seeking to shape common life so much as representatives of a self-conscious technical-social vanguard. A particular variant is the 'expert citizen' who gets caught up in 'affectively fuelled' protests.[79] Engineers, technicians, computer specialists, geographers, biologists, physicists and lawyers frequently embody this type. They are not oriented by political world outlooks, but follow logical, technical and scientific lines of argument, which generate clear guidelines for action from a rationalist foundation. The 'expert citizens' who delegate deci-sions to the specialist are in this way themselves part of the post-democratic process, as they seek to replace by technocratic

77   Ingolfur Blühdorn, writing in *Simulative Demokratie. Neue Politik nach der postdemokratischen Wende* (Berlin: Suhrkamp, 2013), goes so far as to say (with conservative undertones and, in my view, a relatively weak empirical foundation) that the enlightened subject is marketized and liquefied in their identity to the extent that it can no longer be adequately represented—and is ultimately satisfied with a simulative democracy.

78   Niklas Luhmann, *Protest. Systemtheorie und soziale Bewegungen*, Frankfurt: Suhrkamp, 1996, 11.

79   Aaron Sahr and Philipp Staab, 'Bahnhof der Leidenschaften. Zur politischen Semantik eines unwahrscheinlichen Ereignisses', *Mittelweg 36* 20(3), 2011, 23–48, 29.

decision a political deliberation and search for compromise that is necessarily protracted. Among many of those involved, the plebiscitary grassroots-democratic orientation conceals an 'authoritarian impulse' that favours an efficiently run common life with experts in charge.[80] Rank-and-file participation and the desire for an expert in command are not necessarily mutually exclusive.[81]

PEGIDA: THE ANGRY CITIZENS OF THE RIGHT

It is thus unsurprising that another kind of citizens' protest, also not without historic precedent, has become increasingly visible: namely, the exclusionary protest of the privileged. While Occupy shouted: 'We are the 99 per cent!', the right-wing protest formation known in Germany as Pegida ('Patriotic Europeans Against the Islamization of the West') chants: 'We are the people!' The crowds walking the streets of Dresden and Leipzig (it looked more like marching to some) were eerily morose and hurled verbal attacks at the 'Lügenpresse' ('lying press').[82] Since late 2014, their rallies have steadily grown, as if by magic. A split in Pegida's organizing committee led to a temporary decline. But the refugee crisis lent Pegida new momentum, and in December 2015 several thousand people again attended its 'Monday walks'.

There are particular local and regional circumstances that have bolstered Pegida's rise and success in Dresden. In scarcely

80   Walter et al., *Die neue Macht der Bürger*, 323ff.

81   In Max Weber's concept of 'plebiscitary leadership democracy', it is the charismatic ruler who uses the popular vote to defeat the tame, compromise-seeking and bureaucratic apparatus of democracy (cf. Wolfgang Mommsen, *Max Weber and German Politics*, Chicago: University of Chicago Press, 1990).

82   I have already developed the arguments of this section in Oliver Nachtwey, 'Rechte Wutbürger. Pegida oder das autoritäre Syndrom', in *Blätter für deutsche und internationale Politik* 60(3), 2015, 81–90.

any other German state is the political culture so conservative and the citizens so alienated from politics as in Saxony. On top of this, there is a particular fear among men in all parts of eastern Germany that they could again become dependent on public aid (as occurred after unification)—a fear that is fuelled not least by the fact that there has been 'a real destruction of chances of ascent' in the recent past of the new states of the Federal Republic.[83]

Pegida may well be above all an eastern German or Saxon phenomenon, but it is also the expression of a general moral climate in Germany, a neo-authoritarian tendency that has been fermenting for much longer. The fact that this was seething among sections of the population was made clear by the success of books such as Thilo Sarrazin's *Deutschland schafft sich ab* ('Germany Abolishes Itself', 2010) and Akif Pirinçci's *Deutschland von Sinnen* ('Germany Demented', 2014). What was surprising, however, was that this resentment could condense into a local social movement with national reach. Pegida supporters like to be seen as normal citizens with everyday concerns, and this is not completely false. For many people the social world is ever less transparent, indeed heavily laden with fear.[84] And fear for one's own status, as German political theorist Franz Neumann pointed out sixty years ago, can fuel negative affects, regressive historical images and conspiracy theories.[85] Pegida is in this respect the expression of a radicalized middle class beset by fears of downward mobility—and a regressive revolt against a market-conforming democracy.

Pegida had certain forerunners in West Germany, as well. These were first of all the various local 'pro' movements (for

---

83   Olaf Groh-Samberg and Florian F. Hertel, 'Ende der Aufstiegsgesellschaft?', *Aus Politik und Zeitgeschichte* 65(10), 2015, 25–32.

84   Heinz Bude, *Society of Fear*, Cambridge: Polity, 2018.

85   Franz Neumann, 'Anxiety and Politics' [1957], *Triple C: Communication, Capitalism and Critique* 15(2), 2017, 612–36.

example 'pro-North Rhine-Westphalia'), which also presented themselves as citizens' movements but basically expressed anti-Muslim resentment and exhibited clear points of overlap with extreme right-wing organizations. Just a few weeks before the first Pegida 'walk', large far-right mobs paraded through the streets in the 'Hogesa' riots (an abbreviation for 'Hooligans against Salafists'). The 'Monday protests' that broke out in the wake of the Ukraine crisis may not have been a right-wing movement in the narrower sense, but they were full of dubious supporters of obscure and sometimes anti-Semitic conspiracy theories.[86]

Pegida operates differently from these groups. Officially, it has repeatedly distanced itself from extreme right-wing positions. The civic character of its demands is stressed, supposedly derived from Western values such as enlightenment, democracy, freedom, self-determination and the rule of law. In a certain sense, Pegida is a regressive variant of the new political protests. Like Occupy, Pegida supporters on the streets critique the democratic process, the distribution of resources and social hierarchy—but this time it is 'angry citizens' of the right who are expressing these points. Pegida makes sweeping criticisms: politicians, economic leaders and media figures all belong to the supposed establishment of 'those at the top'. Pegida is also an identitarian social movement, concerned with cultural integration and values in a world that is out of joint. In reality, however, it is not about recognizing ethnic difference but rather the relative privileges of those already established in German society. Where Occupy saw a conflict over resources between the '1 per cent' and the '99 per cent', Pegida views the same conflict in terms of natives and foreigners.

86 Cf. Priska Daphi, Dieter Rucht, Wolfgang Stuppert, Simon Teune and Peter Ullrich, '"Montagsmahnwachen für den Frieden" Antisemitisch? Pazifistisch? Orientierungslos?', *Forschungsjournal Soziale Bewegungen* 27(3), 2014, 24–31.

It is unclear who is actually marching with Pegida. Social-scientific surveys conducted in Dresden so far have run up against a barrier, as most supporters refuse to respond. Those participants who were willing to provide information were no longer young; a large majority were men of higher-than-average education levels; in socio-economic terms, many belonged to the (lower) middle class.[87] Unfortunately, these studies do not differentiate economic status sufficiently, but inasmuch as it is possible to conclude from available sources, Pegida attracts those sections of the lower middle class who feel both socially and culturally threatened: the self-employed, those working in the zone between security and precarity, those who have to assert themselves anew each day. The extent to which the traditional working class or the precariat are drawn to Pegida has not yet been closely studied. By 2018, however, it became clear that even the organized workers' movement is not immune to the virus of xenophobic protest, as even some trade union officials and works councils have faced right-wing activists among their ranks.

For the lower middle class, it is a harsh social competition, the struggle for a prosperous life, and the disappointed expectations of ascent and security that lead to a 'brutalization' of social conflict 'stripping the previously morally channelled struggle for respect and recognition of its normative status'.[88] Fear of downward mobility produces a very specific authoritarianism.

---

87 Cf. on this the studies of the Göttingen Institut für Demokratieforschung (Lars Geiges, Stine Marg and Franz Walter, *Pegida. Die schmutzige Seite der Zivilgesellschaft?*, Bielefeld: transcript, 2015) and the Institut für Bewegungsforschung (Priska Daphi et al., 'Protestforschung am Limit. Eine soziologische Annäherung an Pegida', ipb working paper, Berlin, protestinstitut.files.wordpress.com (accessed February 2016)).

88 Axel Honneth, 'Brutalization of the Social Conflict: Struggles for Recognition in the Early Twenty-first Century', *Distinktion: Scandinavian Journal of Social Theory* 13(1), 2012, 5–19.

The most important study of authoritarianism remains that conducted by Theodor Adorno.[89] On the basis of surveys indicating the prevalence of anti-Semitic attitudes in society, Adorno and his colleagues sought to discover what psychological foundations underlay such personality dispositions. For them, an authoritarian personality was the key that led people to become anti-democratic, filled with resentment and potentially fascist. The authoritarian personality, in their view, was characterized by a series of connected symptoms that combined into a syndrome: these included conventionality, obsequiousness combined with aggression, ideas of power, lack of empathy, stereotyping, cynicism, obsessive concern with sexuality, and finally, projectivity (understood as the inclination to believe dangerous things were going on in the world). The essence of authoritarianism specified that aggression was not directed against domination but projected onto others: the authoritarian personality perceives his or her own drives as unacceptable, and transfers these onto others who can thus be condemned for them. For example, contempt for women's rights becomes a basis for criticizing Islam.[90] Most Pegida supporters, for their part, hold firmly to very traditional ideas of gender roles and demand an end to the critique of these, which they label 'genderism'.[91]

The prejudices of Pegida, however irrational they may seem, possess a certain 'meaning': resentment and stereotyping have an orienting function; primitive formulae and conspiracy theories reduce the prevailing lack of transparency

89   Theodor W. Adorno et al., *The Authoritarian Personality*, New York: W. W. Norton, [1950] 1980.

90   In the research, this phenomenon is also described as 'femonationalism' (Sara Farris, *In the Name of Women's Rights*, Durham, NC: University of North Carolina Press, 2017).

91   'Anti-genderism' has recently gained importance in conservative milieus well beyond Pegida. Cf. Sabine Hark and Paula-Irene Villa (eds), *Anti-Genderismus. Sexualität und Geschlecht als Schauplätze aktueller politischer Auseinandersetzungen*, Bielefeld: transcript, 2015.

and bring order to what appears as chaos. This 'logic' then serves to transfer one's own concerns about downward mobility onto foreign groups. It is particularly in the states of former East Germany that people often experience the aforementioned feeling of having been sold short, leading them to defend their own (imagined) privileges and way of life all the more bitterly. Their own conformism thus turns into a devaluation of all those who are different, and of supposedly unproductive 'free riders' in a social system under stress: refugees, immigrants and Muslims.

Authoritarian attitudes are also expressed in the way that conventional ideas and values are lent a different meaning. For example, democracy is criticized for not delivering what it promises—yet the same people are ready to 'exchange it for a system which sacrifices all claims to human dignity and justice'.[92] In this sense, Pegida also turns dissatisfaction with parties, politicians and constitutional bodies into contempt for these people and institutions. Pegida has reshaped the left-wing criticism of the mainstream media using an expression popularized by the Nazis, calling it the 'lying press'. Instead of criticizing democratic representatives for repeatedly undermining the ideal of political equality, authoritarian personalities tend to want to abolish democracy and 'bring about the direct control of those whom they deem the most powerful anyway'.[93] It is only consistent, then, that these demonstrations often ring with praise for Vladimir Putin, hardly an upstanding democrat.

Authoritarian mentalities do not arise in a vacuum. They are the result of people's socialization and their cultural and political milieu, but the market also helps to produce them. Workers suffer from hierarchical relationships in their firms, or under high-handed supervisors; those not economically active

---

92 Adorno, *The Authoritarian Personality*, 678.
93 Ibid., 687.

may experience social hierarchy in the form of economic neces-
sities or constraints, which confront them like an 'anonymous
god'.[94] Today we could say that many people are compelled to
affirm subjectively the forces of the market. Authoritarianism
ultimately rests on the fact that people submit almost with
pleasure to what makes them suffer. Comprehensive empirical
studies show that considerable sections of the middle class have
turned their backs on an 'egalitarian and redistributive' society.[95] Among the population as a whole—somewhat less so in the
middle class, but here as well—something like a 'market-
conforming extremism' has developed, which in connection
with entrepreneurial self-optimizing norms promotes the
devaluation of others.[96] This extremism is especially likely to
appear among those who fear for their standard of living.
Manifest right-wing extremism has returned in recent years,
while resentment has risen. Muslims, Sinti, Roma and asylum
seekers face increasing prejudice.[97] Though some small groups
within the Muslim population, such as Salafists, may pose problems for European society, Islamophobia is undoubtedly the
new matrix of a racism that emerges from the supposed cultural
superiority of the West. This also involves a high degree of
confabulation, or pathological belief in objectively false state-
ments: representative questionnaires show the proportion of
Muslims in Germany estimated at 19 per cent, as opposed to
the actual figure of 6 per cent. In Saxony, they constitute only
0.1 per cent of the local population, yet Pegida supporters fear
a cultural invasion.

94   Max Horkheimer, 'Authority and the Family' [1936], *Critical
Theory: Selected Essays*, New York: Continuum, 2002, 82.
95   Blühdorn, *Simulative Demokratie*.
96   Andreas Zick and Anna Klein, *Fragile Mitte—Feindselige
Zustände. Rechsextreme Einstellungen in Deutschland 2014*, Bonn, Dietz,
2014.
97   Cf. Wilhelm Heitmeyer, *Deutsche Zustände. Folge 1–10*,
Frankfurt: Suhrkamp, 2002–12.

Pegida itself may eventually disappear as a protest movement. An authoritarian crowd can rapidly dissipate if it finds no
new stimulus.[98] Though participation in the Pegida demonstrations has declined since its peak of more than 25,000, 2,000
people still assemble every week. The authoritarian resentment,
however, will not vanish from society so quickly, and the refugee
crisis bears the potential for Pegida to obtain new success with its
mobilization. The Alternative für Deutschland—which, after the
expulsion of its founder Bernd Lucke, changed from a party fluc-
tuating between neoliberalism and national conservatism into a
right-wing populist party—has massively profited from this
development. Pegida and the anti-refugee protests of the recent
past have become the extra-parliamentary arm of the AfD, the
Alternative für Deutschland ('Alternative for Germany') party, a
right-wing and increasingly far-right party founded in early
2013. This constellation has now been made more or less official.
While the AfD maintained its distance and prevented party officials from speaking at Pegida demonstrations in its first years, it
is now formally permitted and even endorsed.

RESISTANCE AND CITIZENS

The Occupy camps have long been cleared, and new struggles at
workplaces remain sporadic so far, despite low wages and precarity. At the same time, it seems far from improbable that the next
decade will see a rise in social conflicts in Europe—Germany
included. Despite the introduction of a legal minimum wage and
a small rise in real incomes, the dynamic of downward mobility
has not been halted—it is merely pausing for breath.

In their basic tendency, Western industrial countries have
become societies of downward mobility, precarity and polarization. In almost all OECD countries, inequality has risen

---

98   Elias Canetti, *Crowds and Power*, London: Phoenix Press, [1962]
2000.

considerably in the past twenty years.[99] New conflicts are arising precisely because upward social mobility remains the central social norm in our society. It is not only young academics with precarious perspectives and stagnating status who have protested; skilled workers and public service employees have also come out into the streets. While young people demonstrate against the lack of job prospects, older citizens protest against the devaluation of their social status and cuts to their pay or pensions.

In post-growth capitalism, ever fewer people find that things are improving; there are too many skilled competitors for good jobs. A society's orientation to upward mobility can become a source of conflict if the ladders of ascent have lost their rungs.[100] The same holds for the performance principle. Many norms that originally ensured stability and legitimacy have reversed in function: they no longer integrate, but have become factors of disintegration. The de-institutionalization of social conflict and injury to normative principles lends new importance to questions of recognition and morality.

Yet this need not necessarily lead to emancipatory movements. The social question has emerged today in a different form. Downward mobility now means that people have something to lose, whereas in the nineteenth century even skilled workers lived scarcely above the threshold of pauperism. A possible source of conflict in the present kind of society lies in the contradictory interests of different groups of workers. Unless trade unions and works councils manage to establish a

---

99   Cf. OECD, *Growing Income Inequality in OECD Countries. What drives it and how can policy tackle it?* Paris, 2011; Thomas Piketty, *Capital in the Twenty-First Century*, Cambridge, MA: Harvard University Press, 2014.

100   Cf. François Dubet, *Injustice at Work*, London: Routledge, 2010; Stephan Voswinkel, *Was wird aus dem 'Fahrstuhleffekt'? Postwachstum und Sozialer Aufstieg*, Working Paper der DFG-Forschergruppe Postwachstumsgesellschaften 08/2013, Friedrich-Schiller-Universität Jena, 2013.

counter-discourse of solidarity, agency workers are seen as a safety buffer and socially devalued. An 'exclusive solidarity' arises with members of one's own status group. Conversely, agency workers accuse permanent staff of resting on their privileges.[101] I have already spoken of the tendency of the middle class to seal themselves off socially. Its members also have a partial interest in the financial markets continuing to expand—since they themselves profit from these through shares and insurance policies.[102] Those whom Wolfgang Streeck has called 'market people' do not stand in strict antagonism to 'state people'; there are important areas in which the two groups overlap.[103]

In many countries—states in crisis such as Spain, but also France and Italy—the German labour-market reforms of Agenda 2010 have been discussed by the elites as a positive example, a way out of the crisis. Transferring the German solution to other countries would amount to 'fighting fire with fire' on a European scale. Revolt in societies of downward mobility would embark on a new and fiercer round.

Many signs indicate that among European protesters, precarity is no longer perceived as an individual fate indicating personal failure, but is rather critically interpreted as a collective social experience. Yet we are (still) not dealing here with new class movements.[104] Social classes arise through collective action that is repeated, governed by material interest and a moral

101   Cf. Klaus Dörre, Anja Happ and Ingo Matuschek, *Das Gesellschaftsbild der LohnarbeiterInnen. Soziologische Untersuchungen in ost- und westdeutschen Industriebetrieben*, Hamburg: VSA, 2013; Klaus Dörre, 'Funktionswandel der Gewerkschaften. Von der intermediären zur fraktalen Organisatione, in Dörre and Haipeter (eds), *Gewerkschaftliche Modernisierung*.

102   Cf. Christoph Deutschmann, *Kapitalistische Dynamik*, Wiesbaden: VS, 2008.

103   Wolfgang Streeck, *Buying Time*, London: Verso, 2014.

104   Göran Therborn, 'New Masses? Social Bases of Resistance', *New Left Review* II(85), 2014, 7–16.

economy.[105] The recent protests and strikes may have the potential to become new class movements, but as of now they remain far removed from this. If there is any such thing as a new class consciousness in Germany, it lies in the diffuse contrast between an elite and the majority of the population. Both international protest and depictions of growing social inequality, such as in Thomas Piketty's bestseller *Capital in the Twenty-First Century*, have shaped public debate in the last few years. The new conflicts, whether at work or in movements such as Occupy, should therefore have met with great sympathy among the population, as they follow a moral economy that is collectively anchored in the '99 per cent' but is trampled on by economic and political elites: the demands for social justice, civil equality, opportunities for upward mobility and above all democracy.[106]

The new emancipatory social movements have placed the rediscovery of democratic practice at their centre. While citizens' protests, as previously described, often focus on technocratic problem-solving, Occupy and the *Indignados* have brought transparent democratic procedures to the forefront. In Greece and still more so in Spain, the 'squares' became new agorae where assembly democracies were constituted. These 'precariat protests' were also democracy protests;[107] they focused on grassroots-democratic alternatives to post-democracy, despite not developing socio-economic counter-proposals to finance capitalism. For the activists, however, the form of protest itself—in

---

105   From different perspectives, cf. Ralf Dahrendorf, *Class and Class Conflict in an Industrial Society*, London: Routledge, 1959, and E. P. Thompson, 'The Moral Economy of the English Crowd'.

106   These norms as so influential because their 'surplus validity' always indicates something beyond their own implementation (cf. Fraser and Honneth, *Redistribution or Recognition?*).

107   Oliver Marchart, *Die Prekarisierungsgesellschaft. Prekäre Proteste—Politik und Ökonomie im Zeichen der Prekarisierung*, Bielefeld: transcript, 2013.

other words, non-hierarchical, non-partisan, solidary discussion—already constituted the essence of a different world, in which equality is rediscovered as political practice.[108] Occupy was only a part of a global protest wave, which began with the Arab Spring, but eventually disappeared as a social movement. It survived, however, as a political symbol. The scientific debate on inequality continues to refer to the distinction between the 1 and 99 per cent, while Bernie Sanders's presidential campaign adopted much of the rhetoric and framing of the Occupy movement.[109]

In the new workplace conflicts, innovative forms of democracy have also been tried. So far unnoticed by public opinion in general, the balance between centralized decision-making and membership participation has shifted to a degree in favour of the latter. The internal renewal of trade unions by strikes and campaigns is proceeding under the paradigm of democratic participation.

The political DNA of today's insurgents lies in their social and political demands; democracy and egalitarian relationships are the prime mover of a new democratic-social conflict. There is still no telos in this conflict, no grand narrative, so far only a 'rebel democracy' beginning to constitute itself in revolts.[110] In this sense, no one is a citizen by simply belonging to a state, but only becomes a citizen by the practice of rebellious subjectivity: 'Democratic citizenship is therefore conflictual or it does not exist.'[111] Downward mobility and regressive modernization are bringing to the fore the previously latent conflict that underlies

----

108   Cf. Costas Douzinas, *Philosophy and Resistance in the Crisis*, Cambridge: Polity, 2013, 176ff.

109   Cf. Craig Calhoun, 'Occupy Wall Street in Perspective', *British Journal of Sociology* 64(1), 2013, 26–38.

110   Miguel Abensour, *Democracy Against the State*, Cambridge: Polity, 2010.

111   Étienne Balibar, *Equaliberty: Political Essays*, Durham, NC: Duke University Press, 2014, 284.

present-day democracy: the tension between freedom and equality among the citizenry.[112]

With the destruction of the welfare state, political citizenship rights are also being curtailed. The new conflict in German society shaped by downward mobility is democratic and social, since both social rights and democratic demands are affected. The current post-democratic constellation, in which the demos is disempowered by economic constraints, is combining with the social conflict characterized by new class structurations[113] to create a dangerous amalgam. Pierre Rosanvallon sees this as extremely disturbing: 'This rending of democracy is the major phenomenon of our time, and an ominous threat to our wellbeing. If it continues, the democratic regime itself might ultimately be in danger.'[114]

For the moment, revolt is often contradictory, individual, emotive and affective. So far, it has generally been enthusiastic but short-lived, and the lines of political conflict remain amorphous. Protests suddenly surge up, only to vanish almost completely a short time later.

The crisis of representation of the established left also holds dangers that should not be underestimated. In the past, traditional left organizations and milieus transmitted knowledge of past social struggles, allowing new actors to understand concrete political problems in the light of historical and political experiences. Today, the new social movements driven by a left-wing impetus see this as a problem, as established interpretations no longer illuminate the everyday reality of many people. Because they no longer trust left-wing activists, protestors bypass

112   Cf. ibid; Pierre Rosanvallon, *The Society of Equals*, Cambridge, MA: Harvard University Press, 2013.

113   Cf. Streeck, *Buying Time*; Frank Deppe, *Autoritärer Kapitalismus. Demokratie auf dem Prüfstand*, Hamburg: VSA, 2013; David Salomon and Oliver Eberl, 'Die soziale Frage in der Postdemokratie', *Forschungsjournal Soziale Bewegungen* 27(1), 2014, 17–26.

114   Rosanvallon, *Society of Equals*, 1–2.

established channels and coordinate via social networks such as Facebook and Twitter—in which small, well-organized 'communities' do indeed play a role.[115]

In some cases, however, the new protest movements have managed to take institutional form. The Spanish *Indignados* and the Greek protest movements, which both had a broader basis than Occupy and were directly confronted with the full severity of austerity policy, may not be as present in the public eye now as they were a few years ago; however, they continue in some city districts, and in the local democratic forums where they protest against housing evictions or seek to build popular infrastructure—precisely those places that the old welfare state no longer reaches. In Spain, local electoral alliances have also arisen. In both Barcelona and Madrid, women active in the anti-eviction movement have been elected mayor.

The traditional left, social and democratic forces in Germany, and in Europe more widely, have so far not succeeded in harnessing this discontent and using the energy it has unleashed for a new democratic beginning. Only Syriza in Greece and Podemos in Spain have been able to establish themselves as parties of revolt. Syriza even spectacularly managed to take over government in Greece, yet in the end did not succeed in implementing the most important points of its programme and had to bend to the demands of European institutions. After a referendum over further cuts, followed by new elections, Alexis Tsipras's party stayed in government, but almost nothing remained of its challenge to austerity policies. In December 2015, not two years after its foundation, Podemos scored a major electoral victory, winning 20.6 per cent of the vote in parliamentary elections. This fell short

---

115   There is also a danger here, however. On the Internet, which demands little control of affects and is not civilized by rational narratives and communications structures, all kinds of noxious weeds can flourish, such as conspiracy theories. This clearly played a part in the 'peace movement' of the 'Monday demonstrations'.

of its goal to overtake the Social-Democratic PSOE (Partido Socialista Obrero Español) as the second-largest party in Spain, yet it effectively broke the two-party system that had existed since the end of the Franco dictatorship.

Yet its success also brought considerable problems for Podemos. The party is no longer an outsider, a fresh challenger to the established parties. The strategy of vote maximization in the vein of anti-establishment populism reached its limits as the party became a crucial factor in national politics. As a result, Podemos was forced to make difficult strategic choices it once easily avoided: should it stick to its winning formula and reject all collaboration with the parties of the old system? Should it align with the left to combat the rising force of nationalism in Spanish politics? The central dilemma, which has alienated quite a few supporters, was the question of collaborating with the PSOE to remove the conservative People's Party from power. Ultimately, Podemos resisted this temptation on the national level, but endorsed and supported PSOE in regional elections. These questions troubled not only the leadership, leading to some serious divisions, but also spawned rifts within the activist base and its supporters. Lastly, the question of national independence for Catalonia further divided the party, as was true for most of the left in Spain.

Aside from Podemos and Syriza, both new and traditional left actors are still pursuing short-term strategies and seeking to stabilize their structures. They are poorly equipped for the present constellation, though, because they have stopped looking ahead. For conservatives, the future is simply a theme to be used in their aim of modernizing society in order to maintain the status quo. The left, on the other hand, always set its sights on the future, once in the form of a teleological perspective on social-ism, the New Jerusalem, and more recently on a 'good'—mean-ing social and democratic—society. It looked forward with high expectations and full of hope. After the catastrophe of the Second World War, and in light of the omnipresent danger of a new state of emergency, it maintained a stable optimism in the post-war years. The conviction was that the future would be better, for ourselves and for our children. These structures of temporality are now broken. Prospects have grown dim, as a society of downward mobility offers no optimistic perspective for a better future. The political left has largely abandoned this hope and become basically a conservative 'rearguard'.[116] The only progress it can see lies paradoxically in the past; it exhausts itself in a more or less lachrymose mantra of 'everything used to be better'. For the future it has no utopias of a better society, or at best only abstract ones. The crisis of representation is accordingly supplemented by a crisis of left imagination: what is lacking are plausible visions and mobilizing utopias;[117] what remain are ideas for the permanent crisis management of an excruciating motionless present.

These retro-normative perspectives are neither particularly helpful nor particularly applicable to reality. There will simply not be a return to social modernity. In the past, some things were perhaps better: greater social security brought real partial emancipation for what used to be the working class. Yet against this were bureaucracy, standardization, discrimination by gender and against immigrants, hierarchy and restrictions on autonomy, as well as an ecologically insensitive industrialism, which were all not just unpleasant epiphenomena, but structural components of society. Thus, rather than yearning for a return to social modernity, we should remember how in regressive modernization, progress and regression are enmeshed in a contradictory manner. Class, gender and ethnicity are intertwined into disparities that cannot simply be reduced to one single factor.

---

116 Herfried Münkler, *Mitte und Maß. Der Kampf um die richtige Ordnung*, Reinbek bei Hamburg: Rowohlt, 2010.

117 For Axel Honneth, the fact that protests are not inspired by visions of a better world is something quite new in the history of modern societies. He accordingly seeks to revitalize the old idea of socialism— interpreted as 'social freedom' (Alex Honneth, *The Ideal of Socialism*, Cambridge: Polity, 2016).

The future of capitalism is also painted in gloomy colours today by other critical observers. Some even see capitalism as heading toward its end, since it can no longer successfully moderate its contradictions. On one hand, it is no longer in a position to generate the growth that is required by the logic of accumulation and the profit interest of corporations. On the other hand, growth itself leads to the intensification of ecological contradictions.[118]

But there is a political danger arising from the society of downward mobility that needs to be taken seriously: that regressive modernization and post-democratic politics lead to an authoritarian current that removes the liberal foundations of our society. This danger is the evil twin of democratic revolt, fuelled by a mixture of anti-democratic and religious-identitarian resentment. The European right seeks to profit from this in its striving to undermine liberal democracy. One of the paradoxical outcomes of European social democracy's neoliberal turn seems be that right-wing populist parties have now become 'new workers' parties', which in some countries (particularly in central and eastern Europe) present themselves as the only opposition to neoliberal capitalism.[119] Though the rebranded Front National in France has stumbled into a severe crisis, Marine Le Pen managed to position herself as the main challenger to Macron's liberal centrism in the French elections. In Germany, the Alternative für Deutschland has become the biggest opposition party, while in Italy Silvio Berlusconi's right-wing Forza Italia party, the post-fascist Lega Nord and the populist Five Star Movement have

---

118   Cf. Wolfgang Streeck, 'How Will Capitalism End?', *New Left Review* II(87), 2014, 35–64; Immanuel Wallerstein et al., *Does Capitalism Have a Future?* New York: Oxford University Press, 2014; David Harvey, *Seventeen Contradictions and the End of Capitalism*, Profile Books, 2015.

119   Cf. Dirk Jörke and Oliver Nachtwey, 'Die rechtspopulistische Hydraulik der Sozialdemokratie. Zur politischen Soziologie neuer Arbeiterparteien', *Leviathan Sonderband 32*, *'Das Volk gegen die liberale Demokratie'*, 2017, 161–186.

become the dominant parties. Not to mention Eastern Europe, where right-wing parties have been in power in Poland and Hungary for several years and have begun dismantling the institutions of liberal democracy.

It is impossible here to discuss alternatives and solutions to the society of downward mobility; the present book has merely sought to analyse wherein lie the problems of contemporary development in the Federal Republic of Germany. Perhaps it can contribute a little to illuminating the present situation and give an impulse to considerations of how the process of regressive modernization might be followed by a solidary modernity.

Afterword
The Crumbling Pillars of Political Stability

Until 2015, Germany was generally viewed as a bastion of political stability in Europe and even the world, and likely would have remained so had the so-called refugee crisis not abruptly exposed the social tensions that had accumulated. During the last decades, the German political party system underwent a largely ignored but profound transformation, which in a paradoxical fashion brought the country in line with European norms as right-wing populism entered the stage of German politics in the form of the Alternative für Deutschland (AfD). The party was now the third-strongest force in the newly elected Bundestag, with 13 per cent of the vote; in the eastern state of Saxony, it was now the strongest party. The Free Democrats (FDP) returned to parliament with 11 per cent, while both the Greens as well as Die Linke fell short of expectations, with roughly 9 per cent each. The latter case is particularly disappointing given that the party began the previous parliamentary term as the largest opposition party, but failed to benefit from or utilize this pole position.

Chancellor Angela Merkel, globally respected and regularly described by the international press as the most powerful woman in the world, was dealt a blow. The Christian Democratic Union (CDU) and its Bavarian sister party, the Christian Social Union

(CSU) together lost almost 9 percentage points, registering at 33 per cent, their worst federal result since 1949. Despite this result, Merkel felt confident enough on election night to remark: 'I can't tell what we ought to do differently now'.[1] The Social Democrats (SPD) received only 20.5 per cent of the vote, their worst result since the Second World War.

Merkel failed to form a government for a good six months. Her original plan to ecologically modernize the German economy in coalition with an increasingly centrist Green Party was no longer feasible, as the necessary parliamentary majority failed to materialize. The neoliberal Free Democrats were unwilling to go along with Merkel's moderate, centrist path and would ultimately break off the long and frustrating negotiations. This represented a novel development in German democracy: the government continued to govern and Merkel remained in office as acting chancellor, but no new government formed.

Merkel was only able to present a new coalition six months after the elections. She had stumbled, but to the displeasure of her increasingly large number of enemies, did not fall. The new government was the old one: a 'grand coalition' between the CDU/CSU and SPD, although the only thing still 'grand' about this government was its label, as both parties combined was only 53 per cent of the electorate. As before, it represented a pure marriage of convenience between two partners who had long grown tired of each other and already filed for a divorce. The fear of fresh elections drove both parties to adapt to the circumstances on election night. This marked a major step for the SPD in particular, given that the party's unfortunate leader, Martin Schulz, had announced that the SPD would join the opposition. Later he would arrange for a decision by the party executive to this effect, but was soon forced

---

1   Berthold Kohler, 'Die Unerschütterliche', *Frankfurter Allgemeine Zeitung*, 26 September 2017.

to relent under pressure from the media and for fear that many newly elected parliamentarians would lose their seats should new elections be held. By entering the grand coalition, the party assumed 'political responsibility for the nation'. The newfound political instability by no means led the political system to anything approaching ungovernability, but demonstrated once again that the pillars of the two main political camps had been filed down to such a degree that neither was strong enough to lead an alternative coalition. Ultimately, the crisis of the German political system stems from the socio-economic and cultural upheavals analysed in this book. Yet it was also a product of the dialectical modernization of the party system, in which the politics of the centre has ultimately led to widespread polarization.

THE POLITICAL SYSTEM OF THE POST-WAR PERIOD

Unlike in the Weimar Republic, political competition in West German post-war society was, historically speaking, oriented toward the centre. Even during great conflict, this essentially consensus-oriented political culture stemmed from the fact that the founding fathers of the Federal Republic equipped the post-war political system with a number of checks and balances (through, for example, federalism), which generally led to a response of the 'middle path' on most political questions.[2]

The West German post-war party system was regarded as especially stable; a high degree of identification with the parties and their strong anchoring in civil society made it difficult for new parties to establish themselves.[3] It thus also proved relatively resistant to disruptive changes, although this by no means meant

2   Manfred G. Schmidt, *Das politische Systems Deutschlands*, 3rd edition, Munich: C.H. Beck, 2016.

3   Klaus von Beyme, *Parteien in westklichen Demokratien*, Munich & Zürich: Piper, 1984.

that nothing happened. The anti-authoritarian revolts of the late 1960s and early 1970s had loosened the country's structural conservatism, and society liberalized itself under Social Democratic leadership. Nevertheless, the Bismarck model continued to apply: repression of the radical left (such as through occupational bans on leftists) was the price of society's liberal modernization. There are limits to democracy in a capitalist society, but these can be extended—the late 1960s and early 1970s represented a period in which such a process occurred. The radical left's talk of a 'formal democracy' at the time thus ultimately failed to reflect reality. The social movements certainly posed a challenge to the major parties, but likewise also served to revitalize them.

The establishment of the Green Party in the early 1980s broke through the stability of the party system for the first time and injected it with the spirit of 1968, after having bid farewell to revolutionary politics. Although other new left-wing formations were founded in the 1980s, they all foundered in the face of the party system's resilience. The late establishment of a right-populist party in Germany, however, ultimately represents little more than a temporal delay. Right-wing parties like Die Republikaner and the Deutsche Volksunion were able to register victories at the state level as early as the 1990s. Their rise could only be 'stopped' by the parties of the centre shifting to the right and agreeing to harsh restrictions on the human right to asylum (and with it, immigration), thereby removing this conflict from the arena of political competition.[4]

THE CRISIS OF THE MAJOR PARTIES

The crisis of the political system in Germany is primarily a crisis of the major parties, which formed after the Second World War

---

4   Cf. Ulrich Herbert, *Geschichte der Ausländerpolitik in Deutschland*, Munich: C.H. Beck, 2001, 315ff.

out of the pre-war ideological mass integration parties—Otto Kirchheimer named this new type of party a 'catch-all party'.[5] For Kirchheimer, the decline of the old ideological mass-integration parties, which had preceded the new major parties, appeared essentially inevitable.[6]

The socialist, denominational and conservative parties were domesticated bit by bit. The fusion of interests and ideas, of ideologies and social models, was abandoned in favour of a de-ideologized pragmatism. The notion of social power structures and even antagonisms was henceforth to be ignored. Parties no longer represented their own clientele, no longer stood exclusively for the interests of their members, but rather focused on maximizing their electoral votes. The consensus vis-à-vis the responsibilities of state, the common good, became a primary focus of the catch-all parties—both the CDU as well as the Social Democrats. This would initially prove quite favourable for both in the 1960s and 1970s. These major parties continued to exhibit noteworthy ideological differences, but they essentially remained parties of the social state well into the 1980s and enjoyed broad trust from the population for their contribution to the building of the welfare system.

In 1969, the CDU/CSU and SPD collectively garnered 87 per cent of the ballots cast. In the following elections in 1972 and 1976, this number would rise to 90 per cent.

This period was by no means shorn of political conflict—in fact, the intensity of such conflict was enormous at times. While the CDU/CSU projected itself as the guarantor of Atlantic anti-communism vis-à-vis the student movement as well as the Eastern bloc, the Social Democrats initiated a new foreign policy

5   Cf. Otto Kirchheimer, 'The Transformation of the Western Party Systems', in Joseph LaPalombara and Myron Wiener (eds), *Political Parties and Political Development*, Princeton, NJ: Princeton University Press, 1966, 177–200.

6   Kirchheimer, 'Transformation of the Western Party Systems', 200.

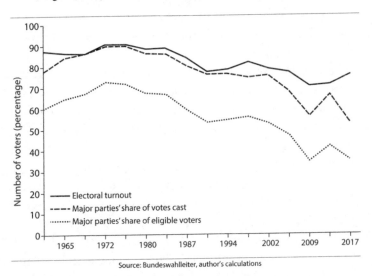

Figure 6.0 Representation of Major Parties in German Political System

Source: Bundeswahlleiter, author's calculations

known as *Ostpolitik*, seeking to ease tensions with the Warsaw Pact countries. After the 1968 wave of revolt broke, its residual elements in the 1970s would provide the Social Democrats with tens of thousands of new members. The SPD counted over 1 million members in the 1970s, while the CDU/CSU claimed nearly 800,000. On the whole, public engagement in party politics grew, while others became active in citizens' initiatives and founded the Greens in the early 1980s.

Despite the drama of some of the social conflicts, this period was characterized by a contested democracy which successfully integrated the majority of society. The policies of the market economy-oriented 'system parties' experienced an extraordinarily high degree of legitimacy. Moreover, these parties were able to retain voters' loyalty precisely because each respective camp exhibited visible differences vis-à-vis the other camp in terms of political order. Yet neoliberalism's triumph would result in, among other things, a transformation of the major parties' logic.

THE PATH TOWARD A FRAGMENTED PARTY SYSTEM

The social-liberal coalition between the SPD and FDP would collapse in 1982 when the Free Democrats, having oriented themselves more sharply toward neoliberalism, refused to continue supporting Keynesian economic policies.[7] The new 'black-yellow' coalition led by Chancellor Helmut Kohl marked a shift in German economic policy toward a supply-side agenda, albeit one which unfolded much more moderately than in Margaret Thatcher's Great Britain or the United States under Ronald Reagan. Yet, while the CDU began calling for cuts to the welfare state as a consequence of supply-side economics and the state budgetary crisis in the 1980s, the SPD in opposition would first shift back to the left—at least internally. The party would ultimately go on to win the 1998 federal elections with a fairly left-wing platform calling for wealth redistribution.

The German party system's orientation would begin to crack in the 2002 elections. The SPD only managed to win through its opposition to George W. Bush's war in Iraq and its stance during the biblical flooding of the Elbe in 2002; each situation allowed it to portray itself as a strong party that defended the vulnerable. The German economy slid into recession in 2003 and unemployment rose above 10 per cent. Encouraged by business associations and the media, politically oriented demands grew louder to address this unemployment through breaking from the German model of a relatively generous welfare state and corporatism (the model of trade union integration dominant since the 1960s). Chancellor Gerhard Schröder decided to seize the opportunity and announced the neoliberal shock therapy campaign known as Agenda 2010 (see Chapters 4 and 5).

The Agenda ended up throwing more fuel onto the smouldering fire of the Social Democrats Dramatic losses would follow in subsequent state elections, further straining the

---

7 However, such elements were already present in the SPD.

party—including a sizeable drop in members, as a sufficiently large segment of erstwhile loyal Social Democrats left the party to form an alternative electoral alliance. In the 2005 snap elections called by the SPD to prevent the consolidation of a left party, the so-called 'Wahlalternative Arbeit und Soziale Gerechtigkeit' (WASG) in an alliance with the primarily eastern Party of Democratic Socialism (PDS) received 8.7 per cent of the vote and became the third largest parliamentary group. The split in the SPD allowed the PDS to expand into a left-wing party encompassing all of Germany, extending far beyond its previous milieus.[8] The three-party system of the 1970s now became a five-party system, and the increasing fragmentation of the party landscape made forming coalitions more difficult. The SPD leadership had moved further to the centre than ever before and sought to defend Agenda 2010 at any cost. Its significantly diminished electoral result made a coalition with the Greens impossible without also Die Linke. The Christian Democrats were likewise harmed by the fact that Angela Merkel kept the party on a radically neoliberal course, expressed in the wildly unpopular Agenda. This cost the party its anticipated majority in 2005 and forced it to form a grand coalition with the SPD.

After this event, Merkel understood that the neoliberal offensive had reached its initial limits—and made a partial U-turn. She was fortunate that German capitalism had recovered a bit since the mid-2000s and overall pressure had subsided. Merkel has not enacted any noteworthy cuts in social policy since 2005— not even between 2009 and 2013, when governing in coalition with the Free Democrats, who had indirectly benefited from the grand coalition in the 2009 elections.

In her coalition with the Free Democrats, Merkel artfully managed to prevent them from pushing through any liberalization

8   Oliver Nachtwey and Tim Spier, 'Political Opportunity Structures and the Success of the German Left Party in 2005', *Debatte. Journal of Contemporary Central and Eastern Europe* 15 (2), 2007, 123–54.

of labour and social policy. Having largely failed to pass any meaningful reforms, the Free Democrats would go into free fall. In the 2013 elections, they failed to re-enter parliament for the first time since 1949 (which they attributed to the role of Angela Merkel, and not without reason). In the renewed grand coalition of 2013, Merkel accepted, alongside marginal social policy re-regulations, the biggest social policy innovation since Agenda 2010: the introduction of a nationwide, statutory minimum wage. The SPD acted as if it were responsible for the law, which was technically correct insofar as the CDU's economically liberal wing and segments of the employers' associations had harboured reservations and softly resisted the measure. Yet Angela Merkel and her trusted advisors had long come to accept the functional view that an economy with a large low-wage sector and weak trade unions (as Germany had now become) needed a minimum wage to prevent the link between work and poverty from growing too strong. The state footed part of the bill, as more than 1 million people still remained entitled to state transfer payments despite being employed. The droning victory cries from the Social Democratic leadership, however, were intended to obscure the fact that the SPD's policies for the lower classes were not particularly sincere. In fact, the party had had a parliamentary majority to pass a minimum wage in the last two legislative terms as well. Die Linke had offered to help pass such a law numerous times but was turned down by the SPD, which neither desired a coalition of the left nor was able to entertain the notion of an alliance with its former leader, Oskar Lafontaine, who had left and since publicly pilloried them. One of the greatest tragedies of the German left's post-war history is its inability to make use of social and parliamentary majorities. In each of 1998 (with 53 per cent) as well as 2002 (51 per cent) and 2005 (51 per cent), the political parties of the left commanded absolute majorities in ballots cast—but failed to make use of them. They have since lost this majority, because the SPD ignored the opportunity and now, in some ways as punishment, the party is so weak that this majority is structurally impossible.

Yet the SPD's aggressive, often rowdy rhetoric does not change the fact that the Social Democrats remain stubbornly tied to their chosen path of 'market social democracy' steeped in neoliberalism.[9] All chancellorship candidates after Schröder's 2005 defeat have belonged to the party's right wing. Long-serving leader Sigmar Gabriel and the last candidate, Martin Schulz, were also aligned with the right.

A double movement took place at the party system level: while the Social Democrats continued to conceive of themselves as supporting a market social democracy, the CDU moderated its more extreme positions in economic policy, where it cultivated a restrained image and adhered to the corporatist tradition. It also began to liberalize itself on social questions: abolishing mandatory conscription, liberalising family policies, boosting women's labour market participation, initiating a phasing out of nuclear energy, and most recently instituting marriage for all. Merkel has stepped back from a number of conservative positions. The logic of the major parties in the new millennium thus acquired a renewed thrust—the Social Democrats and Christian Democrats continued to converge. This logic accelerated as the old connections to organizations and the lifeworld grew thinner.[10] Both parties have lost more than half of their membership since the 1970s. The classical working-class milieus either modernized and no longer stood on the side of the SPD out of tradition, or were driven away by disappointment. The CDU suffered from the crisis of the church, but small businesspeople and traditional conservative circles have also turned their backs.

9   Oliver Nachtwey, 'Market Social Democracy: The Transformation of the SPD up to 2007', *German Politics* 22 (3), 2013, 235–52.

10   Walter Franz, *Im Herbst der Volksparteien? Eine kleine Geschichte von Aufstieg und Rückgang politischer Massenintegration*, Bielefeld: transcript, 2009.

It was a paradox of party politics: the more intense social polarization became, the stronger the major parties were pulled toward the centre, fearing that paying more attention to the issues of the underclasses would fail to yield electoral benefits.[11]

What Kirchheimer predicted fifty years ago would only truly become reality in the twenty-first century. Only now are the major parties truly catch-all parties, primarily focused on occupying the centre after abandoning their former clientele and classical values. Their aim now is solely the pragmatic retention of power.[12] Not only have the old ideological differences largely vanished, but a shared consensus of liberal market economy and liberal social policy has also emerged. Politics has disappeared in this consensus culture insofar as fundamental questions or orientations are no longer at stake, but rather only gradual, small matters of interpretation. However, this has also reopened the system's flanks. Merkel's political style perhaps had a sedative effect in the short term, but would prove provocative over time.

The FDP and the Greens only profited from this development marginally, as they both represented parties of the (better-off) centre.[13] Yet they remained clientele parties insofar as the liberals tend to represent the petit bourgeois and neoliberally inclined milieu of independent businesspeople, while the Greens represent the post-materialist milieu of highly educated service classes. Die Linke was only able to fill this gap in the party system temporarily. Under the leadership of former SPD chair Oskar Lafontaine, one of Germany's few charismatic politicians, it managed to appear as the central opposition party and only serious force

11   Winfried Thaa and Markus Linden, 'Issuefähigkeit—Ein neuer Disparitätsmodus?', in Markus Linden and Winfried Thaa (eds), *Ungleichheit und politische Repräsentation*, Baden-Baden: Nomos, 2014, 53–80.

12   Peter Mair, *Ruling the Void? The Hollowing of Western Democracy*, London: Verso, 2013.

13   Franz Walter, *Gelb oder Grün? Kleine Parteiengeschichte der besserverdienenden Mitte in Deutschland*, Bielefeld: transcript, 2010.

challenging the establishment. But Lafontaine would step down from the leadership in 2010. As a fusion of starkly different currents, the party's varied character would cost it its perception as an anti-establishment force in the public eye over the coming years.[14] After all, the eastern sections of Die Linke play a regional governing role, and at the federal level the party presents itself as a potential government partner.

In its anti-establishment stage, Die Linke had initially helped to channel social resentment to the left. Yet it grew increasingly unable to mobilize those remaining societal groups who no longer felt represented by the major parties. The existence of ever larger sectors of uncommitted voters who primarily sought to cast their ballot against the establishment parties was evidenced by the brief success of the Pirate Party. While Die Linke stagnated, the Pirates managed to enter several state parliaments with impressive results.[15] Yet it soon became clear that they would not succeed as a sustainable anti-establishment force, as they seemed most interested in replacing Green notions of participatory democracy with digital methods. Their star would burn out almost as soon as it began to shine in the political heavens.

GERMANY AND THE INTERNATIONAL CRISIS

Germany has consolidated its already unique position within the eurozone in recent decades. Its strong position in the European currency union yields cumulative economic returns. While the austerity imposed on countries like Greece by German finance minister Wolfgang Schäuble aided the expansion of German capital (such as the selling off of numerous Greek airports to a

---

14   Oliver Nachtwey, 'Die Linke and the Crisis of Class Representation', *International Socialism* 124, 2009, 23–36.

15   Alexander Hensel, Stephan Klecha and Walter Franz, *Meuterei auf der Deutschland: Ziele und Chancen der Piratenpartei*, Frankfurt am Main: Suhrkamp, 2012.

German company), domestic austerity in Germany functioned as a means with which to slow wage development and thereby strengthen German competitiveness vis-à-vis its European neighbours (see Chapter 4). Germany in fact made money off the debt crisis in southern Europe, while also using the European Central Bank's (ECB) low interest rates to lower its own refinancing costs. The German government, however, was forced to pay a price: the debts of the European crisis countries were partially generalized at the European level, imposing greater risk on Germany's budget. This in turn led to several conflicts within the conservative camp. For many representatives of an old-school Deutschmark nationalism, the 'rescue' of the crisis-stricken countries—despite the dramatic savings targets imposed on them by Schäuble—constituted too great a risk. They successfully mobilized concerns about Germany's financial liability, a weakening in international competition due to the ECB's expansive monetary policy, and a kind of 'expropriation' of German savers through low interest rates. There are fears among conservative voters for Germany's economic and political sovereignty. It is here that the AfD was born—before the refugee crisis.[16] That crisis, beginning in 2015, was merely one element accelerating the AfD's mutation into a right-populist party and its subsequent rapid rise, through which it drew on widespread pre-existing prejudice within the German population (see Chapter 5).

The refugee crisis also revealed the uneven development of German society. The country initially displayed its humanitarian side, the 'welcoming culture' of a pro-refugee movement from below, in which a significant portion of the population participated in one form or another. The figures vary considerably, but we can safely assume that millions of people assisted refugees either materially or morally. The welcoming culture movement represented a broad segment of the population, but was

16 Sebastian Friedrich, *Der Aufstieg der AfD. Neokonservative Mobilmachung in Deutschland*, Berlin: Bertz+Fischer, 2015.

simultaneously determined by class structurations. Most of its support came from cosmopolitan members of the educated middle class, for whom refugees posed no threat of competition on the labour market, nor did they move into their neighbourhoods.

The spontaneous humanitarian movement was certainly also one reason why Merkel, who had learned to orient her policy toward social majorities, long neglected to accept a refugee cap. She calculated that this would constitute a lose-lose situation and decided she could better control and limit the losses to her right than she could the possible loss of power through a breakdown of the coalition should she close the borders. Her strength until that point had been based on her shift toward the centre. And this time, unlike in the past when she pragmatically made radical concessions on numerous positions, she was disinclined to allow external pressure to abandon her stance. It would appear that she was also at least somewhat convinced of the humanitarian aspects of her actions—but only somewhat. For it was not always the case that Merkel felt pulled by pure humanitarianism—after all, as an Atlanticist, like her finance minister Wolfgang Schäuble, she had been fairly open to the US invasion of Iraq. She was also taking other, more pragmatic considerations into account: she saw Germany as a leading nation, obligated to save the European common market and political integration. As other European countries and the Visegrad states in particular began to close their borders, it fell to Germany to take in the majority of the refugees prior to Merkel reasserting the Dublin Regulation and pushing through a deal with Turkey to close Europe's outer borders. Following the refugee crisis, Merkel also further restricted the German right to asylum, yet remained—by the standards of international politics—fairly moderate.

Significant portions of the political establishment and media shifted to the right after the crisis. As would soon be revealed, a new line of conflict was beginning to develop which ran through the traditional political camps. Merkel initially had a majority of

Germans on her side but struggled to hold onto her own party. She received support from political opponents, and even Die Linke (with the exception of parliamentary speaker Sahra Wagenknecht) acknowledged its respect for her willingness to hold out against growing public and internal party pressure. In the meantime, the AfD had begun to effectively mobilize those portions of society that not only rejected the welcoming culture, but generally feared that society was being overwhelmed by foreign infiltration. Members of the lower middle class, the underclass and populations outside of the urban centres were particularly receptive to such a message. For those who had spent the last years living under the regime of economic and political austerity, the refugee movement also posed the question of redistribution. Stagnating and even declining real wages, low rates of investment in roads and bridges, and ailing public infrastructure (particularly schools and public swimming pools) drove many to view the refugee crisis as (also) a distribution conflict. Merkel and the political elites, however, clung to the political semantics of claiming that Germans had never had it so good.

This state of conflict was strategically exploited by the AfD, which increasingly integrated anti-Muslim sentiment into its discourse and presented itself as the only anti-establishment party that would represent the interests of 'ordinary' voters. As in many Western democracies where the revolts of 1968 long influenced political culture, right-wing populists' rhetoric focused on the potential collapse of values, the fall of the West and the disappearance of the centre. The AfD not only attracted the nationalistic members of the CDU who no longer saw the party as their political home due to Merkel's centrist approach, but simultaneously drew in the more bourgeois kind of fascist who saw the AfD as a new platform beyond the largely ineffective and publicly shunned National Democratic Party (NPD).

Die Linke then faced the challenge of pursuing a left-wing refugee policy while a portion of its core clientele cultivated a fairly critical attitude toward the welcoming culture. These centrifugal forces within its voting base posed a significant challenge.

WEIMAR IN SLOW MOTION

Grand coalitions have the paradoxical effect of further strengthening the cause of their emergence—namely, growth along the fringes of the political system. Kirchheimer had feared that democracy would grow dull and apathetic, warning that we 'may yet come to regret the passing—even if it was inevitable—of the class-mass party and the denominational party'.[17] This day may now be approaching. An old common saying in West German public life was 'Bonn is not Weimar', and following reunification it was modified to 'Berlin is not Weimar'. Political institutions pursued a moderate path for decades, and their culture was shaped by a continuously challenged democracy, albeit one in which the open rejection of democracy, such as had been the case in the Weimar Republic, was practically absent.[18] This has since changed. The German political system is now a six-party system. The AfD's arrival in the German parliament marks a new degree of fragmentation of the German party system. For the first time since 1933, fascists are seated in the German Bundestag and there is widespread public resentment of parliamentary democracy. A nervous, agitated mood has entered politics.

Generally speaking, there is a crisis of representation and wide-ranging dissatisfaction with the two major parties, which have positioned themselves strategically as parties of the radical centre for the last twenty years. This has effectively intensified political differentiation along the system's fringes and ultimately brought forth a populist constellation that above all lives off attacks on parliamentary democracy. It is a tragedy, as ultimately the democrats of the radical centre caused their own crisis by

17 Kirchheimer, 'Transformation of the Western Party Systems', 200.
18 Cf. Schmidt, *Das politische System Deutschlands*.

robbing democracy of its substance, and lulling it into an economically and socially liberal consensus. This post-political consensus (see Chapter 3) ultimately produced right-wing populism.

The SPD's decision to enter the grand coalition has now made the AfD the main force opposing the established parties. The AfD is currently engaged in an open factional battle between a national-conservative wing that plays with the political style of the alt-right but nevertheless remains bourgeois and would prefer to join the government at some point, and a more or less openly neo-fascist wing that has grown increasingly influential in recent months.

Despite its democratic socialist platform, Die Linke is not an anti-establishment party but rather continues to portray itself as a prospective coalition partner. This has led to deep conflicts inside the party, the outcome of which remains unknown at the time of writing. That said, Die Linke has managed to hold its own while sections of society drift to the right. That is more than nothing, but not much more.

The parties of the grand coalition continue to pursue policies of the economically liberal centre, although they have given in to national and international pressure and sharpened their immigration policies. They also consider deepening fiscal and economic European integration—an eminently neoliberal project.[19]

These catch-all parties, meanwhile, are attempting to revitalize themselves. Often, they try to do everything at once and thereby become even less recognizable as party formations. Some actors still try to respond pragmatically, while others adapt to the right-populist drift occurring in politics more generally. In the CDU, and particularly in its Bavarian sister party, the CSU, a new conservative wing is forming that, in tandem with its Bavarian sister party, strikes a nationalist tone, but whether this will lead to real renewal remains to be seen.

The SPD voted to remain in the grand coalition in the same week that a new study by Oxfam showed that the richest one per cent owned more than did half of the world population. The study also highlighted that increasing financial inequality corresponded to growing political inequality,[20] a fact mentioned at the SPD party conference. The central theme at the gathering was a kind of radical incrementalism, which regarded itself as essentially a shrunken variant of reformism. The SPD's guiding orientation in social policy has long ceased to be democratic socialism; it now pursues the social market economy, despite its rhetorical efforts to distance itself from neoliberalism as if it had not been in government for sixteen of the last twenty years.

The new leadership of the SPD has now promised to renew itself *in government*, and sent chairperson and leading candidate Martin Schulz, along with foreign minister Sigmar Gabriel, into political retirement. This 'renewal' meant that not a single figure from the party's left wing—no one who would oppose another round of government participation—entered the leadership. Andrea Nahles was elected the new chairperson; she had gladly joined the government during the previous term as minister of labour. Nahles is a domesticated ex-left-winger, the only person from the new central party leadership who does not explicitly belong to the right wing. The new finance minister, Olaf Scholz, who made a name for himself as an illiberal law-and-order politician while serving as mayor of Hamburg and maintains a questionable relationship to the truth, assumed the role of Wolfgang Schäuble's worthy successor. Scholz eagerly embraced austerity, kept on his predecessor's secretary and appointed the head of Goldman Sachs Germany as another permanent secretary. This

20 Oxfam Deutschland, '82 Prozent des weltweiten Vermögenswachstums geht ans reichste Prozent der Bevölkerung', 22 January 2018, www.oxfam.de (accessed May 2018).

renewal can really only be understood in a Freudian sense: as a death wish.

Despite all rhetorical efforts, a renewal of the catch-all parties is thus not in sight. Over twenty years ago, conservative German systems theorist Niklas Luhmann assumed that the economic ruptures of a globalized world would make it necessary to found a 'party for industry and labour'.[21] While French president Emmanuel Macron's *En Marche* has formed precisely such a party on top of the ruins of France's old party system, in Germany the grand coalition essentially functions in this way for industry and labour, only it possesses two independent factions joined together against their will. It is thus little surprise that practically all German trade union leaders expressed their support for the formation of the grand coalition. This consensus between industry and labour integrates the most important institutional actors, but likewise potentially accelerates the erosion of the catch-all parties (and also indirectly harms the trade unions). It remains to be seen what will happen to them in the future.

Overall, the development of German politics in the coming years is hard to predict. It is not yet a foregone conclusion if and how the AfD will play a role. It remains possible—although perhaps unexpected, for now—that solidarity will make a comeback in the form of social movements we have yet to encounter. For now, only one thing is certain: there will be no return to stability in the short term.

Basel,
June 2018

---

21 Niklas Luhmann, 'Wir haben gewählt', *Frankfurter Allgemeine Zeitung*, 22 October 1994.

Index